W9-BNX-496

The Tet Offensive

The Tet Offensive:
A Concise History

James H. Willbanks

COLUMBIA UNIVERSITY PRESS

NEW YORK

Columbia University Press
Publishers Since 1893
New York, Chichester, West Sussex
Copyright © 2007 Columbia University Press
All rights Reserved

Library of Congress Cataloging-in-Publication Data

Willbanks, James H., 1947–
The Tet Offensive : a concise history / James H. Willbanks.
p. cm.
Includes bibliographical references and index.
ISBN 0-231-12840-1 (cloth : alk. paper)
1. Tet Offensive, 1968.   I. Title.
DS557.8.T4W54   2006
959.704'342   dc22   2006012721

Columbia University Press books are printed on permanent
and durable acid-free paper
Printed in the United States of America

c 10 9 8 7 6 5 4 3 2 1

References to Internet Web Sites (URLs) were accurate at the time of writing.
Neither the author nor Columbia University Press is responsible for
Web sites that may have expired or changed since the book was prepared.

This book is dedicated to

the members of our armed forces,

then and now, who put it on the line for our nation.

CONTENTS

ACKNOWLEDGMENTS

I would like to thank a number of people and agencies for their assistance in preparing this volume. First of all, I would like to thank James Warren, former executive editor of Columbia University Press, and Marc Jason Gilbert of North Georgia College for their sage advice and willing assistance, which was invaluable. .

Thanks also go to the U.S. Army Center of Military History at Fort McNair in Washington, D.C., the U.S. Army Military History Institute at Carlisle Barracks, Pennsylvania, and the Combined Arms Research Library, Fort Leavenworth, Kansas.

A special thank you goes to the staff of The Vietnam Center at Texas Tech University, and in particular James Reckner and Steve Maxner, not only for the assistance they have given me but also for the important work that they are doing in documenting the nation's longest war.

I am also indebted to my colleagues in the Department of Military History, U.S. Army Command and General Staff College, for their support and advice during the preparation of this volume.

Last, my heartfelt gratitude goes to my wife Diana, who supports and sustains me in everything that I do.

INTRODUCTION

The Tet Offensive of 1968 was the pivotal event of the long Vietnam War. Its outcome and meaning have been the subjects of a debate that has raged for more than thirty years. As historian Marc Jason Gilbert suggests, "To most former allied military officers, some scholars of American history, and much of the American public, the Tet Offensive was a 'last gasp,' a failed all-or-nothing bid to win the war on the ground, which, though stymied in the field, succeeded, largely by accident, in persuading American to throw away the fruits of a major allied victory and start down the road to defeat and humiliation."[1] Other historians and Vietnam-era American policy analysts give more credit to Hanoi and the National Liberation Front for the design, outcome, and effects of the offensive, seeing it as a calculated strategic move that achieved its ultimate objectives—breaking American will and bringing the United States to the negotiating table. Regardless of their differing interpretations on motivations and outcomes, all agree that the Tet Offensive was a decisive moment that forever changed the nature of the U.S. commitment to the war. However, as Richard Falk points out, the Tet Offensive "remains a mirror for restating opposed preconceptions and validating contending ideological biases."[2] This guide seeks to examine the Tet Offensive and explore the various issues and interpretations of this controversial event that changed not only the conduct of the war itself, but that also continues to have an impact on the long-standing debate about the war and its meaning for both the United States and Vietnam.

On January 21, 1968, twenty thousand Communist troops surrounded the Marine base at Khe Sanh and lay siege to it for the next seventy-seven days. Ten days after the initial attack at Khe Sanh, in the early morning hours of January 31, Viet Cong and North Vietnamese forces launched a massive countrywide attack on the cities and towns of South Vietnam.[3] More than eighty thousand Communist troops mounted simultaneous assaults on thirty-six of forty-four provincial capitals, five of six major cities, including Saigon and Hue, sixty-four of 242 district capitals, and more than fifty hamlets.

The ferocity and scope of the offensive stunned both the American public and President Lyndon B. Johnson. The Tet Offensive would destroy any lingering confidence the American public might have had that Johnson's policies were leading to any progress in Vietnam. On March 31, the president spoke to the American people about the course of the war in Vietnam and announced that he was restricting bombing of North Vietnam to the area just north of the demilitarized zone (DMZ). Additionally, he committed the United States to negotiations, naming the veteran diplomat W. Averell Harriman as his personal representative to any such talks. Finally, at the end of his speech, the president shocked the nation by announcing that he would not run for reelection.

The Tet Offensive had effectively driven the president from office. It had provided strength to the war protestors and led other Democrats to challenge Johnson's leadership within his own party. Tet convinced the president that military victory in Vietnam was not attainable and forced a reevaluation of American strategy. The Tet Offensive and its aftermath marked the beginning of a protracted American retreat from Vietnam that would not end until five years later.

The journalist Don Oberdorfer has written, "the Tet Offensive of 1968 was the turning point of the U.S. war in Vietnam, and thus a historic event of lasting importance."[4] Although Oberdorfer was addressing the impact of the offensive on the war in Southeast Asia, the Tet Offensive and its outcome have a much broader meaning. The events of the Tet Offensive demonstrate a vital aspect of contemporary wars: military operations are normally but one aspect of the struggle and may not, as can be seen in the case of the events of 1968 in Vietnam, be the most important factor in determining the war's outcome. This study of the Tet Offensive informs contemporary discussions about the nature of war and its military and political aspects.

The conflict in Vietnam always had a strong political component in addition to the military engagements that raged on the battlefield. The war in the south was about who controlled the population. Recognizing this fact, there was great unity of purpose between the National Liberation Front in the south and the

Central Committee of the Vietnam Workers Party in Hanoi. On the other hand, there was a distinctive lack of unity of effort between the United States and its ally in Saigon. The legitimacy of the South Vietnamese government was always subject to question, and many historians see the troubled relationship between Washington and Saigon and the American military's failure to win hearts and minds of the South Vietnamese people as critical factors that led to the fall of Saigon. In that sense, the Tet Offensive, although usually seen within a military context, had serious political implications, and, in the final analysis, it was in the political arena that the offensive had its greatest impact.

This guide is meant to provide information and resources for further study of the 1968 Tet Offensive. It is not meant to be an exhaustive discussion of the entire war and associated resources for its study; for that, readers should see *The Columbia Guide to the Vietnam War* by David L. Anderson (Columbia University Press, 2002). This guide focuses on the events leading up to the Tet Offensive, the conduct of the offensive itself, and its aftermath. It also seeks to discuss the various tactical, operational, and strategic interpretations of the offensive and the events that took place in its aftermath.

The guide is divided into six major parts. It begins by providing a list of abbreviations and a set of maps as ready references for the reader to use in the rest of the guide. Part I is a historical overview of the Tet Offensive that addresses the prelude to the offensive, the offensive itself (including the battles of Saigon and Hue), the siege of Khe Sanh, and an assessment of the outcomes of the offensive. Part II examines a number of issues and interpretations of the main themes and questions that arose from the Tet Offensive; the objective of this part of the guide is to present the major historiographical threads with regard to the more contentious aspects of the offensive and its aftermath. Part III provides a chronology of action leading up to the offensive, the key events of the offensive itself, and the events that followed in the wake of the offensive. Part IV is a short encyclopedia of key people, places, and events. Part V presents a collection of excerpts from historical documents pertaining to the Tet Offensive. Part VI is an annotated listing of resources for studying the Tet Offensive, arranged topically.

I hope that this volume will provide a useful overview and a guide for further study to provide educators, students, and any other readers a ready reference to aid in the understanding of this crucial event in American history.

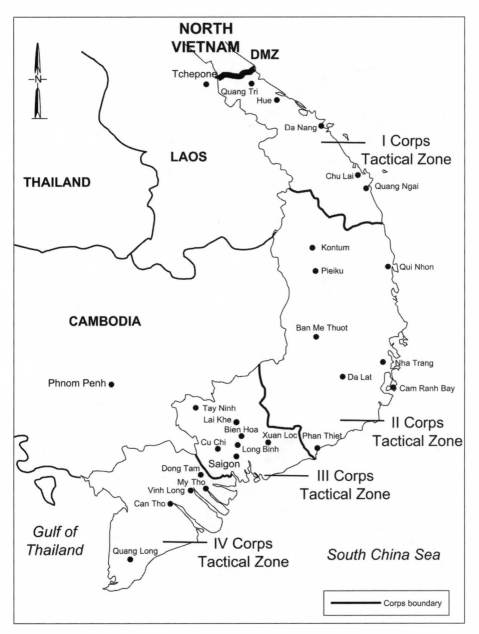

1. Republic of Vietnam Corps Tactical Zones

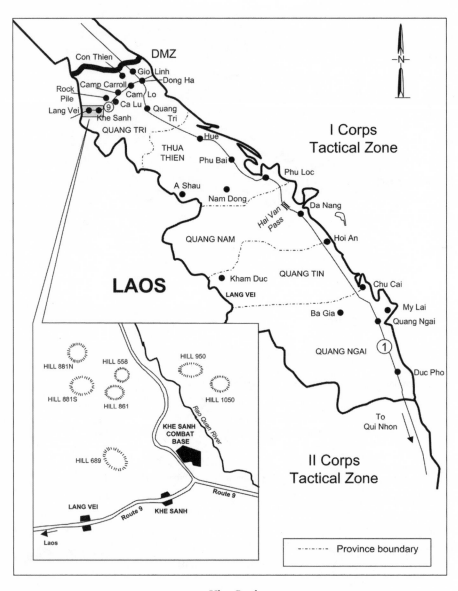

2. Khe Sanh

3. The Tet Offensive, 1968

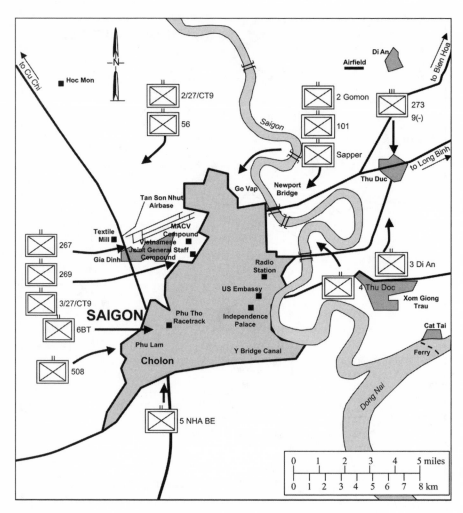

4. The Assault on Saigon

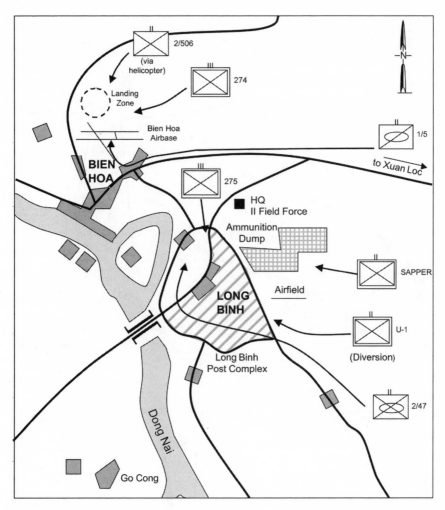

5. The Attack on Bien Hoa - Long Binh

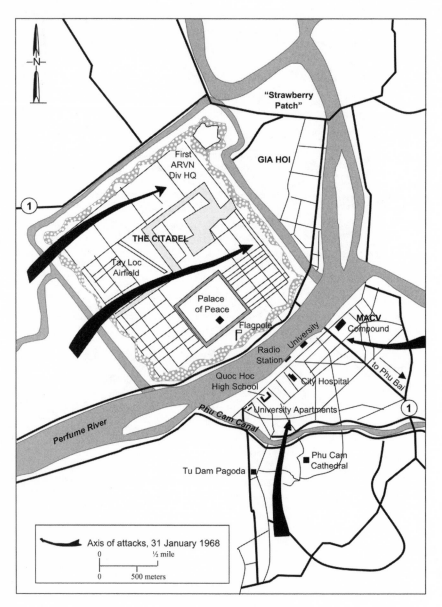

6. The Attack on Hue

ABBREVIATIONS

AAA	antiaircraft artillery
AAR	after action report
AFB	U.S. Air Force base
AID	Agency for International Development
AO	area of operation
APC	armored personnel carrier
ARVN	Army of the Republic of Vietnam
CAP	Combined Action Program
CBU	cluster bomb unit
CG	Commanding General
CIA	Central Intelligence Agency
CICV	Combined Intelligence Center Vietnam
CIDG	Civilian Irregular Defense Group
CINCPAC	Commander-in-Chief, Pacific
CJCS	Chairman, Joint Chiefs of Staff
COMUSMACV	Commander, U.S. Military Assistance Command, Vietnam
CORDS	Civil Operations and Revolutionary Development Support
COSVN	Central Office for South Vietnam
CP	command post
CTZ	Corps Tactical Zone
DCG	Deputy Commanding General
DIA	Defense Intelligence Agency
DMZ	Demilitarized Zone
DOD	Department of Defense
DRV	Democratic Republic of (North) Vietnam
FFV	Field Force Vietnam
FSB	fire support base
GVN	Government of (South) Vietnam
HES	Hamlet Evaluation System
JCS	U.S. Joint Chiefs of Staff
JGS	South Vietnamese Joint General Staff
KSCB	Khe Sanh Combat Base
KIA	killed in action
LAW	light antitank weapon
LZ	landing zone
MACV	Military Assistance Command, Vietnam
MAF	Marine Amphibious Force
MIA	missing in action
MP	military police
NLF	National Liberation Front

NSC	National Security Council
NVA	North Vietnamese Army
OB	Order of Battle
OPLAN	operations plan
PAVN	People's Army of (North) Vietnam
PF	Popular Forces
PLAF	People's Liberation Armed Forces
POW	prisoner of war
PRG	Provisional Revolutionary Government
PSA	Province Senior Adviser
PSDF	People's Self-Defense Force
RD	Revolutionary Development
RF/PF	Regional Forces/Popular Forces
ROK	Republic of Korea
RPG	rocket-propelled grenade
RVN	Republic of (South) Vietnam
RVNAF	Republic of Vietnam Armed Forces
SAC	Strategic Air Command
SAM	surface-to-air missile
SEATO	Southeast Asia Treaty Organization
TOC	tactical operations center
USAID	U.S. Agency for International Development
USARV	U.S. Army, Vietnam
VC	Viet Cong
VCI	Viet Cong Infrastructure
VNAF	Republic of Vietnam Air Force
VNMC	Republic of Vietnam Marine Corps
VNN	Republic of Vietnam Navy
WIA	wounded in action

The Tet Offensive

PART I

Historical Overview

Chapter 1

PRELUDE

On March 8, 1965, elements of the U.S. 9th Marine Expeditionary Force came ashore in Vietnam at Da Nang, initially to provide security for the U.S. air base there. A month later, President Lyndon Johnson authorized the use of U.S. ground troops for offensive combat operations in Vietnam. These events marked a significant change in U.S. involvement in the ongoing war between the South Vietnamese government in Saigon and the Viet Cong (VC).[1] The American goal in Southeast Asia was to insure a free, independent, and prosperous South Vietnam. However, the Saigon government was losing the battle to the Viet Cong, and things worsened when Hanoi began to send North Vietnamese soldiers down the Ho Chi Minh Trail into South Vietnam. Heretofore, U.S. forces had been supporting the Saigon government with advisers and air support, but that approach had proved inadequate in attempting to halt the Communists. With the arrival of the Marines, a massive U.S. buildup ensued; by the end of the year, 184,300 American troops were in Vietnam. This number would rapidly increase until there were more than 485,000 in country by the end of 1967.

The difficulty in achieving U.S. goals in Vietnam was that it was a political problem as well as a military one. The key to making sure that South Vietnam won the war against the Communist insurgents was to win the hearts and minds of the South Vietnamese people. To do this, the people had to believe that the government in Saigon was responsive to their needs. This proved difficult owing to the instability of that government. With the arrival of large number of American combat troops in South Vietnam, the U.S. effort shifted in focus from insuring a viable government in Saigon to conducting military operations to destroy the Communists on the battlefield, essentially a military answer to a political problem.

Eventually, U.S. ground troops were deployed in all four corps tactical zones (see Map 1) and actively conducted combat operations against the Viet Cong and their North Vietnamese counterparts, the People's Army of Vietnam (PAVN).[2] One of the first major battles between U.S. forces and PAVN troops occurred in November 1965 in the Battle of the Ia Drang Valley in the Central Highlands. Over the next two years, U.S. forces under General William C. Westmoreland, commander of U.S. Military Assistance Command, Vietnam (MACV), conducted many large-scale operations designed to find and destroy VC and PAVN forces in a war of attrition meant to wear down the enemy by killing or disabling so many of its soldiers that its will to resist would be broken.

As Westmoreland prosecuted the war of attrition, Hanoi ordered more PAVN soldiers down the Ho Chi Minh Trail to join the forces of the National Liberation Front (NLF) in their fight against the South Vietnamese troops and their American allies. The United States hoped that the continued bombing of North Vietnam and the trail might eventually persuade the Communists to call off the war. However, by late 1967, the bombing seemed to be having little effect, and heavy fighting continued to rage in the south.

The Communists adopted a strategy of protracted war designed to exhaust America's determination to continue its commitment to South Vietnam. General Vo Nguyen Giap, the North Vietnamese defense minister, was confident that Communist persistence would eventually outlast American patience and willingness to sacrifice, much as the Viet Minh had done against the French in the First Indochina War.

In South Vietnam, American troops worked with the Army of the Republic of Vietnam (ARVN) to secure the countryside and drive out the Viet Cong and PAVN. In January 1967, American and ARVN forces attacked into an area known as the Iron Triangle north of Saigon, a region that had long been considered a key Communist sanctuary. Initially, this operation, called Cedar Falls, was successful, and the Viet Cong withdrew from previously safe base areas close to Saigon. From February to May 1967, the allies conducted Operation Junction City, the largest combat operation to that point in the war. During the course of this operation, which was conducted in War Zone C northwest of Saigon, U.S. forces shattered the better part of three VC regiments, but the rest of the VC and PAVN forces in the area withdrew to the sanctuary of their bases in Cambodia.

Although large-scale allied search and destroy operations conducted through-out the 1966–67 dry season such as Cedar Falls and Junction City did not result in the total destruction of PAVN and VC units, they severely disrupted the Communist logistics system and forced the enemy to move its installations and supplies west into sanctuaries in Cambodia. The combination of disrupted logistics and increasing casualties caused many VC and PAVN soldiers to feel that the end of the war was not yet in sight, and this resulted in a decline in the morale and combat capability of some Communist units.[3] Nevertheless, Communist forces continued to conduct effective combat operations from their Cambodian sanctuaries and eventually reoccupied the areas that they had fled in the face of the earlier allied sweeps.

Although some headway was being made militarily, the problem was not purely military in nature. Concurrent with the fighting, there was a significant allied effort to pacify the countryside and spread the control and influence of the Saigon government. By the end of 1967, official U.S. estimates indicated that 67 percent of the South Vietnamese population was living under government control.[4] However, this number was subject to serious question; a 1967 Hamlet Evaluation System (HES) report found in the Pentagon Papers admitted "that to a large extent, the VC now control the countryside."[5]

By the middle of 1967, the war in Vietnam had degenerated into a bloody stalemate. U.S. and South Vietnamese operations had inflicted heavy casualties and disrupted Communist operations, but Hanoi continued to infiltrate troops into South Vietnam, and the Viet Cong still controlled the countryside in many areas in the south. Both the Americans and the North Vietnamese had vastly increased their commitment to the battlefield, but neither side could defeat the other. As the United States poured more troops and firepower into the struggle, the Communist leadership in Hanoi began to debate how to regain the initia-tive in South Vietnam. According to historian William J. Duiker, the party lead-ers acknowledged that total military victory over the combined U.S. and ARVN forces was improbable, but they were convinced that if severe reverses could be inflicted on the enemy's military forces, the United States would be compelled to withdraw from South Vietnam.[6]

AMERICAN PUBLIC OPINION

In the United States, the slow progress in the war and numerous revelations about the government's lack of candor about the conflict combined to erode public support for the Johnson administration's handling of the war and to bolster a growing antiwar movement. Newspapers, magazines, and the nightly television news brought the war home to America. The toll of the fighting in

Vietnam was mounting; the total casualties—dead, wounded, and missing in action—had grown from 2,500 in 1965 and would top 80,000 by the end of 1967. Scenes of the bloodshed and devastation resulting from the bitter fighting convinced increasing numbers of Americans that the price of U.S. commitment in Vietnam was too high. The war was also aggravating social discontent at home. One leading critic, Martin Luther King Jr., criticized the Johnson administration for the cost of the war and the effect it was having on the ability and willingness of the government to redress social ills such as inequality and poverty at home in the United States.

The American people began to mistrust the White House, which, many believed, was not telling them the truth about the real situation in Vietnam. While the reporters covering the war were writing that it had reached a stalemate, President Johnson and his advisers were still publicly saying that the war could be won.

Polls were showing that Americans, who at first had supported the president, were now beginning to turn against him. By June 1967, fully two-thirds of Americans said they had lost faith in President Johnson's ability to lead the country. A public opinion poll in September 1967 showed for the first time that more Americans opposed the war than supported it.[7] At the same time, Johnson's popularity had dropped to below 40 percent, a new low for his term in office.

Antiwar protests had grown in size and violence and garnered considerable media coverage. In October 1967, an estimated 100,000 demonstrators marched on the Pentagon. The American public was becoming increasingly polarized over the war. Even those who supported the war effort were becoming dissatisfied with Johnson's handling of the war and his inability to craft a winning strategy. The president, sensing that his public support had been shaken by the clamor of the antiwar faction and facing reelection in 1968, could ill ignore the growing restlessness of the electorate.

PUBLIC RELATIONS AND
WESTMORELAND'S OPTIMISM

Concerned about public opinion and wanting to show that progress was being made in the war, Johnson ordered a media blitz to reassure the American people and bolster support for his war policies. In what became known as the "Success Campaign," administration officials took every opportunity to try to repudiate the perception that there was a stalemate on the battlefield in Vietnam and repeatedly stressed that progress was being made.

In November 1967, the president called Westmoreland home from Vietnam to make the administration's case to the American public. Stepping off the plane in Washington, an optimistic Westmoreland told reporters, "I have never been more encouraged in the four years that I have been in Vietnam. We are making real progress."[8] The next day he told reporters that the South Vietnamese Army would be able to assume increasing responsibility for the fighting, and that the "phaseout" of U.S. involvement in Vietnam could begin within two years. On November 21, in a speech before the National Press Club, Westmoreland asserted, "We have reached an important point when the end becomes to come into view. I am absolutely certain that, whereas in 1965 the enemy was winning, today he is certainly losing. The enemy's hopes are bankrupt." He assured the reporters and the American public that victory "lies within our grasp."[9] For the time being, Westmoreland's comments helped calm a restive American public. His optimistic predictions would soon come back to haunt him.

TROOP DISPOSITION

By the end of 1967, the Republic of Vietnam Armed Forces (RVNAF) numbered about 350,000 regulars in the Army, Navy, Air Force, and Marine Corps. The South Vietnamese ground forces included eleven army divisions and three marine brigades. About 12,000 American advisers who served as liaison, operations, and logistics specialists accompanied these forces. The 151,000-man Regional Forces and the 149,000-man Popular Forces, which were the equivalent of provincial and local militia, augmented the regular ground forces.

The allied forces also included about 42,000 men who formed the Civilian Irregular Defense Groups (CIDG). These troops, mostly Montagnard tribesmen, were trained and led by American and Vietnamese Special Forces. They normally manned the outposts along the borders with Laos and Cambodia. This put them squarely in the way of Communist troops infiltrating across the border from sanctuaries and base camps in those countries.

There was also a 70,000-man national police force that would be forced to play a combat role once the battle for the cities started in 1968. This was not a role for which the policemen had been trained, and they were ill prepared for the situation that would confront them when the Tet Offensive began.

U.S. forces at the beginning of 1968 included nine divisions, one armored cavalry regiment, and two independent light infantry brigades. This force had one hundred infantry and mechanized battalions numbering 331,000 Army soldiers and 78,000 Marines. The total American military strength reached 486,000 by the end of 1967.

Taken together, the U.S. and South Vietnamese forces included 278 maneuver battalions, 28 tactical fighter squadrons, and 3,000 helicopters.[10] In addition, the allied forces were supported by 1,200 monthly B-52 sorties and a vast array of artillery and logistical support units.

Joining the U.S. and South Vietnamese forces were also troops from several other countries, who were providing military support to Saigon. These were collectively known as the Free World Military Forces and included troops from Australia, New Zealand, South Korea, Thailand, and the Philippines, who fought alongside U.S. and South Vietnamese soldiers.

Facing the Americans, South Vietnamese, and their allies was a formidable combination of PAVN and Viet Cong troops. There were two types of forces within the Viet Cong: main force units that by early 1968 numbered about sixty thousand soldiers organized into regular combat units, and the paramilitary or guerrilla forces. Main force units engaged in full-scale combat and were usually made up of highly motivated, skilled fighters who were adept at ambushes, the use of mortars and rockets, and coordinated attacks on allied defensive positions.

The paramilitary forces of the Viet Cong included regional, or territorial, guerrillas and local guerrillas. They provided logistical support, scouts, and guides and engaged in local hit-and-run tactics such as staging ambushes and laying mines. MACV estimated in October 1967 that there were nearly 250,000 Viet Cong main force and paramilitary forces operating in South Vietnam.[11]

When the war began, the Viet Cong guerrillas did most of the fighting and received only limited support from the North Vietnamese regulars. However, as the war intensified, increasing numbers of PAVN troops traveled down the Ho Chi Minh Trail to join the fighting in the south, serving as fillers in VC units. The first PAVN units had come down the trail in 1964. By early 1968, American intelligence analysts had identified seven North Vietnamese divisions, totaling about fifty-five thousand soldiers, in the south. American intelligence estimated that at the time of the offensive, about half of the 197 main-force enemy battalions in the south were PAVN regulars.[12]

The PAVN was a formidable force organized into divisions, regiments, battalions, and companies. These were armed with modern Soviet and Chinese weapons. They were supported by mortars, artillery, rocket launchers, and, by 1968, tanks. The PAVN soldiers, many of whom sported tattoos that proclaimed, "Born in the North, to die in the South," were well trained and highly motivated.

THE COMMUNIST DECISION TO CONDUCT THE OFFENSIVE

As President Johnson and his advisers wrestled with how to proceed with the war, the Communists were having discussions of their own. According to William J. Duiker, the Communists had earlier decided on a "decisive victory in a relatively short period of time," which was confirmed by the Thirteenth Plenum in late 1966.[13] This led to an aggressive battlefield strategy that achieved only limited results. By mid-1967, the party leaders in Hanoi decided that something had to be done to break the bloody stalemate in the south. However, there followed a contentious debate in the Politburo about how best to do this. By this time, Le Duan, a onetime organizer of the resistance in the south and by 1967 secretary-general of the Lao Dong Party, had become critical of the protracted war strategy. The war was not going as well as the Communists had hoped, chiefly because the commitment of American troops had inhibited PAVN infiltration and imposed heavy casualties. To Le Duan, the aggressive American tactics during the early part of 1967 did not bode well for the successful continuation of a protracted approach toward prosecuting the war. However, two areas of potential allied weakness had emerged. The ARVN still had significant problems, and U.S. public opinion had begun to waiver in its support of the American war effort. For these reasons, Le Duan advocated a more aggressive strategy to conclude the war by destroying U.S. confidence and spreading Communist control and influence in the countryside.

Le Duan was not alone. Chief among those who agreed with him was General Nguyen Chi Thanh, head of the Central Office for South Vietnam (COSVN), which had been initially established in 1951 as the Communist military headquarters in South Vietnam. Thanh also wanted to pursue a more aggressive strategy. He called for a massive attack against the cities of South Vietnam using local guerrillas, main force VC, and PAVN regulars. This would be the advent of the third, and final, stage of the revolutionary struggle—what Communist doctrine termed the General Offensive, General Uprising.

Le Duan and Thanh found other supporters in the Politburo, who were also unhappy with the stalemate in the south. One Communist general later described the situation, saying, "In the spring of 1967 Westmoreland began his second campaign. It was very fierce. Certain of our people were very discouraged. There was much discussion of the war—should we continue main-force efforts, or should we pull back into a more local strategy. But by the middle of 1967 we concluded that you [the Americans and South Vietnamese] had not reversed the balance of forces on the battlefield. So we decided to carry out one decisive battle to force LBJ to de-escalate the war."[14]

Not everyone agreed with Le Duan and Thanh. Some historians and other observers, one of whom described the offensive as "Giap's Dream," ascribe the genesis of the plan to Hanoi's defense minister.[15] However, Giap actually opposed the proposed escalation, because he thought that a major offensive in 1968 would be premature and likely to fail against an enemy with vastly superior mobility and firepower.[16] Long the chief proponent of protracted guerrilla operations against allied communication and supply lines in the south, Giap feared that if the offensive failed, the revolution would be set back years. Giap and Thanh had been longtime rivals for control of the Communists' military strategy in the south. Thanh charged Giap with being old-fashioned, with "a method of viewing things that is detached from reality," insisting that Giap and his followers looked for answers "in books, and [by] mechanically copying one's past experiences or the experiences of foreign countries . . . in accordance with a dogmatic tendency."[17]

In the end, Le Duan and Nguyen Chi Thanh won the argument. After lengthy deliberation, the 13th Plenum of April 1967 passed Resolution 13, which called for a "spontaneous uprising in order to win a decisive victory in the shortest possible time."[18] This was a blow for Giap and his theory of protracted war. However, on July 6, 1967, Thanh died suddenly. The cause of death remains unknown; according to Giap's biographer, Cecil Currey, Thanh fell ill from pneumonia, was wounded by bomb fragments, or suffered a heart attack while on duty in his COSVN tactical operations center.[19] Despite Thanh's death, the Central Committee directed that planning for the general offensive continue. The responsibility for planning and directing the campaign fell to Giap. Although he still thought the offensive was ill advised, Giap swallowed his objections and reluctantly began to put the plan together, warning against expecting quick victory.[20]

It was decided that the offensive would be launched in early 1968 during Vietnam's Tet holiday, which marks the start of the lunar new year. Tet is a time not only of revelry celebrated with feasts and fireworks, but also of worship at the family altar for revered ancestors. For several days the entire countryside is on the move as people visit their ancestral homes, and all business, even the business of war, comes to a halt. Before 1968, both sides in the war had observed Tet cease-fires over the holiday. Therefore, the North Vietnamese reasoned that half the South Vietnamese army and national police would be on leave when Tet began and Saigon would be unprepared for a countrywide attack.

THE PLAN

The plan for the *Tet Mau Than* (New Year of the Monkey) 1968 offensive was finalized in late summer of 1967. North Vietnamese diplomats from around the world were called to Hanoi for consultation in July to discuss the upcoming offensive. This should have been the first indication to allied intelligence that something significant was in the offing, but most allied analysts believed the meeting's purpose was to consider a peace bid.

The Tet campaign was designed to break the stalemate and achieve three objectives: provoke a general uprising among the people in the south, shatter the South Vietnamese armed forces, and convince the Americans that the war was unwinnable. According to William J. Duiker, "Hanoi was counting on the combined offensive and uprising to weaken the political and military foundations of the Saigon regime and to trigger a shift in policy in the United States."[21] To accomplish this, the offensive would target South Vietnamese urban centers.

Dubbed *Tong Cong Kich–Tong Khoi Nghia* (General Offensive–General Uprising or TCK-TKN), the plan, using secrecy and surprise, called for a series of simultaneous attacks against American bases and South Vietnamese cities.[22] Giap specifically targeted previously untouched urban centers such as Saigon in the south, Nha Trang and Qui Nhon in central South Vietnam, as well as Quang Ngai and Hue in the northern part of the country.

Ultimately, Giap's plan was predicated on four assumptions. First, the ARVN would not fight when struck a hard blow. Second, the Saigon government had no support among the South Vietnamese people, who would rise up against President Thieu if given the opportunity. Third, both the people and the armed forces of South Vietnam despised the Americans and would turn on them if given the chance. Fourth, the tactical situation at Khe Sanh in 1967 paralleled that of Dien Bien Phu in 1954.

With these assumptions in mind, Giap devised a three-pronged military offensive. However, in the mind of Giap, this offensive was another step in the long process of *dau tranh*, "the struggle."[23] He later explained his campaign in an interview with journalist Stanley Karnow: "For us, you know, there is no such thing as a single strategy. Ours is always a synthesis, simultaneously military, political, and diplomatic—which is why, quite clearly, the Tet offensive had multiple objectives."[24] For Giap, war was political as well as military, and he recognized that the latter only served to promote the former.

According to General Tran Van Tra, commander of Communist forces in the south from 1963 to 1975, the objectives of TCK-TKN were "to break down and destroy the bulk of the puppet [South Vietnamese] troops, topple the puppet administration at all levels, and take power into the hands of the people; to destroy the major part of the U.S. forces and their war materiel, and render them unable to fulfill their political and military duties in Vietnam; and to break the U.S. will of aggression, force it to accept defeat in the South and put an end to all acts of war against the North."[25] As part of the desire to break the American will, the Communists hoped to convince the United States to end the bombing of the north and begin negotiations to end the war.[26] It is against these objectives, not just the generally accepted military aims, that the offensive must be analyzed.

Giap's plan called for a preparatory phase that would be conducted from September to December 1967. During this period, PAVN forces would launch attacks in the remote outlying regions along South Vietnam's borders with Cambodia and Laos. The purpose of these operations, which were essentially a grand feint, would be to draw U.S. forces away from the populated areas. This would leave the cities and towns uncovered. This phase would have two other objectives. The first was to provide opportunities for Giap's troops to hone their fighting skills, and the other was to increase American casualties. As part of this preparatory phase, main force divisions would begin to move into position around Khe Sanh, an outpost along the Laotian border manned by only a single U.S. Marine regiment.

Although there is some disagreement among American scholars about the phasing of the actual offensive, Tran Van Tra asserted some years after the war that the plan for the offensive called for three distinct phases.[27] Phase I, which was scheduled to begin on January 31, 1968, was a countrywide assault on South Vietnamese cities, ARVN units, American headquarters, communication centers, and air bases to be carried out primarily by VC main-force units. It was hoped that the southern insurgents would be able to infiltrate their forces into the attack positions and target areas before the offensive started.

Concurrent with this phase would be a massive propaganda campaign aimed at coaxing the southern troops to rally to the Communist side. The objective of this campaign was to achieve wholesale defections from the ARVN ranks. At the same time, the North Vietnamese would launch their political offensive, aimed at causing the South Vietnamese people to revolt against the Saigon government. Successful accomplishment of this objective would leave "the American forces and bases isolated islands in a sea of hostile South Vietnamese people."[28]

If the general uprising did not occur or failed to achieve the overthrow of the Saigon government, follow-on operations would be launched in succeeding months to wear down the enemy and lead either to victory or to a negotiated settlement.[29] According to Tra, Phase II of the offensive began on May 5, and Phase III began on August 17 and ended on September 23, 1968.[30] It is clear that to Hanoi and the NLF, the Tet Offensive, which is usually seen to cover a much shorter period by many American historians, was a more prolonged offensive that lasted beyond the action immediately following the Tet holiday.

All of this was unknown to Westmoreland and his intelligence officers at MACV, who thought the sequel to the Tet attacks would be a big set-piece battle designed to defeat American forces decisively, in much the same way that the French had been defeated at Dien Bien Phu, which had precipitated their withdrawal from Vietnam. This perception would prove critical as intelligence reports in later 1967 and early 1968 indicated that the Communists were planning something big. As these reports increased in frequency, Westmoreland would become convinced that the ultimate target of the offensive was Khe Sanh.

PREPARING FOR THE OFFENSIVE

Preparations for the attack began immediately after the decision to launch the offensive was made. Giap masterfully directed an intensive logistical effort focused on a massive buildup of troops and equipment in the south. Men and arms began pouring into South Vietnam from staging areas in Laos and Cambodia. New Russian-made AK-47 assault rifles, B-40 and 122mm rockets, and large amounts of other war materiel were moved south along the Ho Chi Minh Trail by bicycle, oxcart, and truck.

As the PAVN troops infiltrated into the south, VC units were alerted and began preparing for the coming offensive. Guerrilla forces were reorganized into the configuration that would later be employed in attacking the cities and towns. Replacements arrived to round out understrength units. The new weapons and equipment that had just arrived were issued to the troops. Food, medicine, ammunition, and other critical supplies were stockpiled. In areas close enough to the cities to permit rapid deployment but far enough away to preclude detection, VC units conducted intense training for the upcoming combat operations. Some training in street fighting was conducted for special sapper units, but this was limited in order to maintain secrecy. Reconnaissance was conducted of routes to objective areas and targets. Meanwhile, political officers conducted *chin huan*, or reorientation, sessions where they indoctrinated the troops, proclaiming that the final goal was within their grasp and exhorting them to prepare themselves for the decisive battle to achieve total victory against Saigon and its American allies.

To achieve tactical surprise, which Giap considered essential for success, the North Vietnamese instituted a two-part plan of deception to cover preparations for the offensive. The first revolved around passive measures, which primarily relied on secrecy to conceal preparations for the offensive. Operational plans for the offensive were kept strictly confidential and disseminated to each subordinate level only as requirements dictated. Although the executive members of COSVN knew of the plan some time in mid-1967, it was not until the fall that the complete plan was disseminated to high-ranking enemy officials of the Saigon–Cholon–Gia Dinh Special Zone, one of the main target areas of the offensive.[31] Although this secrecy was necessary for operational security, it would add to the customary fog and friction of war once the offensive was launched and have a significant effect on the outcome of the fighting at the tactical level.

The other part of Hanoi's deception plan employed diplomatic maneuvers to obscure the ongoing preparations for the offensive. On December 31, 1967, North Vietnam's minister of foreign affairs declared that if the United States unconditionally ceased its bombings, North Vietnam would be prepared to enter into negotiations. This offer had several objectives. First, it "put a smoke-screen" on Hanoi's preparations for the general offensive to misdirect the attention of American authorities.[32] Second, it was meant to drive a wedge between the Americans and the South Vietnamese, who did not want peace talks of any kind. Last, if the U.S. government agreed to a cessation of bombing, Hanoi could speed up infiltration movements into South Vietnam during the dry season in time for the offensive.

Communist agents also approached prominent representatives of the political opposition in the south in an attempt to sow political dissent against the Saigon government. At the same time, the National Liberation Front initiated a new propaganda effort through "Liberation Radio" to win more converts to the revolution. The Communist hoped these actions would dampen support for the Saigon government and spark a popular uprising, or *khoi nghia*.[33]

The Tet Offensive thus really began in 1967 with the preparatory phase that included the diversionary attacks on the outlying areas in South Vietnam. The bitter fighting that resulted would set the stage for the Tet Offensive that began in January 1968 and lasted into the fall of that year.

Chapter 2

BORDER BATTLES, HILL FIGHTS, AND KHE SANH

During the fall of 1967, the PAVN began to attack allied positions in the northern part of South Vietnam, along the Cambodian border, and just south of the DMZ. These operations served three purposes. They were designed to draw the American troops away from the populated areas.[1] They provided an opportunity to rehearse coordinated operations between troops of the People's Army of Vietnam (PAVN) and Viet Cong (VC) guerrillas. And they served to screen the infiltration of troops and equipment into South Vietnam from Laos and Cambodia before Tet.

Interpreting these moves as an effort to gain control of the northern provinces, General William Westmoreland retaliated with massive bombing raids targeted against suspected PAVN troop concentrations. He also sent reinforcements to the northern and border areas to help drive back PAVN attacks at Con Thien, Loc Ninh, Song Be, and Dak To. The attack on Dak To in the II Corps area in November 1967 was the last of a series of "border battles" that began two months earlier with the siege of Con Thien in the I Corps area and continued in October with attacks on Song Be and Loc Ninh in the III Corps area.[2]

Con Thien was a barren Marine outpost situated ten miles northwest of Dong Ha on the top of Hill 158, overlooking the demilitarized zone (DMZ). It was the easternmost anchor of a line of outposts that extended west to Camp Carroll and Khe Sanh, which were meant to provide a shield to protect the two northern provinces of Quang Tri and Thua Thien.[3] The outpost at Con Thien, occupied by a battalion of Marines, came under ground attack in July 1967 by PAVN forces operating out of the supposedly neutral DMZ. The base was also the target of constant and intense artillery pounding from an estimated 130 PAVN artillery pieces emplaced in well-fortified firing positions north of the Ben Hai River, which bisected the five-mile-wide buffer zone. The Marine defenders conducted a number of spoiling attacks in July and August, turning back several PAVN attempts to take the base.

In September, elements of a PAVN division made a concerted effort to capture Con Thien, but once again the Marines prevailed. Failing to take the base by ground attack, the Communists increased their artillery bombardment of the base. The shelling reached its peak during the week of September 19–27, when more than three thousand mortar, artillery, and rocket rounds struck the Marine outpost. In response, Marine and army artillery, naval gunfire, and massive air strikes, including 790 B-52 sorties, inflicted heavy casualties on the PAVN attackers. By October 31, the Marines had held, and the siege of Con Thien was over.

The Communists followed the attack on Con Thien with new attacks along the borders with Laos and Cambodia. On October 27, a PAVN regiment attacked the command post of a South Vietnamese battalion at Song Be in Phuoc Long province near the Cambodian border in the III Corps area. With the aid of air support, the ARVN soldiers repulsed several PAVN attacks.

Two days later, a VC regiment attacked another South Vietnamese outpost at Loc Ninh, a small rubber plantation town on the Cambodian border in Binh Long province. The Viet Cong penetrated the district headquarters perimeter and gained control of about half the compound, but ARVN reinforcements helped drive back the Viet Cong after bitter fighting. After the first attack was repelled, another VC regiment joined the battle, followed by elements of two other PAVN regiments. The fighting spread into the adjacent plantation areas, and a brigade from the U.S. 1st Infantry Division was inserted into the battle. The combat was intense as both sides fought desperately to overcome the other in heavy fighting that raged from October 29 to November 2. The Communists troops launched repeated human wave attacks against the allied positions, but the defenders inflicted heavy losses on the attackers.[4]

The attack on Loc Ninh represented the first time that the Central Office for South Vietnam (COSVN), the senior Communist headquarters in the southern half of South Vietnam, had staged coordinated attacks by large units from different divisions. It was later discovered that this action was essentially a rehearsal intended to provide VC and PAVN forces with an opportunity to experiment with street fighting techniques, as well as to test South Vietnamese reactions and use of firepower to relieve embattled cities and population centers.[5]

The final "border battle" occurred near a U.S. Special Forces camp near Dak To northwest of Kontum in the mountainous area along the Laotian and Cambodian borders in the Central Highlands. In late October, intelligence indicated that four PAVN main-force regiments were moving into the Dak To region. At the time, there was only one American battalion in the area, but Westmoreland quickly sent in reinforcements. By mid-November as PAVN attack indicators increased, there were a total of nine U.S. and six ARVN infantry battalions in the area. The first engagement between the allied forces and PAVN troops erupted on November 17, and it was followed by a series of pitched battles that ranged over an area of 190 square miles and lasted for twenty-two days. During the bitter fighting, three PAVN regiments were severely crippled, suffering an estimated 1,400 soldiers killed, but allied losses were heavy, too. The ARVN lost 73 men, and 289 Americans were killed during the battles around Dak To; more than 900 American soldiers were wounded.

The attacks on Con Thien, Song Be, Loc Ninh, and Dak To were part of the preparatory phase for Giap's general offensive plan designed to lure U.S. forces away from the cities and into South Vietnam's periphery. In purely tactical terms, these operations were costly failures, and, although exact numbers are not known, the Communists no doubt lost some of their best troops. Not only did the allied forces exact a high toll in enemy casualties, but the attacks also failed to cause a permanent relocation of allied forces to the border areas. The strategic mobility of the American forces permitted them to move to the borders, turn back the Communist attacks, and redeploy back to the interior in a mobile reserve posture. North Vietnamese Colonel Tran Van Doc later described these border battles as "useless and bloody."[6] Nevertheless, at the operational level, the attacks achieved at least part of Giap's intent by diverting Westmoreland's attention to the outlying areas away from the buildup around the urban target areas while also giving the North Vietnamese an opportunity to perfect the tactics that they would use in the Tet attacks.[7]

KHE SANH

U.S. intelligence analysts were puzzled by the Communist moves, which seemed to invite massive American retaliation for no apparent purpose. As the fighting intensified in 1967, Westmoreland received reports that PAVN forces were massing forces to attack the Marine base at Khe Sanh in the northern I Corps area (see Map 2). American Special Forces had originally set up the base in 1962, forming Civilian Irregular Defense Group (CIDG) companies among the Bru Montagnard tribes there to monitor and block activity along the Ho Chi Minh Trail. In 1964, the Special Forces built a new base, which covered an area of about two square miles. Built around an old military base known as the French Fort, it was located on a plateau two miles north of Khe Sanh village. North of the fort, an airstrip had been carved from a piece of level ground among the hills. Special Forces soldiers built strong cement bunkers for the command center and defensive positions.

By 1965, the Special Forces had installed mortars and other weapons to defend the base against the PAVN and Viet Cong who were operating in the area. Nevertheless, the base sustained a major enemy attack on the evening of January 3, 1966, and suffered sixty to seventy casualties among the Special Forces advisers and their Montagnard troops. To strengthen the base, Navy Seabees improved the airstrip, building a 1,500-foot runway of steel planking in the summer of 1966.

The first Marines in the area had come in April 1964 when a communication intelligence unit arrived to monitor VC and North Vietnamese radio communication. Westmoreland visited Khe Sanh for the first time during the period of these early intelligence-gathering operations.

As the war expanded, Khe Sanh gradually grew in importance for the U.S. high command. In mid-1966, the PAVN began to deploy large numbers of forces within the DMZ, in Laos, and in the southern panhandle of North Vietnam. Giap wanted to shorten his supply lines and make infiltration from the north harder for the Americans to detect.[8] With the increased infiltration of PAVN troops from the north, Westmoreland saw Khe Sanh as the key to preventing the North Vietnamese from carrying the fight into the populated coastal regions of northern South Vietnam. Consequently, he ordered a battalion of Marines to the Khe Sanh area in April 1966. In January 1967, the Special Forces troops were displaced from their camp by elements of a Marine regiment, which was ordered to assume operational responsibility for the area in April. The Green Berets moved their camp westward to the Montagnard village of Lang Vei.

Surrounded by a series of mist-enshrouded, jungle-covered hills, Khe Sanh was one of a series of outposts established near the demilitarized zone separating North and South Vietnam. Located just north of Khe Sanh village some seven miles from the border with Laos and about fourteen miles south of the DMZ, Khe Sanh Combat Base (KSCB) was a key element in the defense of I Corps in South Vietnam. Khe Sanh effectively controlled a valley area that was the crossroads of enemy infiltration routes from North Vietnam and lower Laos, which provided natural invasion avenues of approach into the two northern provinces of South Vietnam. To Westmoreland, Khe Sanh was the natural blocking position to block this infiltration in order to protect Quang Tri and Thua Thien provinces.[9] The base also served as a top-secret launch site for vital Special Forces reconnaissance missions into Laos and as an airfield for reconnaissance flights over the Ho Chi Minh Trail. In addition, Westmoreland hoped that he might convince the White House in the near future to approve combat operations into Laos to destroy the North Vietnamese supply routes and sanctuaries.[10] In that case, Khe Sanh would serve as an ideal base for the invasion.

By the end of the summer of 1967, Khe Sanh Combat Base had become the western anchor of a chain of strong points stretching from the border with Laos to the city of Hue in the east that were designed to thwart any PAVN invasion across the DMZ. In addition to the Marines at KSCB and the Special Forces at Lang Vei, there was a small Marine Combined Action Program company and a Regional Forces company in the village of Khe Sanh.[11]

Supported by 175mm guns from two firebases seventeen miles to the east, Camp Carroll and the Rockpile, the Marines began sending out patrols, which soon discovered PAVN bunkers, tunnels, and supply depots. In the meantime, the Marine engineers worked on Route 9, repairing bridges and improving the road so supplies could be brought into the base overland. The PAVN continued to threaten Khe Sanh, and a fierce battle broke out on the night of March 15, 1967, in which the PAVN inflicted heavy casualties on a Marine company.

THE HILL FIGHTS

This battle, along with the others that followed in 1967 and into 1968, became a titanic struggle between U.S. forces and the Communist for control of the high ground in the Khe Sanh area. The base itself was surrounded by several hills that were strategically important to its defense. The most important of these were Hills 881 North, 881 South, and 861 (their names denote their height in meters), within sight of the plateau and overlooking the Rao Quan River. These hills formed a near-perfect triangle, with Hill 881 North at the apex and the other two hills at the base of the triangle. Hill 861 was about 5,000 meters (3.1 miles) northwest of the airstrip; Hill 881 South was approximately 3,000 meters (1.85 miles) west of 861 and 2,000 meters (1.25 miles) south of 881 North. If the PAVN occupied these hills, they would be ideally placed to bombard Khe Sanh Combat Base, thus making aerial reinforcement and resupply virtually impossible. Between April 28 and May 11, 1967, in a series of hard-fought engagements known as the "Hill Fights," two Marine battalions from the Third Marine Regiment wrested control of all three key terrain features from the PAVN, who gave as good as they got in the heavy fighting.

In August, the Marines increased their patrolling activity and extra outposts were established on Hills 558 and 861A, to the east and northwest of 861, respectively, to block the Rao Quan valley. In view of the increasing PAVN activity in the area, the Marines began an effort to improve the defenses of the base and the hilltop outposts. They began to work on building new fortifications

and improving existing fighting positions. At the same time, the Khe Sanh airfield was shut down so the Seabees could make much-needed improvements,
including lengthening and strengthening the runway, using crushed rock from
a nearby quarry and other materials provided by parachute or by a special low-
altitude extraction system.[12] While the airfield was being improved, helicopters
and C-7 Caribou aircraft that could land on short open segments of the runway
supplied the base. The improved airfield would reopen in October to C-123 and
C-130 aircraft. This airfield would prove crucial in the coming siege.

In September, American intelligence reported that two battalions of PAVN
troops, approximately 1,600 men, had moved into the Khe Sanh area. In
November, the PAVN began massing for what appeared to be a major assault.
Under the command of the corps level Route 9 Front, more than 20,000 PAVN
regulars began converging on the Khe Sanh area.

In late November, U.S. intelligence began to receive reports that several
PAVN divisions normally located in North Vietnam were beginning to move
south. By late December it was apparent to U.S. intelligence agencies that two
of these divisions were headed for the Khe Sanh area. One of these divisions, the
304th, was an elite home-guard division from Hanoi that had led the struggle
against the French during the 1950s and participated in the decisive Viet Minh
victory at Dien Bien Phu in 1954. In addition to these two divisions, intelligence
reports indicated that another division and one more regiment were moving to
within easy supporting distance of the PAVN troops converging on Khe Sanh.

The PAVN buildup at Khe Sanh was not unwelcome news to Westmoreland.
For several years, the American commander had hoped to engage the PAVN
and Viet Cong in a traditional set-piece battle on ground of his choosing instead
of having to deal with the usual hit-and-run guerrilla campaign where the
Communists had the initiative. Westmoreland saw Khe Sanh as an opportunity
to use his advantages against Giap's weaknesses. The Communists would have
to mass their forces to take Khe Sanh, and that would make them vulnerable
to the overwhelming firepower at Westmoreland's disposal. The American general was convinced that in such a confrontation, superior U.S. firepower would
destroy the enemy and perhaps win a decisive battle that might turn the tide
of the war.[13]

Already, Westmoreland and his senior commanders believed that the war was
moving in their favor. They seemed to be inflicting heavier casualties on the
Viet Cong, and it was almost impossible to believe that superior American technology could not eventually win a victory in Vietnam. As a result, Westmoreland
and his advisers were not prepared for simultaneous attacks against American
bases and South Vietnamese cities. They did not believe that the Viet Cong
and PAVN had such a powerful military capability, given the casualties that
they had incurred in 1966–67. Ultimately, allied intelligence had failed in its

assessment of Communist strengths and weaknesses, and Westmoreland and his staffers believed their own reports of progress, which would only add velocity to the impact of the Tet Offensive when it finally came.

On January 1, 1968, Radio Hanoi broadcast a poem written by Ho Chi Minh to mark the arrival of the Year of the Monkey, which read:

This Spring far outshines the previous Springs,
Of triumphs throughout the land come happy tidings.
Let North and South emulate each other in fighting the U.S. aggressors!
Forward!
Total victory will be ours.[14]

This was the signal that the general offensive was about to begin. Already, Viet Cong troops had occupied attack positions and infiltrated the major cities, carrying weapons that they would use during the offensive. However, the PAVN and VC forces had not been able to conceal all of their maneuvers from the Americans. Just before the battle at Dak To, a captured enemy document revealed that the attack was to be a prelude to a major PAVN offensive in Kontum province. Other intercepted enemy orders and documents told of impending attacks on Pleiku and Ban Me Thuot.

Although Westmoreland believed the Communists were preparing for a major offensive, he remained convinced that the main battle would be waged at Khe Sanh. He also thought that it would begin sometime before or just after the Tet lunar new year, because he did not believe that the Communists would violate the holiday itself. Apparently, the American commander and his staff did not pay much attention to history. In 1789, the Vietnamese had launched an attack during the Tet holiday against the Chinese troops occupying Hanoi, achieving total surprise and winning a great victory by launching a major attack when it was least expected.

Even though MACV had some indication of an impending offensive, Westmoreland risked uncovering the populated areas in an effort to take the war to the enemy, asserting that he had "no intentions of sitting back to wait the enemy's move."[15] In his mind, the best opportunity to take on the Communists and defeat them was at Khe Sanh, where all indications pointed toward a major buildup of enemy forces.

Although intelligence reports indicated the Communists were planning an offensive operation of some undetermined purpose for late 1968, Westmoreland concluded that the VC effort was probably intended as a diversion to distract allied attention from the main attack by PAVN forces that he was convinced would come at Khe Sanh. He thought that Giap hoped to annihilate a major U.S. force at Khe Sanh just as the Viet Minh had destroyed the French garrison at Dien Bien Phu in 1954. There were several other reasons why Westmoreland focused on Khe Sanh. He was convinced that the PAVN attackers would stay as close as possible to their own territory to reduce the need for long supply lines. He also thought that Giap might try to capture the entire northern part of South Vietnam and incorporate it into his own country.

OPERATION NIAGARA

In January 1968, the possibility of attack loomed larger. On the night of January 2, a Marine advance outpost to the west of the airfield at Khe Sanh spotted six men walking near them. When the Marines told the men to stop, they did not respond. The Marines opened fire, killing five of the men and wounding the sixth. This party turned out to be a PAVN regimental commander and his staff, who were apparently conducting a reconnaissance of the Marine positions. For these officers to be in the area could only mean that the PAVN were planning a major assault.

There were additional signs that there was a major PAVN buildup around Khe Sanh and the surrounding area. Marine patrols discovered fighting positions, widened trails, and even new roads. Additionally, the Special Forces at Lang Vei reported that they were picking up signs of enemy movement eastward during their long-range patrols across the border in Laos.

For Westmoreland, this was all the proof necessary to confirm his belief that Khe Sanh would be the major battle of the coming Vietnam offensive. The MACV commander hoped that the PAVN would make a heavy commitment to the assault there, after which he would hit them with overwhelming U.S. firepower. When the buildup in the Khe Sanh area became apparent, Westmoreland ordered his staff to prepare several contingency plans to deal with the situation. The first was known as Operation Checkers, a contingency plan that called for transferring up to half of the one hundred or so U.S. combat battalions in South Vietnam to the northern provinces if needed.[16] The second plan called for a massive aerial bombardment to counter the increasing threat. This plan, called Operation Niagara "to evoke an image of cascading bombs and shells," was a two-phased operation.[17] Phase I was designed to find the PAVN forces. Phase II, the most concentrated application of aerial firepower in the history of warfare, would destroy them.

Phase I of Operation Niagara began in early January with an intensive intelligence effort to pinpoint PAVN positions around Khe Sanh. U.S. Air Force, Navy, and Marine planes took aerial photographs of the Khe Sanh area, while electronic warfare aircraft listened for PAVN radio traffic. Helicopters also began to drop sophisticated sensor devices onto the ground to detect troop movements.

This included acoustic sensors to pick up voices and seismic devices to record vibrations from marching soldiers and passing trucks and tanks.

For Phase II of Operation Niagara, which would begin once the PAVN opened their attack on Khe Sanh, Westmoreland assembled an impressive armada of more than two thousand strategic and tactical aircraft, ranging from the B-52 Stratofortresses to the propeller-driven South Vietnamese A-1E Skyraiders.

As the Marines of the 26th Regiment under the command of Colonel David E. Lownds made preparations for the coming battle, so did the PAVN, who were rushing additional reinforcements to the area around Khe Sanh.[18] Intelligence reports indicated that a PAVN division was taking up positions northwest of the base, while another was operating to the southwest. In total, Communist forces surrounding Khe Sanh numbered about twenty thousand troops who would be opposed by only about a third of that number of Marines. Other intelligence reports indicated that a PAVN regiment was located inside the DMZ only ten to fifteen miles north of Khe Sanh while another PAVN division was believed to be north of the Rockpile, putting an additional twelve thousand to fourteen thousand enemy soldiers within easy reinforcing distance of the enemy units in the Khe Sanh area.

As the PAVN forces converged on Khe Sanh, the Marines continued to prepare for the coming battle. While the Marines inside Khe Sanh continued to dig additional trenches, build new bunkers, and reinforce the perimeter, additional Marine forces were positioned to control the key terrain surrounding the base.

THE SIEGE OF KHE SANH BEGINS

On 17 January, a Marine patrol was ambushed southwest of 881 North. When another patrol was sent to the same area two days later, it was also ambushed. The PAVN, using the cover of monsoon rain and mist, had quietly retaken 881 North, giving them a position on the high ground that posed an immediate threat to Marine positions elsewhere.

During the afternoon of January 20, a PAVN soldier appeared under a flag of truce at Khe Sanh and surrendered. He turned out to be Senior Lieutenant La Thanh Tonc, commander of the 14th Antiaircraft Company of the 325-C Division. Tonc revealed to the Marines that two PAVN divisions—his and the 304th—were preparing for an attack on Khe Sanh that would begin that night with the initial assault against Hills 861 and 881 South. Once these hills were taken, two PAVN regiments would attack Khe Sanh itself from the northeast and south. According to Tonc, the purpose of the campaign was to gain bargaining leverage at the negotiating table by overrunning the U.S. bases along the DMZ and then subsequently liberating Quang Tri Province. He also claimed that Giap was in the area and directing the campaign personally.[19]

The Marines were not sure whether to believe Tonc, but they went on alert anyway. Tonc's predictions were soon borne out when just after midnight on January 21, following a mortar, rocket, and rocket-propelled-grenade barrage, three hundred PAVN soldiers spearheaded by sappers using satchel charges, bangalore torpedoes, and bamboo ladders breached the perimeter wire and attacked Hill 861. They advanced up the hill, yelling and throwing grenades, and quickly penetrated the Marine defenses and captured the helicopter landing pad in fierce fighting. With supporting fire from adjacent hills, the Marines retook the hill in brutal hand-to-hand combat.

The attack on Hill 881 South that Tonc had predicted never materialized; perhaps a combination of the casualties inflicted by the Marines and the effect of the heavy artillery pounding changed the PAVN plans.

As the attack on Hill 861 wound down, the PAVN began shelling Khe Sanh Combat Base with hundreds of rockets, mortars, and artillery shells. One of the first targets to be hit was the exposed ammunition dump at the eastern end of the runway, setting off an explosion in a Marine bunker containing 1,500 tons of stored ammunition, including bombs, artillery shells, grenades, and small-arms ammunition. The blast destroyed a helicopter and swept away tents, small buildings, and even the landing lights and radio antennae around the airstrip. Another shell hit a cache of tear gas, releasing clouds of choking vapor that soon enveloped the entire base. Secondary explosions from ammunition "cooking off" in the raging fire continued for forty-eight hours. This event was covered by several reporters and cameramen and it rapidly became headline news all over the United States; the situation at Khe Sanh was soon the focus of the evening television newscasts, even after the Communists launched the full-scale Tet Offensive.

Thousands of shells were lost in the explosion of the ammo dump, more than 90 percent of Marines' ammunition. This had to be quickly replaced if the Marines in Khe Sanh were to continue to defend the area. Accordingly, U.S. Air Force C-123 and C-130 cargo aircraft began aerial resupply flights to replenish the destroyed ammunition.

As the ammo dump at Khe Sanh base exploded, hundreds of PAVN troops overran Khe Sanh village along Route 9, forcing the Marines from the Combined Action Company and the South Vietnamese Regional Forces company there to evacuate to KSCB.

After a day of intense fighting and enemy shelling, the Marines had suffered nine killed and seventy-five wounded (thirty-eight of whom were returned to duty). The PAVN had blown up the ammo dump and forced the evacuation of

Khe Sanh village, but the Marines still held Khe Sanh Combat Base and the surrounding hills.

Over the next few days, helicopters brought in a battalion of the 9th Marines and the 37th ARVN Ranger Battalion, the last reinforcements to reach the Marine base until the siege was formally lifted on April 8. The Marines now had about six thousand troops to defend against the twenty thousand to forty thousand PAVN regulars who surrounded Khe Sanh. About half the Marine infantry would be deployed outside the base on the surrounding hills; the recently arrived 1st Battalion of the 9th Marines occupied a defensive position near a rock quarry to guard the western approach to KSCB.

Thus, ten days before the Tet Offensive had formally begun, the Marines at Khe Sanh found themselves virtually surrounded by PAVN troops. When it became apparent that Khe Sanh was in danger of an imminent attack, Westmoreland initiated Operation Niagara II and ordered allied aircraft to begin pounding the PAVN forces surrounding the Marine base. Between January 22 and March 31, a total of 24,000 tactical air strikes would be flown by USAF and Marine fighter-bombers. These strikes were supplemented by 2,700 missions flown by B-52 Stratofortresses as part of Operation Arc Light.

For seventy-seven days, a desperate battle raged between the besieged Marines and the PAVN forces that surrounded them. American print journalists and television reporters covered the intense combat. Despite the obvious differences between Dien Bien Phu and Khe Sanh, the journalists could not resist the comparison. "The parallels are there for all to see," Walter Cronkite informed a CBS radio audience in early February.[20] Perhaps because of that intense coverage, President Johnson remained fixated on the battle. He had a model of the base constructed in the White House and would pore over it for hours, discussing the details with his military advisers. "I don't want any damn Dinbinphoo," he reportedly told the Joint Chiefs of Staff, making them sign a document on January 29 promising that the base could be held.[21] However, as the Marines battled for survival at Khe Sanh, Johnson was presented with a stunning new crisis when the Communists launched the Tet Offensive.

Chapter 3

THE TET OFFENSIVE

As the fighting mounted at Khe Sanh in the first part of January 1968, the Communists were making final preparations for launching the Tet Offensive. Since Tet typically brought a mutual cease-fire, Hanoi assumed that the South Vietnamese would be relaxed and unprepared for an assault. Taking advantage of the situation, the Communists smuggled men and equipment into and around South Vietnam's cities and provincial capitals. Weapons arrived in trucks loaded with flowers, vegetables, and fruit destined for the holiday celebrations. "Mourners" carried coffins filled with weapons and ammunition and buried them at pagodas and churches where they could easily be dug up later. Explosives were concealed in baskets of tomatoes and rice. Viet Cong (VC) soldiers in civilian clothes, some even dressed in South Vietnamese Army (ARVN) uniforms, mingled with crowds of South Vietnamese civilians returning to the cities for the Tet celebrations.

The commander of the VC division charged with conducting the attack on Tan Son Nhut Air Base outside Saigon personally conducted the reconnaissance for his unit's attack. One of his regimental commanders also got a look at the objective when he visited his family's gravesite at a military cemetery just outside the base.

U.S. military intelligence analysts knew that the Communists were planning some kind of spectacular attack but did not believe it would come during Tet or that it would be nationwide. One of the first indications of a change in strategy occurred at Loc Ninh in October 1967. As previously described, the Communists had attacked the district capital and, contrary to normal practice, tried to hold it, suffering terribly when allied air support and artillery drove them out. Intelligence officers were puzzled why the enemy had stood and fought, risking certain heavy losses for a meaningless objective. It would later become known that the Viet Cong had been practicing urban assault tactics.

There were other signs that something unusual was afoot. There had been a flurry of attacks in Dinh Tuong province, where traditionally the Viet Cong tested new tactics. Additionally, intelligence indicated that Communist desertion rates were down, apparently because the enemy troops had been told that victory was near and that the entire country would soon be liberated.

In late November, the CIA station in Saigon compiled all the various intelligence indicators and published a report called "the Big Gamble." This was not really a formal intelligence estimate or even a prediction, but rather "a collection of scraps" that concluded that the Communists were changing their strategy.[1] At first, intelligence analysts at Military Assistance Command, Vietnam (MACV) disagreed with the CIA's assessment, because at the time the command was reducing its estimate of enemy capabilities as part of the effort to show progress in the war.[2]

As more intelligence poured in, MACV commander General William Westmoreland and his staff also came to the conclusion that a major countrywide effort was probable. All the signs pointed to a new major offensive. Still, Westmoreland did not anticipate heavy attacks on cities and towns. On the contrary, he had repositioned forces away from the populated areas to conduct operations along the border with Laos and Cambodia, where he thought the main enemy threat lay.

On December 18, General Earle Wheeler, chairman of the Joint Chiefs of Staff, warned the American public that "there may be a Communist thrust similar to the desperate effort of the Germans in the Battle of the Bulge."[3] President Johnson himself indicated that he was aware that the Communists were planning something unusual when he told the Australian cabinet at Canberra, where he had traveled for the funeral of Prime Minister Harold Holt, that "kamikaze" attacks were expected in Vietnam.[4]

Despite concerns about a potential Communist offensive, the Johnson administration chose not to take any extra measures to prepare the American people for the coming blow. Having spent the previous months trying to convince the public that progress was being made in the war, Johnson was less than enthusiastic about alarming the people. His administration insisted in continuing to paint a rosy picture—and this played right into Giap's hands.

Just before Christmas 1967, intelligence reports indicated a 200 percent increase in truck traffic on the Ho Chi Minh Trail in Laos. The reports were determined to be credible and, together with the other mounting evidence, convinced Westmoreland and his staff that something unusual was afoot. They apparently had no idea that the Communists had the capability to launch such a widespread attack. While predicting that the enemy was planning a major effort to win a spectacular success on the battlefield, Westmoreland, like Johnson, made no deliberate effort to alert the press and the American public for what might be coming. Failing to do so only increased the shock of the enemy offensive once it began.

The indications that the enemy was planning something big continued to pile up. On January 4, 1968, U.S. troops in the Central Highlands captured a document entitled Operation Order No. 1, which called for an attack against Pleiku prior to Tet. A few days later, ARVN soldiers captured a similar order for an assault on Ban Me Thuot, although no date was specified.

Westmoreland became sufficiently alarmed by the situation developing at Khe Sanh and the new intelligence indicators to request that the South Vietnamese cancel the coming Tet cease-fire countrywide. On January 8, the chief of the South Vietnamese Joint General Staff (JGS), General Cao Van Vien, told Westmoreland that he would try to limit the truce to twenty-four hours. South Vietnamese President Nguyen Van Thieu argued that to cancel the forty-eight-hour truce would adversely affect the morale of his troops and the South Vietnamese people. However, he agreed to limit the cease-fire to thirty-six hours, beginning on the evening of January 29.

In mid-January, the 101st Airborne Division captured plans for an attack on the city of Phu Cuong. Because the Communists compartmentalized their plans, there was no mention in the captured documents about a nationwide offensive, and countermeasures were left to local U.S. commanders. Still, there were now many indications that an offensive of unusual proportions was in the offing. There would soon be more.

On January 28, South Vietnamese Military Security Service agents arrested eleven VC cadres in Qui Nhon. The Viet Cong had in their possession two audiotapes containing an appeal to the local population to take up arms against the Saigon government and an announcement that Saigon, Hue, and other South Vietnamese cities had already been liberated.

Toward the end of January, the government of North Vietnam made a strange announcement. Citing an auspicious conjunction of the moon, the earth, and the sun, the government decreed that the Tet holiday would begin not on January 30, as indicated by the lunar calendar, but on January 29 instead. Hanoi, the allies later learned, wanted its people to be able to celebrate Tet before the general offensive was launched.

In the South, the change in the North Vietnamese holiday schedule went unnoticed. By this time in late January, both Westmoreland and the White House were preoccupied with the developing situation at Khe Sanh. Westmoreland remained convinced that the PAVN buildup in the area presaged a Communist attempt to take the northernmost provinces. Accordingly, Westmoreland ordered the U.S. 1st Cavalry Division from the Central Highlands to Phu Bai just south of Hue. Additionally, he sent one brigade of the 101st Airborne Division to I Corps to strengthen the defense of the two northernmost provinces. By the end of January, more than half of all U.S. combat maneuver battalions were located in the I Corps area, ready to meet any new threat.

Not everyone in the U.S. military high command was focused on Khe Sanh. Lieutenant General Frederick C. Weyand commanded the American field forces in III Corps Tactical Zone and was charged with defending the approaches to Saigon. He had fifty-three combat maneuver battalions, most of which had been operating against enemy bases along the Cambodian border in the latter months of 1967.[5] When contact with the Viet Cong in these areas dropped off in December, Weyand became alarmed at the seemingly incoherent pattern of enemy activity and telephoned Westmoreland on January 10 to explain his concern and recommend that forces return from the border. The MACV commander agreed, and fifteen combat battalions were ordered to reposition nearer to Saigon.

When the Communists struck, the number of American battalions within the urban zone had risen to twenty-seven. Their presence made a tremendous difference in the fighting to follow and may have saved the capital city. Although Westmoreland had approved strengthening Saigon's defenses, his attention remained on northern South Vietnam, and not much else was done to strengthen other cities and towns.

The intelligence picture was further clouded on January 30 between midnight and 3:00 a.m., when VC forces apparently launched the offensive prematurely when they attacked eight towns and cities along the coast and in the Central Highlands. A ground attack in battalion strength hit the port of Nha Trang; another struck Hoi An, a district capital near the coast. Mortar and rocket fire preceded a ground attack by two thousand enemy soldiers on the Highlands town of Ban Me Thuot. Farther north, the Viet Cong launched a sapper attack against the headquarters of ARVN I Corps in Da Nang. Additional attacks were made on Kontum, Pleiku, and Qui Nhon.

According to General Tran Van Tra, Giap had called for the offensive to start on "the first day of the Lunar New Year." Apparently there were two different calendars in use: an older version being used in the south and a newer one in the northern areas. Using the older calendar, the lunar new year fell on January 31, but on the newer calendar, it fell on January 30. This "threw off the timing of the opening attacks."[6] Apparently, the fog and friction of war applied to the Communist side as well as to the allied forces.

The premature attacks were not coordinated well, and by daylight all Communist forces had been driven from their objectives. No other towns or cities in South Vietnam were attacked that night. After daylight on January 30, President Thieu, at the urging of General William Westmoreland, canceled the cease-fire throughout the country and alerted all South Vietnamese military units. However, it was too late to call back those ARVN soldiers already on leave, and word of the cancellation of the truce failed to reach many South Vietnamese units until it was too late.

Although the premature attacks provided a warning of the impending offensive and troops were put on alert, few people expected the widespread assaults that followed the next day. However, Brigadier General Philip Davidson, chief of MACV intelligence, looked at the reports and warned Westmoreland, "This is going to happen in the rest of the country tonight or tomorrow morning."[7] The American commander immediately put his forces on alert, but he did not order any change to troop dispositions. Since they had been on alert many times before, most American troops were not prepared for the storm about to break upon them. For Westmoreland, the attacks on January 30 only served to confirm in his mind that the main enemy effort was focused on Khe Sanh. He would soon be proved wrong.

Thus, the premature attacks, the change in alert status and cancellation of the truce had only mixed results. Some ARVN commanders responded with appropriate precautionary measures, but others responded hardly at all. Most American and South Vietnamese commanders thought it was simply out of the question that the Communists would try to capture the cities and towns. Consequently, when the offensive was finally launched, the surprise was almost total.

THE OFFENSIVE BEGINS

The Tet Offensive began in full force shortly before 3:00 a.m. on January 31. More than eighty thousand Communist troops—a mixture of PAVN regulars and VC main-force guerrillas—began a coordinated attack throughout South Vietnam.[8] The PAVN and Viet Cong targeted more than three-quarters of the provincial capitals and most of the major cities (see Map 3). In the north, Communist forces struck Quang Tri, Tam Ky, and Hue, as well as the U.S. military bases at Phu Bai and Chu Lai. In the center of the country, they followed up the previous evening's attacks and launched new ones at Tuy Hoa, Phan Thiet, and the American installations at Bong Song and An Khe. In III Corps Tactical Zone, the primary Communist thrust was at Saigon itself, but there were other attacks against the ARVN corps headquarters at Bien Hoa and the U.S. II Field Force headquarters at Long Binh. In the Mekong Delta, the Viet Cong struck Vinh Long, My Tho, Can Tho, Dinh Tuong, Kien Tuong, Go Cong, and Ben Tre, as well as virtually every other provincial capital in the region. The Communist forces mortared or rocketed every major allied airfield and attacked sixty-four district capitals and scores of lesser towns.

Although the attacks varied in size and scope, they generally followed the same pattern. They began with a barrage of mortar and rocket fire, followed closely thereafter by a ground assault spearheaded by sappers, who penetrated the defensive perimeter. Once inside the cities, the commandos linked up with troops who had previously infiltrated and with local sympathizers, who often acted as guides. Main force units, which quickly seized predetermined targets, followed. They were usually accompanied by propaganda teams that tried to convince the local populace to rise up against the Saigon government. The attackers were both skillful and determined and had rehearsed their attacks beforehand.

The scope of the Tet Offensive was stunning; everywhere there was confusion, shock, dismay, and disbelief on the part of the allies. The carefully coordinated attacks, as journalist Stanley Karnow writes, "exploded around the country like a string of firecrackers."[9] U.S. intelligence had already gathered some information of infiltration into southern population centers and captured documents that outlined the general plan. However, Westmoreland and his intelligence staff were so convinced that Khe Sanh was the real target and that the enemy was incapable of conducting an offensive on such a massive scale that they viewed the captured documents as a diversionary tactic. "Even had I known exactly what was to take place," Westmoreland's intelligence officer later conceded, "it was so preposterous that I probably would have been unable to sell it to anybody."[10] Westmoreland, himself, later admitted that he had not anticipated the "true nature or the scope" of the attacks.[11] Consequently, the U.S. high command had seriously underestimated the enemy's potential for a major nationwide offensive, and the allies were almost overwhelmed initially by the audacity, scale, and intensity of the attacks.

THE BATTLE FOR SAIGON

Some of the bitterest fighting of the Tet Offensive took place in Saigon, which had not seen much combat during the war before 1968. It was the site of a large American air base at Tan Son Nhut, and there were more than 130 U.S. installations in the greater Saigon area. However, because of South Vietnamese sensitivities toward a large American presence in Saigon, the overall defense of the city itself had been turned over to the ARVN, and the installations were guarded only by a thousand-man U.S. military police battalion. Despite the change in alert status, only about one-third of the MPs were at their posts when the Viet Cong struck. The city was protected by a large contingent of ARVN solders and about seventeen thousand South Vietnamese police who patrolled the city streets.

Saigon, a teeming city of more than two million people, had become a safe haven for Vietnamese refugees fleeing the war in the countryside. As more and more people came to the city, its population swelled to nearly three million. Although there was not enough work for all the refugees, at least they had escaped the destructive war that had laid waste to so much of the country. However, the Tet Offensive would soon demonstrate to all South Vietnamese that no area of their country was safe from the Communists.

The plan for the attack on Saigon called for thirty-five battalions to hit six primary targets in the capital city (see Map 4). These objectives included the headquarters of the South Vietnamese Joint General Staff; Independence Palace, which served as President Thieu's office; the American embassy; Tan Son Nhut Air Base; the Vietnamese Navy headquarters; and the national broadcasting station.

During the early morning hours of January 31, the attack on Saigon began from several different directions, with eleven battalions comprising more than four thousand troops focusing on the city's urban center. Prepared by battle-hardened PAVN General Tran Do, the battle plan called for the main force guerrillas to link up with local force troops who had already infiltrated the city in the days just before Tet. Together they were to attack key positions in the city center while other forces from elements of three VC divisions launched simultaneous assaults on the American bases just outside the city to prevent U.S. reinforcements from entering the city. Guided by about 250 men and women from the C-10 Saigon Sapper Battalion, who normally operated in and around Saigon, the initial wave of Communist troops were to seize and hold their objectives for forty-eight hours until additional forces arrived to reinforce them.[12]

Shortly before 3:00 a.m., a small convoy of jeeps and sedans arrived at the government radio station. A group of about twenty armed men dressed in South Vietnamese riot police uniforms dismounted the vehicles, while their leader explained to the guard that reinforcements had arrived. When the guard protested that he knew nothing about reinforcements, they shot him and broke into the station under covering fire from a nearby apartment building. The Communists had prepared a series of audiotapes to be broadcast over the radio throughout South Vietnam, announcing that Saigon had fallen and urging that the people rise up and throw out the government. By controlling the radio station, the Viet Cong hoped to seize the propaganda initiative and motivate the South Vietnamese people to rally to their side.

However, the VC plans were quickly foiled. The ARVN lieutenant colonel in charge of the station had made preparations to take the station off the air if it was ever attacked. As the Viet Cong began their assault, a technician at the station radioed to a transmitting tower several miles away that all communications wires should be cut with Saigon.[13] Without any connection to the tower, radio broadcasts were impossible. Upon realizing what had happened, the sappers destroyed the radio equipment and prepared to defend the building as they waited for reinforcements that were supposed to join them. A company of ARVN paratroopers arrived, and a pitched battle ensued. The Viet Cong held out for six hours before they were all killed; the relief force never showed up.

As the battle for the radio station raged, another contingent of thirty-four sappers from the VC C-10 Battalion wearing ARVN uniforms attacked Independence Palace on Nguyen Du Street. Arriving at 1:30 a.m., they blasted the gates with B-40 rockets, but as the Viet Cong tried to rush through the breach, they were immediately struck with a hail of fire from the defenders inside the palace grounds. The palace security force, comprising the palace guard, national and military police, and two tanks, were too strong for the attackers, who retreated to a nearby apartment building. During the next two days, they tried to hold off ARVN soldiers and American MPs in a desperate last-ditch stand while American TV cameras recorded the action. In the end, all the Viet Cong were killed or captured.

At the Vietnamese Navy headquarters, the Communist plan was to capture both the headquarters and nearby docked ships. The ships would then be used to transport people from rural areas in the Mekong Delta and along the coast to Saigon to participate in the general uprising. The plan rapidly went awry. Twelve VC sappers blew a hole in the security wall but met stiff resistance from the South Vietnamese defenders. Within five minutes, ten of the sappers were dead. As in the other attacks, the attackers had been told to seize and hold their objective while waiting for reinforcements; but, as in most cases, there were no reinforcements and these attacks became suicide missions.

The Viet Cong ran into similar trouble at the compound housing the Armored Command and Artillery Command headquarters on the northern edge of the city. The Communists planned to capture the ARVN tanks and artillery and use them during the remainder of the offensive. However, they soon found out that the tanks had been moved to another base and that the breech locks had been removed from the artillery pieces, rendering them useless.

The attack against the JGS compound began at 2:00 a.m., when VC sappers attacked the ARVN guards on one of the main gates. Additional American MPs arrived on the scene, and the initial VC assault collapsed. The original plan had called for a local force unit to attack one of the other compound gates at the same time, but this unit was delayed en route to their attack position. Nevertheless, when they arrived, they were able to penetrate the weak and disorganized ARVN defenses at that location and get inside the compound. Rather than overrun the entire nerve center of the South Vietnamese armed forces, they dug in and waited for reinforcements. Eventually, ARVN airborne and marine units rooted the Viet Cong out of the compound.

THE BATTLE AT THE U.S. EMBASSY

The most spectacular attack in Saigon was launched against the U.S. embassy in Saigon, located on Thong Nhat Boulevard only a few blocks from the Presidential Palace and the downtown hotels where American reporters and television cameramen were quartered. The embassy, a $2.6 million, six-floor building just opened in September 1967, was the symbol of American power and presence in Vietnam. It was at the center of a fortified compound that covered over four acres and was enclosed by an eight-foot-high wall.

At 2:45 a.m. on January 31, a squad of nineteen VC sappers attacked the embassy. The commandoes had secretly moved weapons and explosives into the city from their base near a rubber plantation thirty miles to the north, concealing the shipments in truckloads of rice and vegetables.

The sappers used a satchel charge to blow a three-foot hole in the compound's outer walls, and then their lieutenant led the way through the breach. The MP guards opened up on the Viet Cong as they came through the hole in the wall, killing the platoon leader and several of his soldiers before they themselves were killed in a hail of return fire from the surviving VC soldiers.

Once inside the compound, the leaderless Viet Cong failed to exploit their initial success. Without orders, they milled around in apparent confusion before taking cover behind some oversized flower tubs. They missed their prime chance, because the embassy building itself was virtually theirs for the taking. The Viet Cong were soon embroiled in a six-hour-long standoff with the guards and military policemen who rushed to the embassy. With the arrival of additional reinforcements from the 101st Airborne Division, who landed by helicopter on the roof of the chancery, the Viet Cong were all killed or captured, and the security of the embassy was reestablished. During the fighting, five Americans were killed.

The Viet Cong never made it inside the main embassy building, but it was left pockmarked by rocket and machine gun fire. The Great Seal of the United States, which had hung over the front door, was blasted by enemy fire and fell to the ground. Although they had only caused minor damage to the embassy and all of them had been wiped out by 3:00 a.m., this small squad of VC sappers had proven in dramatic fashion that there was no place in Vietnam that was secure from attack.

The U.S. media focused on the dramatic assault on the embassy. Reporters and cameramen rushed to the scene immediately, drawn by the pitched gun battle between the U.S. guards and the VC sappers. Confused by the gunfire and darkness, the reporters concluded that the Viet Cong had penetrated the chancery. An AP reporter sent a bulletin saying that the embassy building itself had been taken by the enemy troops. This erroneous report went swiftly over the wire to the United States, where it arrived just before the first-edition deadlines for many influential morning newspapers on the East Coast. The glaring headlines spread the shocking message that the Communists had captured the symbol of American prestige in Saigon. The front-page photograph on the *New York Times* February 1 edition showed three military policemen, rifles in hand, seeking protection behind a wall outside the consular section of the embassy while the bodies of two American soldiers slain by the guerrillas lay nearby. Walter Cronkite, dean of American news broadcasters, is reported to have said, "What the hell is going on? I thought we were winning this war!"[14]

Soon thereafter, photos and film of the fighting on the embassy grounds appeared on the American television evening news programs. The vivid images of dead bodies amid the rubble and dazed American soldiers and civilians dashing back and forth as they tried to flush out the sappers sent shock waves across the United States. The spectacle of U.S. troops storming their own embassy to oust the guerrilla fighters stunned Americans on the home front.

In Saigon, reporters swarmed the grounds of the embassy as military spokesmen tried to explain what had happened. The key question was whether the Viet Cong had actually entered the chancery. Although they clearly had not, AP stood by its claim. Over the years, a confrontational relationship had developed between the military and the press when official pronouncements were often found to be misleading or totally false. This situation came to a head over the issue of the embassy attack.

At 9:20 a.m., Westmoreland arrived at the just-secured embassy compound and held an impromptu press conference. Dressed in starched fatigues, he toured the building with reporters and assured them that no Viet Cong had entered the chancery, exuding an air of extreme confidence. He confidently proclaimed that "the enemy's well-laid plans went afoul."[15] The reporters were stunned. A *Washington Post* writer recalls, "The reporters could hardly believe their ears. Westmoreland was standing in the ruins and saying everything was great."[16] Meanwhile, news was cascading in of VC attacks all over South Vietnam. This situation widened the "credibility gap" almost to the breaking point. Several reporters continued to quote "other sources" denying Westmoreland's assertion that the embassy chancery had not been breached. When the American public read the morning newspapers and watched the evening news, it received two impressions: the Viet Cong had seized the embassy itself, and Westmoreland was lying when he said they had not. While Westmoreland tried to assure them that things were going well for the allies, the American people could see for themselves the carnage wrought by the fighting in Saigon and elsewhere around the country. The severe psychological damage done by these juxtaposed images to the American war effort would not become apparent until later.

The coverage of the embassy attack, coupled with that of the as-yet-unresolved siege of Khe Sanh, gave the false impression that Saigon had been completely overrun and that the whole allied position in South Vietnam was falling apart. Though the attack on the embassy had failed, Communist forces had penetrated to the very heart of American power in South Vietnam, indicating that the war there was much more serious than expected and that U.S. boasts of imminent victory were misguided at best and calculated lies at worst. If the United States could not even protect its own embassy, how could the war have reached a point, as Westmoreland had claimed, "when the end begins to come into view"?[17]

Elsewhere, chaos reigned as fighting broke out all over the city. Small VC squads fanned out and attacked numerous officers' and enlisted men's billets, the homes of ARVN officers, and district police stations. Other groups, carrying "blacklists" bearing the names of ARVN officers, civil servants, and others connected with the Saigon government, conducted house-to-house searches through residential quarters of the city. One civilian witness recalled, "They guarded the street, checked houses and ID cards, and forbade us to leave. Soldiers on leave were arrested and shot on the spot. . . . Ordinary people weren't arrested, but weren't allowed to leave the area."[18]

The Viet Cong conducted ritual burnings of the South Vietnamese flag and held "people's courts" to decide the fate of suspected "traitors." Some of those who were rounded up were shot. By dawn, the Viet Cong had made major penetrations into western and southern Saigon and controlled large areas in the suburb of Cholon.

Brutality begat brutality. On February 1, early in the fight for Saigon, South Vietnamese police captured a Viet Cong soldier in civilian clothes and dragged him before General Nguyen Ngoc Loan, chief of the national police force.[19] The general put a revolver to the man's head and fired. Loan turned to the reporters standing a few feet behind him. "They killed many Americans and many of my men," he said quietly in English. "Buddha will understand. Do you?"[20]

The entire episode, including the man falling to the street with blood spurting from his head, was captured by Eddie Adams, an AP photographer, and Vo

Suu, an NBC television cameraman. The next morning the photograph of the execution dominated the front page of American newspapers; that evening the video tape footage was broadcast on NBC television news. Many Americans were horrified. Former Ambassador to the United States Bui Diem described the situation best in his memoirs when he said that images like this "crystallized the war's brutality without providing a context within which to understand the events they depicted."[21] While that is no doubt true, the impact of this photo and film footage along with the rest of the coverage of the offensive was explosive.

Secretary of State Dean Rusk was furious after watching the NBC news broadcast. "Whose side are you on?" he demanded of the newsmen a few days later, adding, "I don't know why people have to be probing for the things that one can bitch about, when there are two thousand stories on the same day about things that are more constructive."[22]

ATTACKS AROUND THE CITY

Although the fighting in the capital city was spectacular, Saigon was never in danger of falling. The "savior of Saigon," Lieutenant General Fred C. Weyand, commander of II Field Force Vietnam, the corps-level headquarters at nearby Long Binh, was responsible for the defense of the area surrounding Saigon and reacted quickly once the Communist launched their attack on the city.

As previously described, Weyand had sensed in early January that something was afoot. Accordingly, he asked for and got permission to pull his combat forces back from the border areas to within a twenty-eight-mile zone surrounding the city. At his disposal in II Field Force, Weyand had fifty-three maneuver battalions (infantry, armor, and armored cavalry) from four U.S. divisions and two separate brigade-size units. Against his forces were arrayed thirty-five VC and PAVN battalions in the initial assault. As eleven VC battalions attacked Saigon directly, a VC division attacked the supply depots, ammunition dumps, and military headquarters at Long Binh and the nearby U.S. air base at Bien Hoa. A PAVN division blocked the roads to the north and northwest of the city, while three VC battalions attacked the airfield at Tan Son Nhut.

At his headquarters, which was under rocket and ground attack, Weyand tried to make sense of the situation. The map showing the reported attacks around Saigon reminded him of "a pinball machine, one light after another going on as it was hit."[23] Between 3:00 and 5:00 a.m., he shifted some five thousand mechanized and airborne troops to defend the various installations under attack.

The assault on Tan Son Nhut Air Base, just north of the city, was one of the largest actions in the Saigon area. Site of the headquarters of both U.S. Military

Assistance Command Vietnam and the U.S. 7th Air Force, Tan Son Nhut was especially critical to the Viet Cong plans because not only was it the nerve center of the U.S. command, but high-ranking South Vietnamese officials also lived in the area. Around 3:00 a.m. a heavy barrage of rocket and mortar fire hit the air base. Following the barrage, three VC battalions simultaneously assaulted the perimeter from the west, north, and east. They quickly overran an ARVN guard post and penetrated the base. The American command had been caught off guard, and most of the American soldiers, including senior staff, were not even armed. An ARVN airborne battalion, which had been waiting in the terminal for transport to I Corps, took up the fight against the Communists. When the firing broke out, they reacted quickly to block further penetration of the perimeter in that sector.

American officers also joined in the fighting, and the struggle was desperate as the battle raged across the airfield. Meanwhile, an armored relief column rushed from its base at nearby Cu Chi. Arriving at 6:00 a.m., the tanks and armored personnel carriers tanks attacked the Viet Cong from the rear, forcing them to retreat to a textile mill on the outskirts of the base. Allied jets and helicopter gunships pounded the mill, but the Viet Cong stood and fought tenaciously, holding out to the last man.

Fifteen miles north of Saigon was the Long Binh logistical and command complex. This sprawling base, which extended to the enormous Bien Hoa Air Base, was critical to the American war effort and thus provided a lucrative target for the Communist planners. At 3:00 a.m., an intense rocket and mortar barrage pounded the area as soldiers from a VC division prepared to launch the attack. When the signal was given, the veteran VC fighters assaulted the northern perimeter of Long Binh while a local VC battalion launched a diversionary attack against the eastern bunker line. Meanwhile, VC sappers infiltrated the huge ammunition dump just north of Long Binh while another VC regiment attacked the air base and III Corps headquarters at Bien Hoa.

Elsewhere in III Corps Tactical Zone, elements of a PAVN division hit Lai Khe, the headquarters of both the U.S. 1st Infantry Division and the ARVN 5th Division. Meanwhile, troops from a VC division struck the headquarters of the U.S. 25th Division at Cu Chi. These forces were to interdict allied lines of communication and block potential allied reinforcements from the outlying U.S. divisions from reaching Saigon.

Weyand responded to the threat in the Bien Hoa–Long Binh complex by ordering U.S. reinforcements by helicopter and land to relieve the defenders there (see Map 5). The ground relief column had to fight its way through the VC roadblocks. The Americans took heavy losses but were ultimately successful in breaking through the roadblocks and repelling the VC attackers in Bien Hoa. In this action, the Americans were surprised that the Viet Cong stood and fought, rather than withdraw as they had usually done in the past.

THE BATTLE OF CHOLON

Meanwhile, the fighting inside the capital city continued to rage. By this time, the Communist high command had introduced as many as fifteen battalions into the Saigon area. A pitched battle developed in the Phu Tho racetrack area in Cholon, the southwestern suburb of Saigon. A VC battalion had seized the racetrack during the opening hours of the offensive. The racetrack was a strategic location that sat at the hub of several major roads and provided an easily recognizable rallying place for rural VC troops unfamiliar with Saigon. Control of the racetrack itself also denied the allies a potential landing zone for helicopters bringing in additional troops and supplies. Weyand ordered U.S. reinforcements into the area, and bitter fighting ensued for control of the area.

In the fighting in Saigon and the surrounding areas, the Viet Cong used the element of surprise to make initial gains, but they were unable to hold their objectives owing to the quick reaction of powerful U.S. and ARVN forces. Within a few days, allied troops had defeated most of the Communist forces in the Saigon area, but heavy fighting continued for several more days in Cholon. It was a bitter fight that included several large-scale VC counterattacks. Eventually, every VC unit that participated in the Saigon offensive contributed manpower to the battle for the racetrack.

From the roof of the Caravelle Hotel in central Saigon, war correspondents watched the dramatic battle for Cholon unfold. Every night after dinner, the scene was illuminated by the fires burning in Cholon and tracer bullets fired by American gunships hovering over enemy positions. On February 4, residents of Cholon were asked to leave their homes, and the area was declared a free fire zone. U.S. jets subsequently pounded VC positions in and around the racetrack area. A large part of Cholon was devastated by the air strikes, but the Viet Cong, by this time largely leaderless and lacking instructions, still held tenaciously to their positions. Finally, on February 10, troops from an American light infantry brigade destroyed the remaining Viet Cong holdouts. Sporadic fighting continued, but by March 7, the battle for Saigon would be over.

TET COUNTRYWIDE

Saigon was only one objective in the overall Communist plan. As fighting erupted and increased in intensity in and around the capital city, it seemed as if the rest of South Vietnam was also in danger of falling to the Communists. It soon became clear that the Communists had launched a major countrywide offensive involving eighty thousand men, mainly Viet Cong, except in the northern provinces, where PAVN regulars predominated. Communist troops captured Hue and intense battles raged for Quang Tri in the north; Dalat, Kontum, Pleiku, and Ban Me Thuot in the Central Highlands; and Can Tho, My Tho, Soc Trang, and Ben Tre in the Delta. The Communists even rocketed the huge American base at Cam Ranh Bay. They also seized control of scores of district capitals, disrupting the Saigon regime's pacification program.

In Da Nang, South Vietnam's second-largest city, the Communist attack resembled the initial moves in the battle for Saigon. The first assault wave utilized local VC units, sappers, and in-place agents, targeting headquarters and training and logistics bases. As in Saigon, the Communists achieved total surprise, even though a police agent who had infiltrated the local VC organization warned of the coming attack. A reinforced company briefly penetrated the headquarters of the South Vietnamese I Corps on the outskirts of the city, but eventually the South Vietnamese soldiers prevailed and the attack on Da Nang failed.

Fierce fighting also took place in the twelve provinces in II Corps Tactical Zone. Major ground attacks struck seven provincial capitals and three other objectives. Nha Trang was the first city to be attacked in the II Corps area. Just after midnight on January 31, elements of five sapper companies supported by mortar and recoilless rifle teams attacked the Naval Training Center and several targets within the city itself. ARVN Rangers and U.S. Special Forces detachments located in the area reacted quickly and regained control of the city within twelve hours.

At Qui Nhon, a coastal city in II Corps area, the ARVN defenders discovered the Communist plan before the attack began when they captured eleven VC agents. However, the situation was so muddled that the ARVN failed to make any special preparations and the Communist sappers attacked exactly as the captured plan had revealed and still seized their objectives.

In Ban Me Thuot in the Central Highlands, the ARVN division headquarters there also had advance warning when they captured a plan for an attack on the city on January 20. The divisional commander accordingly cancelled his troops' leave and put them on alert. When the PAVN regiment attacked, the South Vietnamese soldiers were ready. The bitter fighting lasted for nine hours, with the city center changing hands four times before the ARVN regained control.

At Dalat, a mountain resort in II ARVN Corps area and also the site of the Vietnamese National Military Academy, VC troops crashed past weak outposts to occupy the southwestern sector of the town. The deputy province chief, leading two regional force security companies and a company of freshman cadets from the military academy, held out against the original VC battalion and one that came to reinforce their comrades.

In the Mekong Delta region, where the Viet Cong attacked thirteen of sixteen provincial cities, the ARVN leadership was less than effective. When the attack struck there, the major general commanding IV Corps did not emerge from his fortified command post for days, leaving the conduct of the defense to his American advisers. Similarly, the ARVN colonel commanding at Vinh Long cracked under the stress of the situation. Another provincial adviser found his province chief wearing civilian clothes under his military uniform—just in case he had to make a quick escape.

Much of the fighting in the Delta fell to the Americans. The Mobile Riverine Force (MRF) was a special American brigade-sized organization equipped to operate in the unique combat environment that prevailed in the Mekong Delta, which was characterized by a vast network of rivers, canals, and rice paddies. The MRF was a joint Army/Navy force consisting of improvised vessels and weapons tailored for the nature of the operational area. Built around a brigade of the 9th Infantry Division and the Navy's River Assault Flotilla 1, the MRF was equipped with specially designed watercraft, including armored troop carriers, barracks ships, gunboats, and sixty-foot-long "monitors" armed with a revolving armored turret housing a 40mm cannon intended for close fire support.

The first attack in the delta came at My Tho, south of Saigon. Three VC battalions and a sapper company had entered the city while one battalion remained on the outskirts. Two MRF battalions rushed to the city to reinforce the units of the embattled 7th ARVN Division. It took three days to recapture My Tho. The battle featured bitter house-to-house fighting, a type of combat far different from the MRF's normal mission and one unsuited to its special weaponry. Nevertheless, the MRF helped secure the city and then rushed off to other threatened positions.

The fighting in the delta was intense and resulted in severe damage to the cities and towns where it occurred. A perfect example of this can be seen in the results of the attack on Ben Tre, a Mekong Delta river city. A reinforced VC regiment numbering about 2,500 men attacked and gained a foothold within the city. To evict the Communists, the Allies had to employ artillery and air strikes, causing extensive damage to the city and producing one of the more unfortunate, but memorable, quotes of the war. While explaining what had taken place, it was reported that an American major said, "It became necessary to destroy the town to save it."[24] In *Reporting Vietnam*, William Hammond observes, "The *New York Times* seized upon the remark as soon as it appeared. So did *Time*. From there it passed into the lore of the war to become one of the most serviceable icons of the antiwar movement."[25] To many, the quote epitomized the seeming futility of the war and the devastation that it wrought. Along with Westmoreland's "light at the end of the tunnel," it turned out to be one of the war's best-remembered phrases.

Day after day and week after week, the Tet Offensive continued to dominate the headlines. The U.S. and South Vietnamese forces had to fight city by city to dislodge the Communist troops. Although the Communists had taken the Americans and North Vietnamese by surprise, their attacks were not as well coordinated as they might have been. Overcoming their initial surprise, the allied forces reacted reasonably quickly in most cases, permitting little time for the attacking forces to establish solid defensive positions. ARVN fought more effectively than most Americans had expected. Generally, the Communists were unsuccessful in maintaining their positions in the cities for very long, and South Vietnamese and U.S. troops inflicted heavy casualties and took many prisoners. Nevertheless, the resolute VC and PAVN troops fought hard and made it difficult for the allied forces.

Despite heavy fighting at some places, in general, the Communist offensive seemed to run out of steam by the end of the first week in February. In most cases, allied control was regained in less than a week and Communist forces were driven out of most of the cities with a few days, with the exceptions being Cholon in Saigon and Hue, the current and ancient capitals of South Vietnam.

Some of the fiercest fighting of the Tet Offensive, and the war, took place in the battle to recapture the old imperial city of Hue, which until 1968 was arguably the most beautiful city in South Vietnam. Two PAVN regiments infiltrated the city before Tet; with support from other PAVN troops stationed outside, they seized control on January 31. By the second week in February, with the fighting beginning to wind down elsewhere, U.S. attention turned to the north, where U.S. Marines found themselves confronted with retaking Hue while at the same time holding off the PAVN at Khe Sanh.

Chapter 4

THE BATTLE FOR HUE

The longest and bloodiest battle of the Tet Offensive occurred in Hue, the most venerated place in Vietnam. The city, six miles (10 km) west of the South China Sea coast and sixty miles (100 km) south of the demilitarized zone (DMZ), was the capital of Thua Thien Province and South Vietnam's third-largest city, with a wartime population of 140,000. Hue was the old imperial capital and served as the cultural and intellectual center of Vietnam. It had been treated almost as an open city by both sides and thus had remained remarkably free of war. Although there had been sporadic mortar and rocket attacks in the area, Hue itself had been relatively peaceful and secure before 1968.

Hue was one of the keys to the northern provinces of South Vietnam. The city sits astride Highway 1, which in 1968 was one of the main land supply routes for the allied troops occupying positions along the DMZ to the north; the city also served as a major unloading point for waterborne supplies that were brought inland via the river from the coast.

Hue was really two cities divided by the Song Huong, or Perfume River, which flowed through the city from the southwest to the northeast on its way to the sea. Two-thirds of the city's population lived north of the river within the walls of the Old City, or Citadel, a picturesque place of gardens, pagodas, moats, and intricate stone buildings. Just outside the walls of the Citadel to the east was the densely populated residential district of Gia Hoi.

Once the residence of the Annamese emperors who had ruled the central portion of present-day Vietnam, the Citadel covered three square miles and was protected by an outer wall thirty feet high and up to forty feet thick, which formed a square about 2,700 yards on each side. Three sides were straight, while the fourth was rounded slightly to follow the curve of the river. The three walls not bordering the river were encircled by a zigzag moat that was ninety feet wide at many points and up to twelve feet deep. Many areas of the wall were honeycombed with bunkers and tunnels that had been constructed by the Japanese when they occupied the city during World War II.

The Citadel included block after block of row houses, parks, villas, and shops, along with various other buildings and an airstrip. Within the Citadel was another enclave, the Imperial Palace compound, where the emperors had held court until 1883, when the French took control of Vietnam. Located at the south end of the Citadel, the palace had twenty-foot high walls that measured 765 yards per side. The Citadel and the Imperial Palace were, as one observer put it, a "camera-toting tourist's dream," but would prove to be "a rifle-toting infantryman's nightmare."[1]

South of the river and linked to the Citadel by the six-span Nguyen Hoang Bridge, over which Route 1 passed, lay the modern part of the city, which was about half the size of the Citadel and in which resided about a third of the city's population. The southern half of Hue contained the hospital, the provincial prison, the cathedral, and many of the city's modern structures, including government administrative buildings, the U.S. Consulate, Hue University, the city's high school, and the newer residential districts.

The South Vietnamese Army (ARVN) 1st Infantry Division was headquartered in Hue. The division headquarters was located at the northwest corner of the Citadel in a fortified compound, but most of its combat units were outside the city, spread out along Highway 1 north of Hue toward the DMZ. The only combat element in the city was the division's Hac Bao Company, known as the "Black Panthers," an elite all-volunteer unit that served as the division reconnaissance and rapid reaction force. Security within the city itself was primarily the responsibility of the National Police.

The only U.S. military presence in Hue when the battle began was the Military Assistance Command, Vietnam (MACV) advisory compound, which housed two hundred American soldiers and a handful of Australians who served as advisers to the 1st ARVN Division. This lightly fortified compound lay on the eastern edge of the modern part of the city about a block and a half south of the Nguyen Hoang Bridge. The nearest U.S. combat base was Phu Bai, eight miles south along Route 1, which was a major Marine Corps command post and support facility that was the home of Task Force X-Ray, which had been established as a forward headquarters of the 1st Marine Division. The task force, commanded by Brigadier General Foster C. "Frosty" LaHue, assistant commander of the 1st Marine Division, was made up of two Marine regimental headquarters and three battalions. Most of these troops had only recently arrived in the Phu Bai area, having been displaced from Da Nang, and they were still getting acquainted with the area of operations when the Communists launched their attack on Hue.

Opposing the allied forces in the Hue region were eight thousand Communist troops, a total of ten battalions, including two People's Army of Vietnam (PAVN) regiments and six Viet Cong (VC) main-force battalions.[2] During the course of the battle for Hue, the total Communist force in and around the city would grow to twenty battalions when three additional infantry regiments were dispatched to the Hue area from the Khe Sanh battlefield.

Before the Tet Offensive began, the Communists had prepared extensive plans for the attack on Hue, which called for a division-size assault on the city, while other forces cut off access to Hue to preclude allied reinforcements. The senior PAVN commanders believed that once the city's population realized the superiority of the Communist troops, the people would immediately rise up to join forces with the VC and PAVN against the Americans and the South Vietnamese, driving them out of Hue. Possessing very detailed information on civil and military installations within the city, the Communist military planners had divided the city into four tactical areas and prepared a list of 196 targets within the city. They planned to use more than five thousand soldiers to take the city in one swift blow.

Documents captured during and after the Tet offensive indicate that VC and PAVN troops received intensive training in the technique of city street fighting before the offensive began.[3] Adept at fighting in the jungles and rice paddies, the PAVN and VC soldiers required additional training to prepare for the special requirements of fighting in urban areas.

While the assault troops trained for the battle to come, VC intelligence officers prepared a list of "cruel tyrants and reactionary elements" to be rounded up during the early hours of the attack.[4] This list included most South Vietnamese officials, military officers, politicians, American civilians, and other foreigners. After capture, these individuals were to be evacuated to the jungle outside the city, where they would be punished for their crimes against the Vietnamese people.

The PAVN commanders had carefully selected the time for the attack. Because of the Tet holiday, the ARVN defenders would be at reduced strength. In addition, bad weather that traditionally accompanied the northeast monsoon season would hamper aerial resupply operations and impede close air support, which would otherwise have given the allied forces in Hue a considerable advantage.

The city's defense hinged in large part on the leadership of Brigadier General Ngo Quang Truong, commander of the 1st ARVN Division, who was regarded by many U.S. advisers as one of the best senior commanders in the South Vietnamese armed forces.[5] A 1954 graduate of the Dalat Military Academy, he had won his position through ability and combat leadership and not because of political influence or bribery, as was the case with many other South Vietnamese generals.

On the morning of January 30, the beginning of the Tet holiday, Truong received reports of VC attacks on Da Nang, Nha Trang, and other South Vietnamese installations during the previous night. Sensing that something was amiss, he gathered his division staff at the headquarters compound and put them and his remaining troops on full alert. Unfortunately, over half of his division was on holiday leave and out of the city. Believing that the Communists would not attack the "open" city directly, Truong positioned his available forces around the city to defend outside the urban area; he assigned the only regular ARVN troops in the city, the Hac Bao "Black Panther" reconnaissance company, to defend the airstrip at the northeastern corner of the Citadel.

THE BATTLE BEGINS

Unbeknown to Truong as he made his preparations for whatever was to come, there were clear indications that there would be a direct attack on his city. On the same day that the South Vietnamese commander put his staff on alert, a U.S. Army radio intercept unit at Phu Bai overheard Communist orders calling for an imminent assault on Hue. Following standard procedure, the intercept unit forwarded the message through normal channels. Winding its way through several command layers, the intercept and associated intelligence analysis did not make it to the Hue defenders until the city was already under attack.[6]

Even as the intelligence report made its way slowly through channels, the Viet Cong had already infiltrated the city. As in other target cities, Communist troops wearing civilian garb had mingled with the throngs of people who had come to Hue for the Tet holiday. They had easily transported their weapons and ammunition into the city in wagons, truck beds, and other hiding places. In the early morning hours of January 31, these soldiers took up initial positions in Hue and prepared to link up with the PAVN and VC assault troops. At 3:40 a.m., the Communists launched a rocket and mortar barrage from the mountains to the west on both the old and the new sectors of the city. Following this barrage, the assault troops began their attack. The VC infiltrators had donned their uniforms, met their comrades at the gates, and led them in the attack on key installations in the city.

Two PAVN battalions of infantry and a VC sapper battalion launched the main attack from the southwest and moved quickly across the Perfume River into the Citadel toward the ARVN division headquarters in the northeastern corner (see Map 6). The PAVN troops rapidly overran most of the Citadel, but Truong and his staff held the attackers off at the division compound, while the Hac Bao Company managed to hold its position at the eastern end of the airfield. By daylight on January 31, the PAVN controlled the rest of the Citadel, including the Imperial Palace.

The situation was not much better for the Americans and Australians south of the river in the new city. A PAVN battalion twice assaulted the MACV compound, but the attackers were repelled each time by rapidly assembled defenders armed with individual weapons. Failing to take the compound, PAVN tried to reduce it with mortar and automatic-weapons fire from overlooking buildings. The defenders held their ground and waited for reinforcements. Meanwhile, two VC battalions took over the Thua Thien province headquarters, the police station, and other government buildings south of the river. At the same time, other PAVN forces occupied blocking positions on the southern edge of the city to prevent reinforcement from that direction.

Thus in very short order, the Communists had seized control of virtually all of Hue. When the sun came up on the morning of January 31, nearly everyone in the city could see the gold-starred, blue-and-red National Liberation Front flag flying high over the Citadel. It was clear that the VC and PAVN troops were now in charge in Hue.

Having captured most of the city, the VC cadre instituted a new political regime and established Revolutionary Committees to control the various neighborhoods. While the NVA and VC assault troops roamed the streets freely and consolidated their gains, political officers began rounding up the South Vietnamese and foreigners on the special lists. They marched through the Citadel, reading out the names on the lists through loudspeakers and telling them to report to a local school. Those who did not report were hunted down.[7] Most of the detainees were never seen alive again.

As the battle erupted at Hue, fighting raged elsewhere in cities and towns from the DMZ to the Ca Mau Peninsula in the south, and allied forces had their hands full all over the country. The northern provinces were no exception, and it would prove difficult to assemble sufficient uncommitted combat power to oust the Communists from Hue. Additionally, U.S. and South Vietnamese forces had been moved to the west to support the action in and around Khe Sanh, thus reducing the number of troops available in the entire northern region.

General Truong, who by this time had only a tenuous hold on his own headquarters compound, ordered one of his regiments, reinforced with two airborne battalions and an armored cavalry troop, to make its way into the Citadel from their positions northwest of the city. En route, these forces encountered intense small arms and automatic weapons fire as they neared the Citadel. They fought their way through the resistance and reached Truong's headquarters late in the afternoon.

As Truong tried to consolidate his forces, another call for reinforcements went out from the surrounded advisors at the MACV compound. This plea for assistance was almost lost in all the confusion caused by the simultaneous attacks going on all over the I Corps Tactical Zone. Lieutenant General Hoang Xuan Lam, commander of the South Vietnamese forces in I Corps, and Lieutenant General Robert Cushman, III Marine Amphibious Force (MAF) commander, were not sure what exactly was happening inside the city. The strength and the scope of the Communist attack was less than clear during the early hours of the battle, but the allied commanders realized that additional forces would be needed to eject the Communists from Hue. Accordingly, Cushman ordered TF X-Ray to send reinforcements into the city to relieve the besieged MACV compound.

While both ARVN and U.S. commanders tried to assess the situation and prepared to move more troops to Hue, PAVN forces quickly established additional blocking positions to prevent those reinforcements from reaching the beleaguered defenders.

THE MARINES RESPOND

General LaHue, commander of Task Force X-Ray, dispatched a company of Marines to move up Route 1 from Phu Bai by truck to relieve the surrounded U.S. advisers. LaHue, having received no reliable intelligence to the contrary, believed that only a small enemy force had penetrated Hue as part of a local diversionary attack; little did he know that almost a full enemy division had seized the city. He therefore sent only one company to deal with the situation. LaHue later admitted, "Initial deployment of force was made with limited information."[8]

Not knowing exactly what to expect when they reached the city, the Marine company headed north as ordered, joining up with four Marine tanks en route. As they approached the city, they encountered stiff resistance from the PAVN defenders and became pinned down between the river and the Phu Cam canal, just short of the MACV compound they had been sent to relieve.

With the first company unable to continue the attack, a reaction force was hastily organized and began to move up the highway, reinforced with two self-propelled twin-40mm guns. The force met little resistance along the way and linked up with the original relief force. With the aid of four tanks and the self-propelled guns, the combined force fought its way to the MACV compound, reaching the beleaguered defenders at about 3:15 p.m. The cost, however, was high: ten Marines were killed and thirty were wounded.

Having linked up with the defenders of the MACV compound, the Marines were ordered to cross the Perfume River and break through to the ARVN division headquarters in the Citadel. Leaving the tanks on the southern bank to support by fire, the Marines attempted to cross the Nguyen Hoang Bridge leading into the Citadel. As the infantry started across, they met a hail of fire from a machine gun position at the north end of the bridge. According to one Marine, the PAVN were well dug-in and "firing from virtually every building in Hue city" north of the river.[9] After two hours of intense fighting, the Marines were forced to pull back. The attempt by the Marines to force their way across the bridge had been costly; the Marine company lost one-third of the unit killed or wounded "going across that one bridge and then getting back across the bridge."[10]

At Phu Bai, despite detailed reports from his troops in the city, LaHue and his intelligence officers still did not have a good appreciation of what was happening in Hue. He later explained, "Early intelligence did not reveal the quantity of enemy involved that we subsequently found were committed to Hue."[11] The intelligence picture of what was happening in Hue was just as confused at MACV headquarters in Saigon; General William Westmoreland cabled General Earle Wheeler, chairman of the Joint Chiefs of Staff, that the "enemy has approximately three companies in the Hue Citadel and Marines have sent a battalion into the area to clear them out."[12] This repeated gross underestimation of enemy strength in Hue resulted in insufficient forces being allocated for retaking the city in the early days of the battle.

With the South Vietnamese forces fully occupied in the Citadel north of the river, Lieutenant General Lam, I Corps commander, and General Cushman decided to divide responsibility for the battle. They agreed that ARVN forces would be responsible for clearing the Citadel and the rest of Hue north of the river, while the Marines would clear out the southern part of the city. This situation resulted in what would be, in effect, two separate and distinct battles that would rage in Hue, one south of the river and one north of the river.

The ancient capital was almost sacred to the Vietnamese people, particularly so to the Buddhists. The destruction of the city would result in political repercussions that neither the United States nor the government of South Vietnam could afford. Cushman later recalled, "I wasn't about to open up on the old palace and all the historical buildings there."[13] As a result, limitations were imposed on the use of artillery and close air support to minimize collateral damage. Eventually these restrictions were lifted when it was realized that both artillery and close air support would be necessary to dislodge the enemy from the city. However, the initial rules of engagement played a key role in the difficulties incurred by the allies in the early days of the bitter fighting.

Having divided up the city, Cushman, with Westmoreland's concurrence, began to send reinforcements into the Hue area in an attempt to seal off the enemy inside the city from outside support. Beginning on February 2, elements of the U.S. Army 1st Cavalry Division entered the battle with the mission of blocking the enemy approaches into the city from the north and west. While these U.S. Army units saw plenty of heavy action in these outlying areas and contributed greatly to the eventual allied victory at Hue, the fighting inside the city was to remain in the hands of South Vietnamese troops and U.S. Marines.

FIGHTING IN THE NEW CITY

As the ARVN and Marines made preparations for counterattacks in their assigned areas, the weather took a turn for the worse when the temperature fell into the fifties and the low clouds opened up with a cold drenching rain. As the rain fell, the Marines launched an attack to seize the Thua Thien Province headquarters building and prison, a distance of six blocks west of the MACV compound. The fighting was immediately joined. One Marine later recalled, "We didn't get a block away [from the MACV compound] when we started getting sniper fire. We got a tank . . . went a block, turned right and received 57mm recoilless which put out our tank." The attack was "stopped cold" and the battalion fell back to its original position near the MACV compound.[14]

By this time, LaHue had finally realized that he and his intelligence officers had vastly underestimated the strength of the Communists south of the river. Accordingly, he called in Colonel Stanley S. Hughes, new commander of the 1st Marine Regiment, and gave him overall tactical control of U.S. forces in the southern part of the city. Assuming command of the battle, Hughes ordered a new attack. By the afternoon of the next day, the Marines had reached the Hue University campus, but only after intense fighting.

On the afternoon of February 2, Colonel Hughes moved his command group into Hue, where he could more directly control the battle. Once in the city, he wasted no time in taking charge of the situation. He ordered one of his units, the 1st Battalion, 1st Marines, to keep the main supply route into the city open and directed his other battalion, 2nd of the 5th Marines, to attack south from the university toward the provincial headquarters, telling the battalion commander, Lieutenant Colonel Ernest C. Cheatham, to "clean the NVA out."[15]

From the MACV compound to the confluence of the Perfume River and the Phu Cam Canal was almost eleven blocks, each of which had been transformed by the PAVN troops into a fortress that would have to be cleared building by building. The Marines began their attack toward the treasury building and post office, but they made very slow progress, not having yet devised workable tactics to deal with the demands of the urban terrain. As the Marines, supported by tanks, tried to advance, the PAVN troops hit them with a withering array of mortar, rocket, machine gun, and small arms fire from prepared positions in the buildings.

The Marines just did not have enough men to deal with the PAVN soldiers entrenched in the buildings. By the evening of February 3, they had made little progress and were taking increasing casualties as they fought back and forth over the same ground against a fiercely determined foe.

Early in the morning of February 4, the Marines renewed their attack. It took twenty-four hours of bitter fighting just to reach the treasury building. Attacking the rear of the building after blasting holes through adjacent courtyard walls with 106mm recoilless rifle fire, the Marines finally took the facility, but only after it had been plastered with 90mm tank rounds, 106mm recoilless rifles, 81mm mortars, and finally tear gas. The PAVN forces fought well, making the Marines pay dearly for their advance, but the Marines resolutely pressed the attack.

In rapidly deteriorating weather, the Marines found themselves in a room-by-room, building-by-building struggle to clear an eleven-by-nine-block area just south of the river. Fighting in such close quarters against an entrenched enemy was decidedly different from what the Marines had been trained to do. Accustomed to fighting in the sparsely populated countryside of I Corps Tactical Zone, nothing in their training had prepared them for the type of warfare demanded by this urban setting.

It was savage work—house-to-house fighting through city streets—of a type largely unseen by Americans since World War II. Fighting in the winding, narrow confines of Hue's streets negated the allied edges in mobility and firepower. Ground gained in the fighting was to be measured in inches, and each city block cost dearly, as every alley, street corner, window, and garden had to be paid for in blood. Correspondents who moved forward with the Marines reported the fighting as the most intense they had ever seen in the war.

The combat was relentless. Small groups of Marines moved doggedly from house to house, assaulting enemy positions with whatever supporting fire was available, blowing holes in walls with rocket launchers or recoilless rifles, then sending fire teams and squads into the breach. Using M-16 rifles and grenades, the Marines had to clear each structure room by room. Making skillful use of Hue's numerous courtyards and walled estates, the PAVN fought back every step of the way.

Progress for the Marines was slow, methodical, and costly. On February 5, there was a particularly bloody battle when one Marine company captured the Thua Thien province headquarters building. Using two tanks and 106mm recoilless rifles mounted on "mechanical mules" (a flat-bedded, self-propelled carrier about the size of a jeep), the Marines advanced against intense automatic weapons fire, rockets, and mortars. Responding with their own mortars and tear gas, they finally overwhelmed the PAVN defenders in mid-afternoon.

The fighting continued, but it was not until February 11 that the Marines captured the province headquarters and reached the confluence of the river and the canal. Two days later, they crossed into the western suburbs of Hue, aiming to link up with troopers of the 1st Cavalry Division, who were moving in toward the city. By February 14, most of the city south of the river was in American hands, but mopping up operations would take another twelve days as rockets and mortar rounds continued to fall and isolated snipers harassed Marine patrols. The Marines had recaptured the new city, but they had sustained 38 dead and 320 wounded in doing so. It had been even more costly for the PAVN, who had fought desperately as they gave ground to the Marines; the bodies of more than a thousand VC and PAVN soldiers were strewn about the city south of the river.

THE FIGHT FOR THE CITADEL

While the Marines had fought for the southern part of the city, the battle north of the river had continued to rage. By February 4, the ARVN advance had effectively stalled among the houses, alleys, and narrow streets adjacent to the Citadel wall to the northwest and southwest, leaving the PAVN still in possession of the Imperial Palace and most of the surrounding area.

On the night of February 6–7, the PAVN counterattacked and forced the ARVN troops to pull back to the Tay Loc airfield. At the same time, the North Vietnamese rushed additional reinforcements into the city. Truong responded by sending reinforcements of his own into the battle. However, the ARVN troops still failed to make any headway against the dug-in PAVN, who had burrowed deeply into the walls and tightly packed buildings.

With his troops stalled, an embarrassed and frustrated Truong appealed to the Marines for help. On February 10, LaHue ordered one of his battalions into the old city to help recapture the Citadel. At the same time, two battalions of Vietnamese Marines moved into the southwest corner of the Citadel with orders to sweep west. This buildup of allied forces inside the Citadel put intense pressure on the PAVN forces, but they stood their ground and redoubled efforts to hold their positions.

Once in the old city, the Marines from Major Robert H. Thompson's 1st Battalion, 5th Marines launched the attack down the east wall of the Citadel toward the river. Under heavy enemy fire, the advance did not get very far, with the Marines losing fifteen killed and forty wounded. A fresh company replaced the lead unit, but once again, heavy small arms, machine gun, and rocket fire that seemed to come from every direction raked the Marines. Nevertheless, they managed to inch forward, using air strikes, naval gunfire, and artillery support. The fighting proved even more savage than the battle for the new city on the south bank.

The next day another Marine company was inserted into the battle by boat. After making preparations, the new company launched their attack the following morning to take a key tower on the east wall. For the next twenty-four hours, the battle seesawed back and forth while much of the Citadel was pounded to rubble by close air support, artillery, and heavy weapons fire. The bitter hand-to-hand fighting went on relentlessly. The Marines were attacking a defender's paradise—row after row of single story, thick-walled masonry houses jammed close together up against a solid wall riddled with spider-holes and other fighting positions. The Marines discovered that the PAVN units in the Citadel employed "better city-fighting tactics, improved the already formidable defenses, dug trenches, built roadblocks and conducted counterattacks to regain redoubts which were important to . . . [their] defensive scheme."[16] It was a battle fought inch by inch; each PAVN strongpoint had to be reduced with close-quarter fighting. No sooner had one position been taken than the PAVN troops opened up from another, exacting a deadly toll on the Marines as they inched their forward.

By February 17, the Marines attacking the Citadel had suffered 47 killed and 240 wounded in just five days of fighting. On February 18, with what was left of his battalion completely exhausted and nearly out of ammunition, Major Thompson chose to rest his troops in preparation for a renewal of the attack. The following morning, the Marines resumed the attack toward the Imperial Palace. After twenty-four more hours of bitter fighting, they secured the wall, but had virtually spent themselves in doing so against the dug-in PAVN defenders who fought desperately to hold their positions. Meanwhile, troops from the U.S. 1st Cavalry Division had taken up positions west of the Citadel to seal off the city from North Vietnamese replacements and supplies.

For the final assault on the Imperial Palace itself, a fresh unit, Company L of the 3rd Battalion, 5th Marines, was brought in. By February 22, the PAVN held only the southwestern corner of the Citadel. The Marines breached the outer perimeter of the palace, but once inside, they were faced by intense fire from the entrenched PAVN defenders.

As the Marines girded themselves for the next assault on the Imperial Palace, MACV decided that it was politically expedient to have the palace liberated by the South Vietnamese.[17] On the night of February 23–24, an ARVN battalion launched a surprise attack westward along the wall in the southeastern section of the Citadel. A savage battle ensued, but the South Vietnamese pressed the attack. The PAVN, suffering from a lack of ammunition and supplies, fell back. Allied forces overran some of the last positions; VC and PAVN troops abandoned the others as they withdrew westward to sanctuaries in Laos.

On March 2, 1968, the battle for Hue was declared officially over. "The twenty-five day struggle for Hue was the longest and bloodiest ground action of the Tet offensive," said the *Washington Post's* Don Oberdorfer, who witnessed it firsthand, "and, quite possibly, the longest and bloodiest single action of the Second Indochina War."[18] It had been a bitter ordeal, and the casualties on both sides had been high. In the twenty-six days of combat, the ARVN lost 384 killed and more than 1,800 wounded, plus 30 missing in action. The U.S. Marines suffered 147 dead and 857 wounded. The U.S. Army sustained 74 dead and 507 wounded in the battles that raged in the area surrounding the city. The allies claimed over 5,000 Communists killed in the city and an estimated 3,000 killed in the fighting in the surrounding area. Actual figures of VC and PAVN casualties are not known, but it is clear that the Communists forces had paid dearly in the bitter fighting.

In the end, the U.S. and ARVN forces had retaken the city, but the costly battle had demonstrated that the Communists could occupy an important city, thought to be safe from the war and under the control of the allies. The American high command had been completely surprised by the audacity of the enemy attacks. American intelligence had failed to pick up the danger signs of impending Communist assault until it was too late. According to allied intelligence before the battle, PAVN units that fought in the Hue were not even supposed to have been in the area; they had very stealthily surrounded the city, eluding allied intelligence efforts. Once in the city, they fought skillfully and tenaciously to hold it, inflicting heavy casualties on the Marines and South Vietnamese soldiers.

The cost of the battle for the people of Hue was catastrophic. During the twenty-five days of intense fighting to retake the city, Hue was reduced to rubble, block by block. Although the U.S. command had tried to limit damage to the city by relying on extremely accurate 8-inch howitzers and naval gunfire, much of the once beautiful city lay in rubble. Estimates tallied ten thousand houses either totally destroyed or damaged, roughly 40 percent of the city, and 116,000 civilians were made homeless (out of a pre-Tet population of 140,000). One observer described the destruction after the fighting, "The beautiful city . . . was a shattered, stinking hulk, its streets choked with rubble and rotting bodies."[19]

Aside from this battle damage, the civilian population suffered terrible losses from the fighting: some 5,800 were reported killed or missing. Many of the dead and wounded were trapped in the rubble of their homes and courtyards. The exact extent of the battle's toll on the civilians in Hue would not become clear for some time. In late February, soldiers moving through the Gia Hoi schoolyard came across freshly turned earth; upon investigation, the soldiers discovered the hastily buried bodies of a number of civilians, most of whom had been bound and shot. This proved only the first instance of such graves, and more bodies would be found over the course of the next several months. In total, South Vietnamese authorities uncovered nearly three thousand corpses in mass graves in the Hue area. Most had been shot, bludgeoned to death, or buried alive, almost all with their hands tied behind their backs. The victims included soldiers, civil servants, merchants, clergymen, schoolteachers, intellectuals, and foreigners. South Vietnamese investigators charged that VC cadres had rounded up the victims and executed them after the Communists had seized the city in early February. Others were apparently killed as the PAVN withdrew from the Citadel.

Chapter 5

THE SIEGE OF KHE SANH

On the morning of January 31, 1968, when the Tet Offensive was launched, General William Westmoreland remained convinced that the enemy's real goal was the conquest of the U.S. Marine base at Khe Sanh, even though the enemy's real intentions were unclear. The attacks on Saigon and other cities, he declared, were designed to create "maximum consternation" in Vietnam and were "diversionary" to the main effort still to come at Khe Sanh and the northern part of the country.[1]

The Marines were less convinced that holding Khe Sanh was a good idea. Senior commanders thought that Khe Sanh was too isolated and too hard to support. The assistant commander of the 3rd Marine Division summed up this sentiment by saying, "When you're at Khe Sanh, you're not really anywhere. You could lose it, and you really haven't lost a damn thing."[2] But Westmoreland did not see it that way. Khe Sanh was a linchpin in his future plans for operations in Laos, and any Communist buildup there threatened his strategy.

Westmoreland had good cause to be concerned with the worsening situation at Khe Sanh. The Marines had been under heavy shelling and living in a state of siege since January 21, ten days before the start of the Tet Offensive. For the next seventy-seven days, the Marines would endure a daily bombardment while enemy assault units probed for a soft spot in the defenses.

Some American political leaders had begun to fear that Khe Sanh might turn into another Dien Bien Phu. The People's Army of Vietnam (PAVN) had successfully closed Route 9, isolating Khe Sanh and precluding ground resupply of the Marines defending the base. On several levels, the situation was reminiscent of the 1954 battle that had ended in French defeat. However, in truth, conditions at Khe Sanh were decidedly different from those at Dien Bien Phu. The French position had been in a valley, and the North Vietnamese had controlled the surrounding hills. At Khe Sanh, the Marines had a much stronger position; they controlled the critical high ground that surrounded the base. In addition, American forces possessed a much stronger air force than the French had at Dien Bien Phu. With those air assets, Westmoreland was convinced that he could pound the enemy from the air and at the same time continue to support the Marine base completely by aerial resupply even if it remained surrounded by the PAVN on the ground.

It must also be pointed out that Khe Sanh, while surrounded by enemy forces, did not meet the strictest definition of "siege" in the historical sense. The Marines conducted constant patrols from the base, often as far as a third of a mile from their own lines.[3] The intent was to keep the PAVN off balance and to gather intelligence. Thus, given the ability to conduct patrols outside the wire and the fact that helicopters and fixed wing aircraft could get into and out of Khe Sanh, it was not truly besieged in the traditional sense, as Dien Bien Phu most definitely had been.

Despite the differences between Khe Sanh and Dien Bien Phu, the Marines knew that the Communists might try to replicate their earlier victory and they were clearly aware of how critical their mission was. The Marine commander told his men that they were "going to be remembered in American history books."[4] He told them that their mission had been ordered by the highest authority and that they were to hold Khe Sanh "at all costs." The Marines were aware that Westmoreland wanted to turn the area around Khe Sanh into a killing ground where the often too-illusive enemy could be drawn into a set-piece battle and destroyed by American firepower. One of the Marine artillery officers at Khe Sanh described the situation best when he said, "Our entire philosophy [is] to allow the enemy to surround us closely, to mass about us, to reveal his troop and logistic routes, to establish his dumps and assembly areas, and to prepare his siege works as energetically as he desires. The results [will be] an enormous quantity of targets . . . ideal for heavy bombers."[5] One Marine who survived the siege put it in more personal terms, saying, "the marines at Khe Sanh were bait; chum liberally spread around the Khe Sanh tactical area to entice large military forces of North Vietnam from the depths of their sanctuaries to the exposed shallows of America's high-technology killing machine."[6]

One of those most concerned with the worsening situation at Khe Sanh was Lyndon Johnson. On February 2, at a press conference in the White House, the president had announced that the Tet offensive was a "complete failure." However, after pointing out that the Communists had already suffered staggering losses estimated at more than ten thousand killed, he sounded a note of caution, saying that the third phase of the Communist campaign—a "massive attack" across the demilitarized zone (DMZ) in the area of Khe Sanh—was "imminent."[7] Thus, despite the fact that the fighting continued in Hue, the attention of both the White House and Westmoreland remained fixed on Khe Sanh.

Before the Tet offensive began, there had been some discussion in the White House about the advisability of continuing to defend Khe Sanh, but with the Communist attack on the Marine base on January 21, the debate about whether to hold Khe Sanh came to an abrupt halt. General Maxwell Taylor later recalled, "It was apparent that the die was cast and we would have to fight it out on this line . . . we ourselves had done a great deal to build up the importance of Khe Sanh in the minds of the public, and it was going to be difficult to explain to our people or anyone else that Khe Sanh was a minor outpost and the outcome of the battle unimportant."[8]

With the decision to hold Khe Sanh, both the White House and the Pentagon focused on the six thousand Marines there and the twenty thousand PAVN soldiers who surrounded them. Concerned about the ability of the Marines to hold, General Earle Wheeler, chairman of the Joint Chiefs of Staff, cabled Westmoreland to raise the possibility of "whether tactical nuclear weapons should be used if the situation in Khe Sanh should become that desperate." Acknowledging that their use was unlikely, he nevertheless requested a list of targets in the area "which lend themselves to nuclear strikes, whether some contingency nuclear planning would be in order, and what you would consider to be some of the more significant pros and cons of using tac [tactical] nukes in such a contingency."[9] Westmoreland replied that he did not think the situation would require the use of nuclear weapons, but that they should not be ruled out if the North Vietnamese launched a major invasion south across the DMZ, and therefore contingency planning was ongoing. Johnson later vehemently denied that nuclear weapons had ever been considered (and Westmoreland was quietly told to discontinue planning for their use). This episode indicates the mind-set in the White House and Pentagon as the situation at Khe Sanh worsened. Politically, as well as militarily, Khe Sanh had to be held at all costs.

Events would soon increase that concern. On the night of February 3, the American sensors that had been dropped during Operation Niagara detected heavy enemy troop movement. Two days later, in the early morning hours of February 5, Hill 861A was attacked. To MACV, it appeared that the

Communists, taking advantage of the fact that the nationwide Tet Offensive had diverted attention away from Khe Sanh, were renewing their efforts to capture the combat base and the surrounding area. At 3:05 a.m., heavy shelling began on Khe Sanh Combat Base and several of the outlying positions. At the same time, wave after wave of PAVN riflemen from the 325C Division struck the Marines on Hill 861A. The skillful and determined attack quickly gained a foothold on the northern edge of the American perimeter, but there was a brief lull in the fighting as the PAVN soldiers "stopped to sift through the Marine positions for souvenirs."[10] Taking advantage of the lull, the Marines rallied and launched a counterattack. The fight degenerated into hand-to-hand combat as the Marines forced the PAVN troops back. Shortly after dawn, the PAVN made another concerted assault to take the Marine position, but the Marines, supported by mortars from the surrounding hills, prevailed in the bitter fighting.

THE FALL OF LANG VEI

As PAVN forces completed their encirclement of the Marines at Khe Sanh, they made preparations for a major assault on the nearby Special Forces camp at Lang Vei. Twenty-four members of the American Special Forces team and their Montagnard troops, as well as some Laotian soldiers who had fled their homes just across the border during a Communist attack some days earlier, manned the base. The total allied force numbered about four hundred troops.

The shelling of Lang Vei began in the early morning hours of February 7. Then, at first light, the PAVN struck in force spearheading their attack with eleven Soviet-made PT-76 amphibious light tanks, marking the first time that tanks had been used by the Communists in South Vietnam. Although the defenders received artillery support from Khe Sanh, Camp Carroll, and the Rockpile, they were soon overrun. Calling down artillery and air strikes on top of their own position, the commander of the camp, thirteen of his Green Berets, and some sixty Montagnards managed to break out to the east. Marine helicopters picked them up later that afternoon, but half the original garrison was unaccounted for, and ten of the twenty-four Americans at Lang Vei had been killed.

The appearance of tanks at Lang Vei rightfully concerned many of the Marines at Khe Sanh. With tanks, they reasoned, the PAVN could take Khe Sanh anytime it wanted. Still the Communists made no direct move on the combat base. However, they continued to apply pressure on the base while ground and artillery and mortar attacks continued against the Marine positions in the surrounding hills.

It appeared to the Marine defenders that the enemy was preparing for another major attack on Khe Sanh. Based on the previous enemy activity in the area, they thought that the PAVN would attack the Marine outposts to the north of the base and then make a direct attack on the main base from that direction. They also believed that another PAVN division would attack along the axis of Lang Vei–Khe Sanh village and then make its final assault on the base from the south and east.

While the Marine defenders waited for the next attack, they were unaware that the Communists had encountered serious problems elsewhere that would have an impact on the situation at Khe Sanh. As the fighting in Hue increased in intensity, Giap began to withdraw PAVN units from the Khe Sanh area to reinforce his beleaguered troops, who were trying desperately to hold on to the old imperial capital. Around February 10, five PAVN battalions began moving from the Khe Sanh area to join their comrades in Hue.[11] Although the PAVN had thinned their forces in the area, they still had sufficient troops to keep Khe Sanh encircled and continuously bombard it with rockets, mortars, and artillery.

Such tactics had proved successful against the French at Dien Bien Phu in 1954. However, as noted, there were some crucial differences between the situation at Dien Bien Phu and the one at Khe Sanh in 1968, not the least of which was that Khe Sanh was never truly besieged in the classic sense of the term. Whereas the Viet Minh had been able to sever virtually all outside support from the French defenders at Dien Bien Phu, the Marines at Khe Sanh were never cut off, and U.S. forces never lost the ability to reinforce and resupply the base. In addition, the Marines held the vital hill positions to the north and west of Khe Sanh and actively conducted patrols in the areas surrounding the combat base.

Consequently, the PAVN appeared content for most of the seventy-seven days to hold their positions and bombard the defenders with 122mm rockets and 82mm and 120mm mortars from positions in an arc about two thousand to three thousand yards north and west of the base, while long-range 130mm and 152mm guns fired on the Marines from concealed positions on Co Roc Mountain across the border in Laos. The defenders received an average of 2,500 rounds a week in an area little more than 1,750 yards long and 875 yards wide.

In the United States, the U.S. media continued to report on the situation at Khe Sanh, implying that it was in imminent danger of being overrun by the Communists. On February 27, Walter Cronkite intoned that "Khe Sanh could well fall, with terrible loss in American lives, prestige, and morale."[12] No doubt influenced by such gloomy reports, some of Johnson's advisers had begun to question the wisdom of continuing to hold Khe Sanh in the face of the continued siege, but Westmoreland remained convinced that the Marine base was critical and was steadfast in his insistence that Khe Sanh be held.

RESUPPLYING THE MARINES

The key to the survival of Khe Sanh combat base was the airfield. If the PAVN could close it and cut off supplies to the base, they would win an enormous victory. The Marine commander estimated he needed 160 tons of supplies a day to sustain his Marines as they defended against the PAVN. With Route 9 cut by the Communists, the airfield and aerial resupply became the lifeline for the defenders. Although Communist mortar, rocket, and artillery fire hit the field repeatedly, the Marine defenders were able to repair it each time.

The PAVN tried to isolate the Marine base from outside aerial support by an intensive umbrella of air defense artillery, but U.S. Air Force and Marine pilots and crews braved heavy fire to keep the Marines on the ground resupplied with ammunition, food, water, and other combat necessities. Despite intense enemy ground fire and deplorable weather conditions, these airlifts insured that supply levels never became dangerously low and precluded Khe Sanh from becoming a repeat of Dien Bien Phu. As Marine historian Captain Moyers S. Shore observed, "the Marine and U.S. Air Force transport pilots, helicopter crews, loadmasters, and ground personnel kept open the giant umbilical cord which meant life for the combat base."[13] This effort was not without cost; seventeen helicopters and four fixed-wing aircraft were lost to enemy gunners.

TACTICAL AIR SUPPORT

While the helicopter and cargo aircraft crews exerted uncommon efforts to keep the Marines resupplied, U.S. Air Force, Navy, and Marine Corps pilots, as well as airborne and ground controllers, provided close air support to keep the PAVN at bay. Marine and Air Force controllers coordinated the air strikes, acting as the link between the fighter-bombers and the Marines on the ground. Tactical aircraft—F-4 Phantoms, A-4 Skyhawks, and A-6 Intruders—flew approximately three hundred sorties per day over Khe Sanh. Constant air strikes pounded the PAVN. Even more devastating were the B-52s flying from their bases in Guam, Thailand, and Okinawa. The big bombers each carried a 27-ton payload of 108 mixed 500- and 750-pound bombs, which was devastating on enemy troop concentrations, supply depots, and bunker sites. During the siege, it is estimated that B-52s dropped at least 50,000 tons of ordnance on the NVA forces surrounding Khe Sanh. These air strikes were critical in the defense of the combat base and surrounding Marine positions.

In addition to the massive airpower brought to bear, the defenders' own artillery at Khe Sanh was supplemented from firebases at Camp Carroll and the Rockpile. Fire support coordinators at Khe Sanh had a tremendous amount of firepower at their disposal. Several innovative methods were used to maximize this firepower. One was known as the "Mini Arc Light." This strike involved plotting a 550-by-1,100-yard block around a reported PAVN position. Then, two A-6 Intruders, each carrying twenty-eight 500-pound bombs, would be called in; thirty seconds before they arrived, the 175mm guns from Camp Carroll or the Rockpile would hit one half of the block, firing about sixty rounds. The A-6s would then go for the middle of the block, while 155mm and 105mm howitzers, plus 4.2-inch mortars from Khe Sanh, would saturate the other half. All the rounds would be timed to strike simultaneously. The effect on the enemy was devastating.[14]

A NEW ATTACK

During the early evening hours of February 29, acoustic and seismic sensors along Route 9 indicated a major troop movement toward the combat base from the east. Colonel Lownds, the Marine commander, thought this might be the big attack everyone had been anticipating and immediately called for maximum fire against the area indicated by the sensors. In response, artillery, fighter-bombers, and B-52s struck the area. This devastating firepower broke up the attack, destroying the better part of two battalions. Undeterred, at 9:30 p.m. the PAVN launched a large-scale attack against the ARVN ranger positions on the southeast corner of Khe Sanh base. With the aid of mortars, artillery, and tactical air support, the South Vietnamese Rangers beat back the PAVN attack, but the Communists made another attempt at 11:30 p.m. This, too, was stopped cold before they made it to the defensive wire. A third wave came at 3:15 a.m., but the result was the same. These failed attacks seemed to mark a turning point in the battle for Tet; the PAVN never again mounted a sizable attack against the base.

At the end of February, a Marine patrol discovered that the PAVN were digging trenches. Later patrols revealed that these trenches were moving closer and closer to the perimeter of the main base at Khe Sanh and that the PAVN were sometimes completing as much as ninety-five yards a night. From these advanced positions, they might be able to launch a powerful assault that could overrun the base before the Marines had time to mount a successful defense, as had happened at Dien Bien Phu. The Marines knew that the anniversary of the first attacks on the French stronghold was only two weeks away, and they were concerned that the trench digging indicated that the enemy might be preparing for a new attack to commemorate that historic day.

Since the situation looked like it was entering a new and potentially more dangerous phase, Westmoreland turned again to airpower, including B-52 raids on suspected Communist troop concentrations near the base perimeter. This was a risky move, because up until this time, the American forces had usually tried to avoid B-52 bombing of enemy positions if they were in close proximity to U.S. troops. There was just too much chance that Americans might be killed by "friendly fire" from the bombs dropped from an altitude of thirty thousand feet. However, Westmoreland decided that using the big bombers so close to the base was the only way to drive the enemy from the Khe Sanh area. Adding additional motivation were more intelligence reports that the Communists were again building up their troop strength for one more big push. Beginning at the end of February and continuing into early March, B-52s repeatedly hammered the PAVN positions around Khe Sanh.

Unbeknown to the Marine defenders, the PAVN had actually begun withdrawing their forces from the area, and on March 10 the Communists stopped repairing their trenches.[15] On March 13, the anniversary of the start of the battle at Dien Bien Phu passed without incident. The sporadic shelling continued, but Marine patrols soon discovered that some of the PAVN trenches had been abandoned.

On March 30, a company of Marines fought a three-hour battle with North Vietnamese troops near where two patrols had been decimated on February 25. This time the Marines prevailed, counting 115 enemy dead on the battlefield. It was the last big battle in the Khe Sanh area. Small firefights with the enemy in the surrounding hills continued, and the Marines were still harassed by enemy rocket and artillery fire, but the base at Khe Sanh had held.

LIFTING THE SIEGE

On April 1, elements of the 1st Cavalry Division reinforced with an ARVN airborne battalion began Operation Pegasus, the relief of Khe Sanh. Landing zones were established along Route 9. As the helicopters of 1st Squadron, 9th Cavalry reconnoitered the way ahead, the 1st Cavalry troopers landed along the road and pushed westward until the head of the relief column, 2nd Battalion, 7th Cavalry, linked up with the Marines at Khe Sanh on April 8, officially bringing the siege to an end. On April 18, the Marines who had endured the siege were airlifted out of the area. They had suffered 199 killed in action and 830 wounded, while the Pegasus relief force had lost 92 killed and 629 wounded. ARVN forces had lost 34 killed and 184 wounded.

The PAVN and Viet Cong had lost an estimated 10,000 to 15,000 killed during the desperate fighting for Khe Sanh, many to the Marine and Army artillery (over 150,000 rounds) and the 100,000 tons of bombs dropped during Operation Niagara. Two PAVN divisions had suffered badly, and the Marines claimed a resounding victory with the end of the siege. Local Montagnard tribesmen later told of finding large numbers of PAVN dead in the jungle surrounding Khe Sanh; many were found in groups of two hundred to five hundred at a time along the various avenues of approach to the Khe Sanh base, apparently killed by B-52s and close air support.[16]

A look at the respective casualty figures perhaps points out the difference in results between Dien Bien Phu and the outcome at Khe Sanh. Approximately eight thousand Viet Minh and two thousand French soldiers died at Dien Bien Phu. However, at the battle at Khe Sanh, the Communists lost more than ten thousand soldiers at a cost of fewer than two hundred U.S. Marines killed in action. According to Stanley Karnow, a Communist veteran of the battle later admitted that PAVN and VC units suffered as much as 90 percent losses in the relentless downpour of American bombs, napalm, and artillery shells.[17]

On April 11, four days before Pegasus came to an end, Westmoreland flew to Washington to confer with the president. Standing on the White House lawn, he announced that Route 9 was open again and that the battle of Khe Sanh was over. He lavished praise on everyone involved with the successful defense of the combat base: the Marines for their "heroic defense," the combat engineers for their "herculean" efforts in reopening the main road to the base, and the supply units for having performed "the premier logistical feat of the war." He saved his highest accolades for those who had contributed to "one of the heaviest and most concentrated displays of firepower in the history of warfare." Army and Marine artillery units fired 158,891 round during the siege. The Air Force flew 9,691 bombing sorties over Khe Sanh, the Marines 7,078, and the Navy 5,337. Yet the "key to success, the big gun, the heavy weight of firepower, was the B-52 strikes."[18] As Westmoreland later told B-52 crewmen stationed on Guam, "Without question, the amount of firepower put on that piece of real estate exceeded anything that had ever been seen before in history by any foe, and the enemy was hurt, his back was broken, by airpower . . . basically the fire of the B-52s."[19]

Despite all the doomsday prophets in the media, the greatly outnumbered Marines supported by massive American firepower had survived seventy-seven days of intense fighting and shelling. Perhaps an editorial in the *Washington Post* best sums up the epic battle at Khe Sanh: "To be sure, Khe Sanh will be a subject of controversy for a long time, but this much about it is indisputable: It has won a large place in the history of the Vietnam war as an inspiring example of American and Allied valor."[20]

From the Vietnamese perspective, the PAVN could also point to their own valor; they had more than held their own in the desperate fighting. Whatever their intentions, which will be discussed later, their soldiers had stood fast under a devastating bombardment for two and a half months. Although their losses were huge, they, as Khe Sanh veteran Peter Brush points out, "were willing to absorb losses of this magnitude in order to continue, and win, their struggle."[21] In describing the fighting capability and dedication of the PAVN, perhaps the words of a Marine at Khe Sanh provide the best appreciation: "You'll never hear Marines say the North Vietnamese aren't tough. They're probably the toughest fighters in the world as far as I am concerned. They knew what they were fighting for. They understood why they were there and they were there for the duration."[22] The same can be said of the Marines.

Chapter 6

THE IMPACT OF THE TET OFFENSIVE

In most American accounts of war, the Tet Offensive lasts only a few weeks, and the end date is usually placed somewhere around the end of March when the siege is lifted at Khe Sanh. However, the fighting continued into the fall as Hanoi and the Central Office for South Vietnam (COSVN) pressed the attack. According to General Tran Van Tra, writing after the war, the fighting from May to the end of September was a continuation of the original General Offensive–General Uprising. He acknowledged that the initial phase of the offensive had not gone as well militarily as planned and that the People's Army of Vietnam (PAVN) and Viet Cong (VC) "were not able to destroy a significant number of the enemy forces," but he maintained that their "attacks sent shudders through the enemy's vital points, and destabilized its military, political, and economic foundations throughout South Vietnam."[1] He further acknowledged that the "enemy" had responded strongly, but in so doing had betrayed many "weaknesses." Accordingly, the situation provided the Communists with "an opportunity . . . to continue strong assaults and compensate for . . . earlier shortcomings in order to win even bigger victories."[2]

To replace the heavy losses incurred in the earlier fighting, Hanoi sent eighty thousand to ninety thousand replacements down the Ho Chi Minh Trail by the end of April. In the first week of May, they launched a new round of attacks, which the South Vietnamese and Americans referred to as a "Mini-Tet." According to most Communist histories, however, this action was a continuation of the overall 1968 General Offensive.[3]

In the renewed offensive, they struck 119 cities and bases, including Saigon. Unlike during the earlier phase of the offensive, when VC units bore the brunt of a large part of the heaviest fighting, the PAVN conducted almost all of the May attacks. Otherwise, the new attacks resembled those of the initial Tet Offensive. Unfortunately, however, for the Communists troops, this time they failed to achieve surprise. Allied intelligence had clear indications that the PAVN would launch a new round of attacks and allied forces were ready. The attacks planned for Hue and elsewhere in the I Corps area in May, as well as those in the Central Highlands, were preempted by allied attacks on the gathering forces.

The new assault on Saigon began in the early morning hours of May 5, when a barrage of rockets and mortars slammed into the heart of the city. Heavy fighting raged in parts of Saigon, including the vital Tan Son Nhut area, but U.S. ground and air cavalry units repelled the PAVN forces. It looked as if the battle was over, but two days later, the Communists renewed their attack, and intense fighting once again broke out in Cholon and around the Phu Tho racetrack. By May 13, the Communists were defeated once again, but the fighting in some places had been as bitter as that in the first days of the Tet Offensive.

Two weeks later, the Communists launched yet another assault on Saigon. This time two PAVN regiments captured the densely populated northern suburbs while a local-force battalion reoccupied the Cholon area, where they raised a National Liberation Front (NLF) flag over the central post office. It took until the first week in June for South Vietnamese Army (ARVN) brigades to root out the PAVN soldiers, using tear gas and helicopter gunships.

Still that did not mean a respite for Saigon, because the Communists initiated a daily barrage of 122mm rockets on the city. Twenty-five times in thirty-eight days, rockets pounded the capital, killing hundreds of civilians and wounding nearly a thousand more. In addition, the new round of fighting produced 180,000 new refugees whose homes had been destroyed.

In Saigon and most of the other areas attacked, the Communist forces were destroyed or driven into the countryside. However, television coverage reinforced the impression that the enemy was once again knocking at the gates of the most heavily defended cities in South Vietnam.[4]

The fighting during the subsequent phases of Tet was intense. The United States lost 562 dead in the week ending May 11, the highest weekly total of the war; with the loss of nearly 2,000 dead during that month, May 1968 became the bloodiest month of the war for U.S. troops. The Communist forces had clearly demonstrated that they had not been destroyed during the earlier Tet fighting.

The fighting continued for several more months, entering yet another phase of the offensive. The Viet Cong attacked a number of ARVN positions in the Mekong Delta in August, and the PAVN launched a major attack on U.S. forces forty miles northwest of Saigon in September. PAVN colonel Bui Tinh acknowledged that these attacks were very costly.[5] Accordingly, in late September, COSVN ordered PAVN and VC main-force units to withdraw to their sanctuaries across the border with Cambodia.

POLITICAL FALLOUT

While the fighting continued in South Vietnam, Johnson wrestled with what to do with the deteriorating political situation at home. Though General William C. Westmoreland, the commander of U.S. forces in Vietnam, characterized Tet as a great victory for the allies, the nature of such a victory was difficult for many Americans to understand. The only sign of success was the high "body count," but it seemed that the Communists had a limitless supply of manpower. Tet proved to many Americans, stunned by the scope and ferocity of the offensive, that their government had been misleading them about allied progress in the war. Part of the impact of the offensive on public opinion can be traced back to Westmoreland's optimistic predictions in the fall of 1967. Richard Falk writes, "The public relations urge to build confidence on the home front by exaggerating battlefield prospects subsequently helped create a vulnerability to abrupt disillusionment with the war effort. . . . The dynamics of hopes raised in such circumstances can quickly shift to the dynamics of hopes crushed."[6]

Walter Cronkite, the CBS Evening News anchorman and perhaps the most trusted journalist in the nation, had flown to South Vietnam in mid-February and visited Hue while the battle still raged. He interviewed Marines during the fighting and concluded that victory was not possible. In a special half-hour report broadcast after his return to the United States in late February, Cronkite, as the camera panned over the battle damage in Saigon, said that the ruins "in this burned and blasted and weary land . . . mean success or setback, victory or defeat, depending on who you talk to." He went on to say:

> We have been too often disappointed by the optimism of the American leaders. . . . To say that we are closer to victory today is to believe, in the fact of evidence, the optimists who have been wrong in the past. . . . To say that we are mired in stalemate seems the only realistic, yet unsatisfactory conclusion. . . . It seems now more certain than ever that the bloody experience of Vietnam is to end in a stalemate. . . . It is increasingly clear

to this reporter that the only rational way out then will be to negotiate, not as victors, but as an honorable people who lived up to their pledge to defend democracy, and did the best they could.[7]

Cronkite's report had a significant impact on the president. Watching the program, Johnson reportedly remarked to his press secretary, George Christian, "If I've lost Cronkite, I've lost middle America."[8] This sentiment was pretty close to the truth, because the media had a significant impact on the perspectives of mainstream Americans and Cronkite's comments reflected the widespread dissatisfaction with the administration's policies that many in the American media felt. Previously, Cronkite and many of his colleagues had generally accepted the optimistic reports of government authorities, but like most other Americans, they were stunned by the level of combat and the ability of the Communists to launch such a widespread offensive.

The correspondents in Vietnam only had to look around to see the impact of the offensive. "Covering the war was easy," observed Ron Steinman, head of the NBC News bureau in Saigon. "It was like springtime with buds of fire popping out wherever you chanced to turn your head."[9] Able to see the fighting and its effects firsthand, the reporters found the military's claims of victory less and less credible. In the wake of Tet, the media took an increasingly unfavorable view of U.S. policy, and the reporting on the situation in South Vietnam during and after Tet had a significant impact on public opinion.

When the offensive first began, however, Americans rallied behind the flag in a predictable display of patriotic fervor; journalist Don Oberdorfer reported that there was a "sudden jump in public hawkishness" in the wake of the early television reports of the offensive.[10] In fact, a public opinion survey in early February revealed that 55 percent of those polled favored a stronger military response to the situation in Vietnam. However, as journalist Stanley Karnow points out, the American people's "mood of despair quickly returned as the fighting dragged on, and their endorsement of the conflict resumed its downward spiral."[11] Given the extensive media coverage, the American public was able to see for itself the widespread bloodshed and devastation wrought by the heavy fighting. These images contradicted all of the optimistic claims of the previous fall. It was clear that America's foe remained much stronger than the politicians and generals had led them to believe.

Westmoreland claimed that the failed Communist efforts during Tet represented the "last gasp" of a losing cause, but few Americans believed him. In November 1967, Westmoreland had reported that American forces were winning the war in Vietnam, but the surprise and ferocity of the Tet attacks strained his credibility to the breaking point. Many Americans could not reconcile Westmoreland's new claims with what they had seen on their TV screens. After

Tet, it was impossible for most Americans to believe Westmoreland's renewed promise that victory was just around the corner.

THE REQUEST FOR ADDITIONAL TROOPS

Johnson's deteriorating public support would soon get worse over one of the most controversial issues to develop in the aftermath of the offensive. This issue, which began to play itself out in the days right after the offensive began, involved a request for an increase in U.S. troops in South Vietnam. Although Westmoreland is generally credited for making the additional troop request, the situation was actually much more complex than that. On February 3, General Earle Wheeler, chairman of the Joint Chiefs of Staff, expressing the president's continuing concern about Khe Sanh, sent a message to Westmoreland asking if he needed additional reinforcements. Westmoreland replied that the defense of Khe Sanh was solid and that he did not need anything except a few more supply aircraft and the additional troops he had already been promised, about ten thousand. The following day, Wheeler sent another cable saying that the president was considering diversionary attacks north of the demilitarized zone (DMZ) or in eastern Laos to relieve the pressure on Khe Sanh. The next day, Westmoreland received a message from Admiral U.S. Grant Sharp, commander-in-chief of the U.S. Pacific Command, reiterating the same message and adding that there might be some inclination in Washington toward relaxing the ceiling on U.S. troops in Vietnam.

Westmoreland was not sure what was going on. He had repeatedly reported that he had the situation at Khe Sanh in hand and he was not sure why Washington was so concerned.[12] Still, Westmoreland had been urging the president for several years to remove the constraints on the conduct of the war, advocating operations not only in eastern Laos, but also against North Vietnam itself. Accordingly, he notified Wheeler that an additional U.S. division would be needed if and when operations in Laos were authorized. Wheeler responded, somewhat testily, that Westmoreland should focus on his "immediate requirements stemming from the present situation in Vietnam," not his "longer range" needs.[13] A following message from Wheeler to Westmoreland urged the MACV commander to ask for more troops if he needed them.

Fear of a defeat at Khe Sanh was not the real factor motivating Wheeler. The issue of an additional troop request for Vietnam was intertwined with a much larger issue. Wheeler was concerned that American forces around the world were stretched too thin. There were also problems elsewhere that concerned Wheeler and his fellow chiefs of staff. North Korea had recently seized the U.S. communications ship *Pueblo*; trouble in Berlin or the Middle East might flare up again at any moment. The Army's strategic reserve consisted of one division, the 82nd Airborne at Fort Bragg, North Carolina. In the wake of the Tet offensive, Wheeler saw an opportunity to use the situation in Vietnam to get President Johnson to call up the reserves in order to replenish the strategic reserve.

As part of this plan, Wheeler coaxed Westmoreland to submit a new assessment of the situation in Vietnam. Westmoreland responded with a message that was in total opposition to his earlier confident claims. Although he continued to claim victory in the Tet Offensive, he told the Joint Chiefs of Staff that he needed reinforcements not only to replace his losses during Tet but also to deal with the growing power of the PAVN throughout South Vietnam. Intelligence reports indicated that Hanoi was sending in more soldiers to fill the ranks that had been reduced during Tet. The MACV commander said that the situation was one of great opportunity, but also one fraught with danger. This was completely opposite in tone from the message traffic that had been coming out of his office for Washington.

A somewhat perplexed president dispatched Wheeler on a fact-finding mission to South Vietnam to confer with Westmoreland on future needs. Upon his return to Washington, Wheeler's report to President Johnson was filled with bad news. On February 27, he told the president, "There is no doubt that the enemy launched a major, powerful nationwide assault. This offensive has by no means run its course." In fact, the battle for Khe Sanh was still underway. Wheeler went on to say that the ARVN had suffered huge losses, and the Communists were largely in control of the countryside. He added that Tet "was a very near thing. . . . We suffered a loss, there can be no doubt about it." Wheeler predicted a renewed Communist offensive and contended that more troops were necessary unless the United States was "prepared to accept some reverses."[14]

According to historian George Herring, Wheeler's pessimism may have been sincere, but it appeared "that by presenting a gloomy assessment he hoped to stampede the administration into providing the troops needed to rebuild a depleted strategic reserve and meet any contingency in Vietnam."[15]

Accordingly, Wheeler brought a request from Westmoreland for 206,000 more troops for South Vietnam. The troop increase would be in three increments. The first would total 108,000 troops that would deploy to Vietnam by May 1. The second and third increments totaled 42,000 and 55,000 troops, respectively. These troops would not deploy to Vietnam unless the Communists had made substantial gains on the ground or the White House approved a more aggressive ground strategy. Otherwise, these forces would be earmarked for rebuilding the strategic reserve.

Although Wheeler maneuvered Westmoreland into asking for more troops, Westmoreland did not need much urging; he thought he had the Communists on the run and could use the additional troops to pursue them into their hiding places and sanctuaries. He wanted to drive the Communists from their border sanctuaries in Cambodia and to cut the Ho Chi Minh Trail by a thrust into Laos. He thought that calling up the reserves would convince the North Vietnamese that the United States was serious about pursuing victory in the war. However, Wheeler's report did not reflect any of these considerations and did not mention the idea that part of the additional forces would be used to augment the strategic reserve. In his memoir *A Soldier Reports*, Westmoreland implies that Wheeler deliberately concealed why he wanted the additional troops in order to force the issue of the strategic reserve.[16]

Wheeler's ploy did not work. In fact, as Richard Falk writes, the troop request "significantly hardened the impression among the hesitant in Washington and the media that Tet was an enormous, unacknowledged American defeat, and that the war, if seriously resumed, would be an even greater drain that it already was, and this the United States could not long afford either politically or economically."[17]

For his part, Johnson was taken aback by Westmoreland's request for such an enormous increase in troop strength. He knew that such a proposed troop deployment would necessitate calling up the reserves, requiring a national call to war. Johnson realized that such a move would threaten the American economy and the future of his Great Society programs, in addition to energizing the antiwar movement.

Charging him to "give me the lesser of evils," the president asked Clark Clifford to form a task force within the Defense Department to evaluate the situation in South Vietnam and come back with a recommendation on Westmoreland's request for more troops in Vietnam.[18] Clifford had replaced Secretary of Defense Robert S. McNamara, who had privately turned against the war and left the administration in January 1968. Clifford had directed Johnson's election campaign in 1964 and was for several years a leading supporter of the war effort, but he had begun to develop doubts very similar to those that had led McNamara to resign.[19]

Clifford's task force assessed U.S. strategy in Vietnam and reviewed the proposal for additional troops. The group examined the implications of any new escalation and concluded that the existing policy was failing. Additional troops offered no guarantee that the war could be turned around; increasing the forces in Vietnam promised "no early end to the conflict, nor any success in attriting the enemy or eroding Hanoi's will to fight."[20] While the task force report did not openly challenge continued U.S. involvement in Vietnam, it did warn against committing additional troops to the war and suggested a more cautious military strategy in Vietnam than the search-and-destroy operations that Westmoreland favored. Clifford's group advised the president to send approximately 22,000 additional troops and approve a call-up of 245,000 reservists, but to link any further increases in troop strength to the performance of the Saigon government and its armed forces. Privately, Clifford told the president, "The major concern of the people is that they do not see victory ahead. The military has not come up with a plan for victory. The people were discouraged as more men go in and are chewed up in a bottomless pit."[21]

While Johnson and his advisers debated about what to do in Vietnam, his poll numbers plummeted. By late February, surveys showed that only 32 percent of the American people endorsed Johnson's handling of the war, down from 51 percent in November 1967. Gallup Poll data suggest that between early February and the middle of March 1968, nearly one person in five switched from "hawk" to "dove" on the war.[22]

The president's policies were also under attack in Congress, where the response to Tet was immediate and intense. Senator Robert Kennedy claimed that Tet had "finally shattered the mask of optical illusion with which we have concealed our true circumstances, even from ourselves." For Senator Mike Mansfield, long an opponent of the war, Tet was the disaster that he had been anticipating. "From the outset," he said, it "was not an American responsibility, and it is not now an American responsibility, to win a victory for any particular Vietnamese group, or to defeat any particular Vietnamese group." Senator George Aiken of Vermont summed up the situation for many Americans when he said, "If this is a failure, I hope the Viet Cong never have a major success."[23]

Adding to Johnson's political woes was the deteriorating American economy. Inflation had been growing rapidly since 1966, and the costs of running the war in Vietnam while also financing the programs of the president's Great Society were more than the United States could afford. To remedy the situation, the president had proposed a 10 percent surtax on income, but Congress had refused to pass it until the tax hike was accompanied by cuts in domestic spending.

The situation for the administration worsened considerably when the *New York Times* ran a story on March 10 revealing that Westmoreland had requested that an additional 206,000 troops be sent to Vietnam. The other media quickly picked up the story. NBC News reporter Frank McGee told the nation that 206,000 more troops would only result in more destruction, not peace and victory. Echoing the earlier story from Ben Tre, he said, "We must decide whether it is futile to destroy Vietnam in an effort to save it."[24] The *Times* story and the subsequent reports were incomplete and misleading because they did not say that Wheeler wanted half of the force to shore up America's strategic reserve. Nevertheless, they added to the fears of Americans that the war was going nowhere—if the Tet battles had been a defeat for the Communists, as

Westmoreland and the administration insisted, why then did they need 200,000 more troops in Vietnam?

With this new blow to Westmoreland's credibility, the president's own popularity increased its downward spiral. By late March, a new poll revealed that 78 percent of Americans surveyed felt that the United States was not making any progress in the war, and only 26 percent of the American public approved Johnson's handling of the war.[25] During the two months following Tet, one in every five Americans switched from supporting the war to opposing it. For much of the American public, the Tet Offensive had been a rude awakening to the realities of the war that prompted a reevaluation of the nation's commitment. Having been repeatedly told by leading administration spokesmen and military leaders that the Communists were fading and that there was light at the end of the tunnel, the public was shocked to find them still capable of such an effort. Vivid coverage of close-quarter fighting appeared on their television screens and in newspapers and magazines, reminding them once again of the escalating human costs of the war. Presidential advisor Walt Rostow said that the additional troop request story "churned up the whole eastern establishment and created a false issue. It caused an unnecessary crisis and distorted things. It overrode the hopeful news and had quite substantial effects on public opinion."[26]

THE NEW HAMPSHIRE PRIMARY

Two days after the news of the 206,000 additional troops issue broke, the Democratic primary election was held in New Hampshire. Senator Eugene McCarthy of Minnesota, who had announced his decision the previous fall to challenge the president in the 1968 primaries, charged that the Tet Offensive demonstrated that "the Administration's reports of progress [in Vietnam] are the products of their own self-deception."[27] McCarthy, relatively unknown outside his state and running on an antiwar platform as the "Peace Candidate," astonished the nation by coming within a few hundred votes of defeating Johnson in the primary. Most in the media attributed the president's poor showing in the primary to an antiwar protest by voters. Not all who voted for McCarthy did so because they opposed the war; some wanted to register a protest against Johnson's apparent failure to take a firmer stand following the Tet offensive.[28] Nevertheless, the vote revealed Johnson's political vulnerability and the growing lack of confidence in the president's handling of the war. It was clear that the incumbent president, who four years earlier had been elected by the widest margin in American history, was in desperate political trouble.

Four days after the New Hampshire primary, a potentially much stronger Democratic candidate, Robert Kennedy, convinced to run by the administration's handling of the Tet Offensive, the president's low ratings in the polls, and the results of the primary, announced his decision to enter the race. Kennedy, like McCarthy, made opposition to the war the central issue of his campaign.

In trouble on the campaign trail, the president soon found himself under increased pressure from Congress. Senator J. William Fulbright, a Democrat from Arkansas, opened new hearings in the Senate Foreign Relations Committee on the administration's conduct of the war. In the House, 139 members signed a petition asking Johnson for a complete review of Vietnam policy. These responses reinforced the Johnson administration's belief that additional escalation would prove increasingly divisive.

On March 25–26, a beleaguered Johnson called for a meeting of a group of fourteen unofficial senior advisers he referred to as the "Wise Men"—former cabinet officers, presidential aides, ambassadors, generals, and others who had advised him on other occasions. The Wise Men included former secretary of state Dean Acheson, former ambassador Henry Cabot Lodge, former national security adviser McGeorge Bundy, and retired generals Omar Bradley, Matthew Ridgway, and Maxwell Taylor.

Johnson had gone to the Wise Men for counsel before, and as late as November 1967, they had recommended that the president stay the course in Vietnam and press ahead with his current program, rejecting de-escalation of the war. Now, in the wake of the Tet Offensive, Johnson turned again to the group for advice.

The Wise Men met on March 25, with two members of Johnson's cabinet, Secretary of State Rusk and Secretary of Defense Clifford, in attendance. Military and CIA officials briefed the group, saying that even with reinforcements it might take the United States another five to ten years to defeat the Communists in Vietnam. At the end of two days of meetings, the Wise Men met with the president and delivered their verdict: the war was unwinnable with present policies, and it was time for the United States to begin reducing its role in South Vietnam. Though there was some disagreement, the consensus of the Wise Men was that no additional troops should be sent to Vietnam, that the bombing of North Vietnam should be halted, and that the United States should move toward a negotiated settlement and disengagement.

Johnson was shocked by this shift in opinion among these solidly anticommunist elder statesmen and military leaders, some of whom had helped shape the policies that had gotten the United States involved in Vietnam in the first place. Although the antiwar movement had not been able to change Lyndon Johnson's policies directly, it had an effect on the Wise Men, and they in turn pushed Johnson in a new direction. As Johnson noted in his memoirs, the Wise Men "expressed deep concern about the divisions in our country. Some of them felt that those divisions were growing rapidly and might soon force withdrawal from Vietnam."[29] Although the president did not wholeheartedly subscribe to the advice of the Wise Men—"The establishment bastards have bailed out," he bitterly noted—their recommendations, clearly a repudiation of his war policies, greatly influenced Johnson as he prepared to make a major speech on the war to the nation.[30] He later wrote in his memoirs that he had asked himself at the time, "If they [the Wise Men] had been so deeply influenced by the reports of the Tet offensive, what must the average citizen in the country be thinking?"[31]

On Sunday, March 31, 1968, the beleaguered president spoke to the American people in a nationally televised broadcast. That night he announced that the Tet Offensive had been a failure for the Communists, but he did not offer any optimistic predictions. Instead, he announced a halt to the bombing raids in North Vietnam except for the area just north of the DMZ and called upon North Vietnamese leaders to join the United States in peace talks. And at the end of the speech he paused and said, "With America's sons in the fields far away, with America's future under challenge right here at home, with our hopes and the world's hopes for peace in the balance every day, I do not believe that I should devote an hour or a day of my time to any personal partisan causes or to any duties other than the awesome duties of this office—the Presidency of your country." Then he stunned his listeners by declaring, "I shall not seek, and I will not accept, the nomination of my party for another term as your president."[32] The Vietnam War had finally destroyed Johnson's presidency.

Three days after Johnson's speech, North Vietnamese leaders announced their willingness to accept his invitation to take part in peace negotiations. American and North Vietnamese diplomats began meeting a few weeks later in Paris to discuss how the talks would be arranged. It turned out to be a long discussion, since the United States initially objected to the participation of the Viet Cong in the peace talks, and the Communists objected to the participation of the Saigon government.

The first formal meeting of the negotiations began on May 13 at the Majestic Hotel in Paris. Ambassador-at-large W. Averell Harriman, representing the U.S. side, met with Hanoi's representative, Xuan Thuy, secretary of the Lao Dong Party. These negotiations were extremely contentious from the very beginning and would last for the next five years.

Having essentially forced a president out of office, the Tet Offensive claimed another major victim in June 1968 when Westmoreland, who had commanded the Military Assistance Command, Vietnam (MACV) for four and a half years, was replaced and promoted to fill the position of U.S. Army Chief of Staff. Johnson had actually made the decision to replace Westmoreland with his deputy, General Creighton Abrams, in mid-January before the Tet offensive was launched, but the delayed announcement enabled Westmoreland's critics to maintain that the president had become disenchanted with the general because of the Tet offensive and had "kicked him upstairs."

On June 17, the Marines began to take down the base at Khe Sanh and evacuate the area. The American press criticized the decision, especially after the number of casualties that had been sustained there. To walk away from a site that so recently had been proclaimed a vital position further strained the president's credibility with the public and emphasized the war's irrationality.

On November 1, Johnson halted all bombing of North Vietnam (U.S. planes had continued since March to pound targets up to 225 miles north of the DMZ). President Nguyen Van Thieu of South Vietnam still objected to peace negotiations, apparently trying to delay any talks until after what he hoped would be the election of Richard Nixon to the presidency. All the while, the year's death toll in Vietnam continued to mount. American losses in the war by the end of 1968 stood at 30,610 killed. Of these, 14,589, nearly half the total number, had been killed in the past year.

THE PRESIDENTIAL ELECTION OF 1968

While American troops were trying to stabilize the situation in South Vietnam, a bitter election campaign was being waged in the United States. Former vice president Richard Nixon received the Republican nomination for the presidency, implying that he had a "secret plan" to end the war in Vietnam if elected. Meanwhile, the Democratic Party splintered over the war issue. Eugene McCarthy and Robert Kennedy won most of the primaries in the spring, but Kennedy was assassinated in early June after winning the California primary. Vice President Hubert Humphrey entered the race for the presidency in April with President Johnson's support. In August, he won the Democratic Party's nomination at its national convention in Chicago, which was marred by bloody street battles between antiwar protesters and Chicago police. Humphrey was too closely identified with Lyndon Johnson's failed policies in Vietnam to unite his party in the remaining weeks before the November election. On November 5, 1968, Richard Nixon was elected president of the United States, and on January 20, 1969, he was inaugurated. It was now Nixon's war.

Following his inauguration in January 1969, Nixon began to implement a new policy in South Vietnam. Called Vietnamization, it included improved training and a vast modernization effort for the South Vietnamese armed forces. Concurrently, Nixon began to withdraw American troops, a process that continued until almost all U.S. ground soldiers had left. In 1972, U.S. advisers and massive American airpower helped the South Vietnamese beat back a North Vietnamese invasion. After months of secret negotiations with the North

Vietnamese and a stepped-up bombing campaign, the Paris Peace Accords were signed in January 1973, and a cease-fire was initiated soon thereafter. By March of that year, all American military forces had been withdrawn from South Vietnam. The cease-fire proved to be only a momentary lull in the fighting, which continued for two more years until a final Communist offensive overran the South Vietnamese forces in fifty-five days. On April 30, 1975, PAVN tanks crashed through the gates at the presidential palace in Saigon, and the war was over. All of Vietnam fell under Hanoi's control, and Saigon was renamed Ho Chi Minh City.

Chapter 7

ASSESSING THE TET OFFENSIVE

Any assessment of the Tet Offensive must begin with the critical question of "Who won?" For some, such as historian David F. Schmitz, the Tet Offensive clearly "represented a defeat for the United States and its policy in Vietnam."[1] However, the question is very complex. An assessment of the Tet Offensive must be considered on a number of levels; as historian William J. Duiker suggests, it must be viewed in "highly qualified terms and not simply as a victory or defeat for either side."[2] Militarily, Tet was largely a failure for Hanoi and the National Liberation Front (NLF). By attacking the major cities, the Communists had hoped to win a huge symbolic victory. They wanted to prove to the South Vietnamese people that they could not depend on the Saigon government or the American army, even with its huge firepower advantage, to protect them. The Communists also hoped that the people of South Vietnam, especially the Buddhist activists who were opposed to the regime in Saigon, might rise up and begin a revolt. Combined with pressure from the Viet Cong (VC) and People's Army of Vietnam (PAVN) troops, a popular uprising might have toppled the South Vietnamese government and led to an immediate American withdrawal. When this uprising did not materialize, the government in Saigon and the American command claimed a great victory.

Militarily, there is clear justification for such claims. Tactically, the Tet Offensive was a catastrophe for the Viet Cong and PAVN. General Vo Nguyen

Giap's plan failed to achieve the hoped-for decisive victory on the battlefield for a number of reasons.

First, he underestimated the tactical and strategic mobility of the American forces in South Vietnam. His opposite, General William Westmoreland, was able to take advantage of this mobility and could react to the enemy thrusts across South Vietnam's borders and still pull his forces quickly back when the Communists launched their assault on the cities and towns. Thus, Giap's preparatory attacks along the borders failed to draw the U.S. forces to those areas permanently. The mobile American troops fought the border battles but were still available to react rapidly to the offensive once it was launched.

Second, Giap's plan was too complicated and difficult to coordinate. The strict secrecy required to insure surprise prevented coordination between units that had never worked together. Each unit knew only its small piece of the plan and had no feel for the overall campaign objectives. Thus, while achieving numerous isolated initial successes, once in position the Communist troops had to fend for themselves and often appeared not to have any real idea of what to do next.

Additionally, the secrecy and coordination problems contributed to the confusion that may have led to the premature attacks on January 30, 1968. Thus, the offensive was launched piecemeal over two days rather than in one simultaneous decisive blow. As Dave Richard Palmer suggests, "Had all the battles commenced as planned that first night, the outcome might well have been different. As it turned out, most Allied forces were granted from a few hours to a few days to brace for the storm."[3]

Third, Giap's plan violated the principle of mass. The PAVN and Viet Cong had tried to hit too many places at once. By attacking virtually everywhere, they were strong nowhere, spreading their forces too thinly; thus, they did not have enough troops to do much more than make some spectacular attacks that were soon defeated by allied forces. Only in Hue and Saigon did Giap have enough forces to make a significant impact.

Ultimately, the plan called for the Communists to attack the strength of the American and South Vietnamese (ARVN) forces. Turning away from their previously very successful hit-and-run tactics, the Communists attacked headlong into vastly superior firepower. Even when the attacks were successful, there were no plans for what to do next and upon attaining their initial objectives, the Communists became immobilized or were forced to retreat for lack of follow-up orders or reinforcements.

The greatest failing of Giap's plan at the tactical level lies in the assumptions upon which it was based, all of which proved to be absolutely wrong in the end. The Communists had expected the ARVN to crumble under their attacks, but the South Vietnamese army did not collapse, nor did the ARVN soldiers desert in large numbers to join the Viet Cong as the Communists had predicted.

Despite instances of poor leadership, troop indiscipline, and excessive reliance on American firepower, the South Vietnamese responded fairly well to the demands of the situation.

As for the anticipated general uprising, there had been no spontaneous revolt by the South Vietnamese people against the Saigon government. On the contrary, the devastation resulting from the fighting caused many South Vietnamese to rally behind Saigon.

The price of Giap's miscalculations and flawed assumptions was high. The Tet Offensive resulted in huge casualty figures for the Communist forces. Estimates range from a total of 40,000 dead out of 80,000 Communists engaged to as high as more than 72,000 Communists dead, according to U.S. military records.[4] While these numbers are certainly subject to debate, it is clear that the Communists failed to hold on to any of the major objectives that they had attacked and suffered horrendous casualties in the process; this situation undermined the Viet Cong's "reputation of invincibility."[5]

Most historians agree that the National Liberation Front never completely recovered from Tet. The Viet Cong was badly crippled as a fighting force, and the NLF political organization was seriously damaged.[6] In 1981, Dr. Duong Quynh Hoa, a prominent Communist, told journalist Stanley Karnow that the Viet Cong had borne the brunt of the heavy fighting in the cities and towns; she admitted mournfully, "We lost our best people."[7] Militarily, the Viet Cong were never again able to field full main-force battalions (with some exceptions, such as in the Mekong Delta). From this point on in the war, the war became more conventional and was fought mainly by PAVN forces controlled directly from Hanoi. Journalist Don Oberdorfer remarks, "The Viet Cong lost the best of a generation of resistance fighters, and after Tet increasing numbers of North Vietnamese had to be sent south to fill the ranks. The war became increasingly a conventional battle and less an insurgency. Because the people of the cities did not rise up against the foreigners and puppets at Tet—indeed they gave little support to the attack force—the Communist claim to moral and political authority in South Vietnam suffered a serious blow."[8]

PAVN General Tran Van Tra writes, "We did not correctly evaluate the specific balance of forces between ourselves and the enemy, did not fully realize that the enemy still had considerable capabilities and that our capabilities were limited, and set requirements that were beyond our actual strength. . . . We suffered large sacrifices and losses with regard to manpower and material, especially cadres at the various echelons, which clearly weakened us. Afterwards, we were not only unable to retain the gains we had made but had to overcome a myriad of difficulties in 1969 and 1970 so that the revolutionary could stand firm in the storm."[9] According to Duong Quynh Hoa, "Hanoi was guilty of grievous miscalculation, which squandered the strength of the Southern forces."[10]

U.S. and South Vietnamese forces had indeed defeated VC and PAVN forces on the tactical level, recovering quickly from the surprise and fighting courageously; fifteen Americans were awarded the Medal of Honor for bravery during the Tet battles. However, the allied victory had been very costly. More than 1,100 Americans were killed and wounded in the first two weeks of Tet, along with several thousand South Vietnamese soldiers. By the end of March, the casualties had risen to 1,001 American dead and 2,082 ARVN and other allied forces killed.[11]

On the upside for the allies, the South Vietnamese troops had displayed better fighting capability than most observers expected, and government control was reestablished in most areas following the heavy fighting in the late spring and early summer. Recruiting by the Saigon government flourished, and ARVN morale was much higher than before Tet. The government was soon able to arm thousands of volunteers for a nationwide self-defense force.

Still, the Tet Offensive had damaged allied pacification efforts in the rural areas. The offensive weakened the government's standing in the countryside. Historian Richard A. Hunt remarks, "Nearly five hundred of the five thousand RF/PF [Regional Forces/Popular Forces] outposts were abandoned or overrun, and the government moved RF/PF units out of rural villages and into besieged towns and cities to provide additional defensive forces."[12] The withdrawal of government soldiers and police contributed to a drop in security, and many villages reverted to revolutionary control when the allied troops who normally operated in those areas were withdrawn to handle the fighting in the population centers. However, Hunt points out that the setback to the pacification program was not as drastic as depicted in the American press and that allied forces recovered very quickly. However, Westmoreland's request for additional troops seemed to confirm the gloomy reports in the American media.[13]

In the cities, there was much ambivalence on the part of the citizenry. A study conducted in Saigon in late 1968 revealed that many South Vietnamese in the city remained passive and might be led to accommodate to the Viet Cong movement.[14] The South Vietnamese and American troops had turned back the Communist onslaught in 1968, but there was much concern among South Vietnamese, particularly the elite in Saigon, that the ARVN would not be able to stand up to future attacks if the Americans left.[15] Such attitudes would have a great impact on the success of the Vietnamization effort after Nixon took office. Thus, Tet, according to a study by Leslie Gelb and Richard Betts, "exposed the extreme vulnerability of the GVN [Government of Vietnam] that lay beneath the veneer of military progress."[16]

The Tet Offensive was never a purely military campaign, and any analysis of the operation must include an assessment of the outcome of its strategic political objectives. Although the allies won most of the Tet battles and inflicted horrendous casualties on the Communist forces, the Tet Offensive "broke like a clap of thunder on an astonished world" and resulted in a stunning strategic victory for the Communists.[17] In the words of a former VC colonel, Bui Tin, "the *Mau Than* Offensive caused a disastrous turnabout in U.S. policy that gave Hanoi breathing room at just the moment when we were hardest-pressed in South Vietnam! So, on the political, strategic, and psychological fronts, we had won a major and spectacular victory!"[18]

However, Stanley Karnow and others maintain that the outcome of the Tet Offensive may not have been as clear-cut to the Communist planners as Bui Tin and his comrades would have it. Karnow quotes a top North Vietnamese general, Tran Do, who commented after the war, "In all honesty, we didn't achieve our main objective, which was to spur uprisings throughout the south. Still, we inflicted heavy casualties on the Americans and their puppets, and this was a big gain for us. As for making an impact in the United States, it had not been our intention—but it turned out to be a fortunate result."[19]

Such statements have contributed toward the claim by many that a decisive tactical defeat was turned into a psychological victory at the strategic level, almost by happenstance. A perfect example of this line of thought can be seen in most discussions of the results of the VC attack on the U.S. embassy. Historian James R. Arnold spoke for many when he wrote of the embassy attack, "Here was the paradox of the war: a small, ill-conceived, tactically flawed attack against an insignificant military objective, designed to impress the South Vietnamese, proved the decisive action of the war because of its impact on the American public."[20]

Some American historians of the war, most of the senior leaders who participated in the war, and much of the American public maintain that the reaction to the Tet Offensive in the United States was a fortunate coincidence for Hanoi and the NLF—that the impact of this attack and the rest of the Tet Offensive was a result of "a meddling new media" and "weak-willed leaders" and not because of any design by the Communists.[21] The implication is that the war was lost in Washington and not in Vietnam.

General Tran Van Tra finds this assessment of the outcome of the Offensive to be "an example of blind xeno [xenophobia]."[22] To Tra, the Tet Offensive was a strategic victory "won by blood" that achieved the objectives that it was designed to accomplish. He wrote:

> The Tet Offensive was still a great victory, creating the most important strategic turning point of the war, eventually leading us to total victory. Tet, Tet Mau Than in fact, shook the enemy's aggressive will to its foundation and put an end to the U.S. dream of achieving "victory" by escalating the war; it awakened the United States to the fact that might, resources,

and money have their limits; and it highlighted the conclusion that the United States was not strong enough to force another nation—even a smaller and weaker one—to kneel down and surrender if that nation's desire for independence and freedom was strong.[23]

For Giap, the Tet Offensive had vindicated North Vietnam's war strategy. Speaking of the Americans, he claimed, "Until Tet they had thought they could win the war, but now they knew that they could not."[24] There was a lot of truth in what Giap said. Part of the impact of the Tet Offensive lay in its timing. It occurred just before the first presidential primaries and thus, in the words of Don Oberdorfer, "caught the American political system at its moment of greatest irresolution and potential for change."[25] According to Townsend Hoopes, one of President Johnson's advisors, the Tet attacks left the White House in a state of "troubled confusion and uncertainty."[26] This situation would prove fatal for the Johnson administration and represented the turning point in the war for the United States. Political scientist Bernard Brodie maintains that the Tet Offensive "does not simply mark but actually caused the beginning of the end of American participation in the Vietnam War, with all the strategic and political consequences that flowed from that withdrawal."[27]

On one level, the Tet Offensive was an ill-advised and comprehensive military defeat at the tactical level for the Communists. But, as Brodie suggests, Tet, whether by design or not, was "unique in that the side that lost completely in a tactical sense came away with an overwhelming psychological and hence political victory."[28] According to historian David Schmitz, the Tet Offensive was decisive because of its impact on senior officials in the Johnson administration, who then helped bring about Johnson's dramatic decision to change policy.[29] The offensive had shaken the will of both the president and the American public, convinced Johnson to institute a unilateral bombing halt, resulted in the opening of negotiations in Paris, and ultimately led to the president's leaving office. The Viet Cong and PAVN had paid a high price, but, as Tran Van Tra writes, they were prepared to make such sacrifices since the Tet Offensive was meant to be the "decisive phase" of the revolutionary "road to victory."[30]

The Tet Offensive played a key role in the subsequent events that led to the long, protracted U.S. withdrawal under Richard Nixon. It marked the beginning of the end of U.S. involvement in Southeast Asia. In the final analysis, as Oberdorfer writes, "The North Vietnamese and Viet Cong lost a battle. The United States Government lost something even more important—the confidence of its people at home."[31] It is correct that the Vietnamese foe lost the bloody battles of the Tet Offensive and that, as many historians point out, the allied forces made progress in the aftermath of the offensive, but in the long run, the tactical successes and the advances in pacification achieved during the years following the offensive eventually proved irrelevant. At the strategic level, the offensive was not a "desperate gamble," but rather a calculated campaign that won a great political victory that turned the tide of the war. It proved to the United States that the war was unwinnable, effectively toppled a president, convinced the new president to "Vietnamize" the war, and paved the way for the ultimate triumph of the Communist forces in 1975.

PART II

Issues and Interpretations

Chapter 8

MOTIVATIONS AND OBJECTIVES OF
THE TET OFFENSIVE

Scholars disagree about what motivated the Tet Offensive. As historian Edwin Moise has pointed out, "It is not entirely clear to what extent this extraordinary gamble was based on hopes it could achieve its maximum goals—causing a real collapse of the Republic of Vietnam, and drawing the population of the cities into a general uprising—and to what extent it was based on a reasonable assurance of achieving more modest disruptions of the U.S. and ARVN war effort, and of U.S. public support for the war."[1] The question remains a source of debate among historians of the war. Some argue that the North Vietnamese Communist government and the National Liberation Front (NLF) were worried about mounting losses and pursued a conventional assault as a desperate measure to stay in the war. Most, however, believe that the leaders in Hanoi, despite the difficulties incurred in the south, remained optimistic about their ultimate success and their ability to improve the military situation or even achieve a knockout blow on the South Vietnamese armed forces. Other observers maintain that the offensive was an attempt to improve the position of the North Vietnamese in future negotiations by placing the two northernmost South Vietnamese provinces under Communist control. Still others claim that the attitudes of the American public and members of the Johnson administration were the ultimate targets of the offensive. All of these perspectives are subject to debate. The Communists have been less than forthcoming with explanations of their motives for the offensive, which remain obscured by propaganda and the difficulty in gaining access to North Vietnamese records.

The Communists clearly hoped to stimulate a popular uprising and the formation of a coalition government. Some might have looked for the collapse of Nguyen Van Thieu's regime and perhaps even an American withdrawal. According to historian George Herring, a majority more likely expected a less decisive change, such as a halt to the bombing or a weakened government in Saigon, and viewed the offensive as part of a long-term strategy of "fighting while negotiating."[2]

Historians James Owens and Randy Roberts maintain that North Vietnamese strategist Nguyen Chi Thanh, head of the Central Office for South Vietnam and one of the primary advocates for launching the general offensive, believed that the offensive could alter the entire outcome of the war. The success of a widespread offensive could undermine the Thieu regime, force the South Vietnamese Army (ARVN) to surrender, secure a military foothold in the major cities and provincial capitals, and inflict heavy casualties on Americans while bringing the war home to the South Vietnam to demonstrate that Viet Cong (VC) power was everywhere.[3]

Other sources make it clear that some Communist leaders in Hanoi were not sure of the likely outcome; one, Le Duan, is reported to have said that they "must fight and then see."[4] Historian Ngo Vinh Long, having done extensive research in Vietnam, has written that the most important objective of the Tet Offensive was to force the United States "to de-escalate the war in North Vietnam and to begin negotiations."[5] Similarly, historian Marilyn Young maintains that the leaders in Hanoi hoped for a collapse of the South Vietnamese government, followed by popular demands for a coalition government that would include the National Liberation Front, and the consequent withdrawal of the United States.[6]

The picture became somewhat clearer in 2002 when an English translation of *The Official History of the People's Army of Vietnam, 1954–1975* was published. In discussing the planning for the Tet Offensive, the official history quotes the Party Central Committee resolution that called for the general offensive and general uprising, enumerating the following objectives:

- To break down and destroy the bulk of the puppet troops, topple the puppet administration at all levels, and take power into the hands of the people.
- To destroy the major part of the U.S. forces and their war materiel and render them unable to fulfill their political and military duties in Vietnam.

- On this basis, to break the U.S. will of aggression, force it to accept defeat in the South, and put an end to all acts of war against the North. With this, we will achieve the immediate objectives of our revolution—independence, democracy, peace, and neutrality for the South—and we can proceed to national reunification.[7]

Historians writing before the publication of the official history were aware of this resolution, but, as one can see, the general language of the document is indirect and does not spell out the specific objectives of the offensive. Extrapolating from the resolution and comparing it with what happened once the fighting started, some historians have asserted that Hanoi's aim was to undermine the confidence of the South Vietnamese civilians living in the cities as well as the peasants who had fled there from the countryside. By attacking the cities, the North Vietnamese hoped to prove to the people that there was no safety anywhere in South Vietnam, with the result that they would lose all confidence in their government, which would eventually be toppled by the Communists. In addition, according to the historians who hold this view, Hanoi believed that the American people, whom the Johnson administration had assured that their troops were winning the war, would be shaken in their support of the war effort. The peace protests in America would grow, and pressure would therefore build on the U.S. government to rethink the war and begin to disengage from South Vietnam. The North Vietnamese were doubtless hopeful that the offensive would lessen American support for the war. Still, Pham Van Dong, North Vietnam's prime minister, told the American reporter David Schoenbrun in 1967 that the North Vietnamese were "grateful for the help of the American peace demonstrators, but, in the final analysis we know that we must count mainly on ourselves."[8]

An additional objective for the offensive can be gleaned from an examination of a series of articles by Giap entitled "The Big Victory, the Great Task," broadcast by Radio Hanoi on September 17–20, 1967. The Communists were aware that a new offensive might have an explosive impact during an American election year. In Giap's words, the offensive would become a partisan issue that "will make the American people more aware of the errors and setbacks of the Johnson administration in the aggressive war in Vietnam."[9]

It appears that the Communist leaders believed that a catastrophic military defeat of allied forces in an American election year, an immense increase in American and South Vietnamese casualties, and a demonstration that the South Vietnamese were incapable of shouldering the burden of the war together might prove the equivalent of a Dien Bien Phu. The U.S. government might then decide that there was no way to victory except at a cost that most Americans were unwilling to pay.[10]

William J. Duiker, author of *The Communist Road to Victory in Vietnam*, maintains that while the North Vietnamese were quite confident before the offensive, they hedged their bets with a contingency plan "in case the uprising did not succeed in achieving the total overthrow of enemy power, it would be followed by a series of military offensives during succeeding months to wear down the enemy and lead either to victory of to a negotiated settlement."[11] That explains the follow-on phases in the summer and early autumn of 1968, after the earlier fighting had failed to achieve all of their goals.

Another interpretation ascribes a wholly different goal for the North Vietnamese in 1968. Norman Podhoretz, author of *Why We Were in Vietnam*, and Harry Summers, author of *On Strategy*, assert that one objective of the Tet Offensive was the elimination of the Viet Cong in order to insure that South Vietnam would be controlled by North Vietnam after the war was over.[12] This is highly debatable, and other historians argue that it is unlikely that North Vietnam, locked in a life-or-death struggle with the United States, would have willingly squandered that many military forces in the interest of postwar internal politics.

Some have attributed great military genius to Giap, asserting that he knowingly set out to achieve the great psychological victory against the United States. Other historians suggest that there is little evidence to indicate that Giap had any idea how great the impact of the offensive would be on both the White House and the American public. Tran Do, a top North Vietnamese general, acknowledged that the Communists had failed to spur the general uprising in the south but still managed to inflict heavy casualties on both the Americans and the South Vietnamese. As for achieving a decisive psychological victory in the United States, Do admits that "it had not been our intention—but it turned out to be a fortunate result."[13]

Given the stated and implied objectives of the Tet Offensive, perhaps the best assessment of how the Communists did in achieving them can be found in a 1988 article in a Vietnamese military journal written by General Tran Van Tra, who was commander of the Communist B-2 Front in the south for a major part of the war against the United States. He reveals that he and his comrades failed to achieve the goals enumerated in the Central Party Committee resolution because they "surpassed our actual capabilities by many times."[14] That may be true, but in the end, the offensive had such an impact on the White House, media, and the American people that the Communists' failure to achieve their original goals at the tactical and operational levels proved irrelevant. In the end, they won a great political victory at the strategic level.

Chapter 9

MILITARY INTELLIGENCE AND
SURPRISE AT TET

One of the lingering debates about the Tet Offensive centers on how the Communists were able to achieve the level of surprise that they did when they launched the offensive. As historian John Prados has written, "Whether the attack at Tet represented a surprise—and intelligence failure—has ever after remained a fervid question, often lurking in the wings of Vietnam discussions, provoking numerous arguments."[1]

The Viet Cong (VC) and People's Army of Vietnam (PAVN) skillfully used both active and passive deception to fool the allied intelligence apparatus. By using passive measures such as operations security to achieve secrecy, they were effectively able to mask preparations for the offensive. By using active deception measures such as the offensive operations in the border areas, they successfully drew the allies' attention away from the urban target areas.

Nevertheless, there were numerous signs that the Communists were up to something. Vo Nguyen Giap had written a series of articles broadcast over Hanoi Radio, which also appeared in part in PAVN newspapers in September 1967 and were later published collectively as *Big Victory, Great Task*. In one of the broadcasts, Giap acknowledged the U.S. troop buildup in South Vietnam while noting that an opportunity presented itself to confront Washington with a dilemma because "the present mobilization level has far exceeded initial U.S.

forecast and is at sharp variance with U.S. global strategy."[2] Then Giap outlined how the Communists planned to take advantage of that opportunity.

In retrospect, these articles provided a pretty good blueprint for what Hanoi was planning, but the beliefs many U.S. commanders and analysts embraced diverged from Giap's description of the situation, and thus they dismissed his claims and recommendations as unrealistic.[3] Such dismissals of new intelligence would continue even as indicators of an impending offensive began to mount.

On October 16, 1967, South Vietnamese Army (ARVN) units in the Mekong Delta found a three-page memorandum from the regional party committee, dated September 2, that used the phrase "winter-spring campaign" and discussed preparations for it. On October 25, an important enemy document fell into allied hands in Tay Ninh Province. Dated September 1, 1967, the document contained instructional material on how "to help better understand the new situation and our new task."[4] It further defined a three-pronged offensive designed to defeat the South Vietnamese forces, destroy U.S. political and military institutions, and instigate a countrywide insurrection of the popular masses. According to the captured document, this projected offensive bore the abbreviated designation TCK-TKN for *Tong Cong Kich–Tong Khoi Nghia* (General Offensive–General Uprising). At about the same time, ARVN troops captured another document that discussed sapper training and preparations for VC and PAVN personnel to use against ARVN mechanized equipment.

Over the next two months, several other captured documents indicated that a new offensive was in the offing. Perhaps the best known of these documents was a military directive issued by COSVN B-3 Front Command, which controlled Communist operations in the central part of South Vietnam. This document fell into allied hands in mid-November 1967. It called for "many large scale, well-coordinated combat operations" to "destroy or disintegrate a large part of the Puppet [ARVN] army." Of particular note were directions to "annihilate a major U.S. element in order to force the enemy to deploy as many additional troops to the Western highlands as possible."[5]

On November 19, the picture became clearer when U.S. troopers from the 2nd Battalion, 327th Airborne, operating in Quang Tin Province, captured a thirteen-page notebook containing a document entitled "Ho Chi Minh's Order for Implementation of General Counteroffensive and General Uprising during 1967 Winter and 1968 Spring and Summer." This document was translated and disseminated to both U.S. and South Vietnamese intelligence agencies in the form of a detailed memorandum from the Defense Intelligence Agency. The U.S. embassy in Saigon even put out a press release containing a number of details from the notebook and document. Still, the dissemination of this intelligence appears not to have had a major impact on allied thinking or preparations.

On November 25, 1967, allied forces in Tay Ninh province captured a ten-page document. Dated September 1, 1967, it was essentially a training manual entitled "Clearly Understand the New Situation and Mission: Take Advantage of Victories to Surge Forward and Complete Defeat the U.S. and Puppet Enemy." It contained a general outline of the strategy and objectives of a new offensive.

Captured documents were not the only indications that a new offensive was impending. Although enemy troop-infiltration levels did not appear to be out of the ordinary in late 1967, reports of more than twenty thousand enemy troops moving south in January represented a drastic increase and indicated that some sort of increased enemy action was probable. Additionally, truck traffic detected on the Ho Chi Minh Trail in late 1967 far exceeded earlier periods, further indicating that a major push was coming.

Thus, there was a good deal of fairly explicit intelligence available to U.S. and South Vietnamese decision makers in the last few months leading up to the offensive, intelligence that gave indications of significant action pending by the Communists. According to John Prados, "The indicators were numerous. . . . The stream of them began relatively early in the cycle of preparation for the offensive and that many of the reports were complementary and built upon each other."[6]

So, then, the question is, why the surprise? The Tet Offensive represented, in the words of National Security Council staff member William Jorden, writing in a February 1968 cable to presidential advisor Walt Rostow, "the worst intelligence failure of the war."[7] Nevertheless, after the war, some of those officers who held posts as commanders and intelligence officers in Vietnam at the time of the Tet Offensive asserted that Military Assistance Command, Vietnam (MACV) headquarters was fully aware that there had been a change in North Vietnamese strategy, but was surprised only by the actual scale and level of coordination of the Tet attacks.[8]

Many historians and other observers discount such claims and have endeavored to understand how the Communists were able to achieve such a stunning level of surprise. There are a number of possible explanations. First, allied estimates of enemy strengths and intentions were flawed. Part of the problem was that MACV, in an effort to show progress in the war, had purposefully downgraded the intelligence estimates about VC/PAVN strength. CIA analyst Sam Adams charges that MACV actually falsified intelligence reports to show progress in the war.[9] Whether this accusation is true is subject to debate, but it is a fact that MACV changed the way it counted the enemy, revising enemy strength downward from almost 300,000 to 235,000 in December 1967.[10] U.S. intelligence analysts apparently believed their own revised estimates and largely disregarded the mounting evidence that the Communists not only retained a significant combat capability but also planned to use that capability in a dramatic fashion.

Former South Vietnamese Colonel Hoang Ngoc Lung, in a postwar monograph written for the U.S. Army about the 1968 offensive, observes that "intelligence theory taught us that in estimating the enemy's probably course of action we should be primarily concerned with his capabilities and not his intentions."[11] Having said that, he asserts that South Vietnamese intelligence analysts dismissed many of the captured documents as so much wishful thinking on the part of the Communists—that the documents represented merely an expression of the intention of the Communists, rather than something they clearly had the capabilities to accomplish—at least as those capabilities were known and assessed by allied commanders and intelligence analysts.

Thus, the allies greatly underestimated the capabilities of their enemy and dismissed new intelligence indicators because they too greatly contradicted prevailing assumptions about the enemy's strength and capabilities. It was thought that enemy capabilities were insufficient to support a nationwide campaign. As Marilyn Young, author of *The Vietnam Wars*, writes, "To have taken other signs of the coming offensive seriously—captured document, rumors, warnings given American civilians by Vietnamese friends—would have meant revising the view of the war to which Americans, civilian as well as military, were firmly wedded."[12] Therefore, the influence of entrenched beliefs about the enemy and the nature of the war colored the perceptions of allied commanders and intelligence officers when they were presented with intelligence that varied with their preconceived notions.

In the same vein, documents and other evidence were discounted because the analysts did not think that the Communists would want to incur inevitable heavy losses for such questionable objectives. Even if the Communists could occupy any cities, did they have the strength to hold them against the strong reaction of the allied forces? Thus, the reports did not pass the logic test for allied intelligence analysts. Such an evaluation depends, of course, on who is defining what is logical.

Some of the South Vietnamese analysts even believed that the enemy was actually reverting to the first or defensive phase of his revolutionary war strategy. They thought that U.S. search-and-destroy operations conducted in 1967 in War Zones C and D and the Iron Triangle, the critical areas between Saigon and the Cambodian border, had forced the Communists to return to a more defensive posture and that the enemy did not have the capability to go from there to a general offensive.[13] Even when the analysts agreed that there was a general offensive being planned, they thought it would come in the distant future, because Giap had always talked about the war lasting for a protracted period. These perceptions overshadowed information suggesting indications of an impending escalation.

Another problem that had an impact on the intelligence failures in Tet deals with what is known today as "fusion." The data collected was never assembled into a complete and cohesive picture of what the Communists were doing. The analysts often failed to integrate cumulative information, even though they were charged with the production of estimates that should have facilitated the combination of different indicators into an overall analysis. Part of this problem can be traced to the lack of coordination between allied intelligence agencies. Most of these organizations operated independently and rarely shared their information with each other. That was true even within the military intelligence structure.

Ronnie Ford, author of *Tet 1968: Understanding the Surprise*, argues that bureaucratic infighting over order-of-battle issues among the American intelligence agencies led to the lack of coordination and information sharing, impeding both the synthesis of all the intelligence that was available and the ability to predict when and where the offensive might come. Ford writes, "The substantive disagreements and bureaucratic infighting that were to follow in Washington and in Saigon over enemy strength would preclude the fusion of intelligence necessary to prevent the surprise of the 1968 Tet Offensive."[14]

Even if the allied intelligence apparatus had been better at fusion, it would still have had to deal with widely conflicting reports that clouded the issue. While the aforementioned intelligence indicated that a general offensive was in the offing, there were a number of other intelligence reports indicating that the enemy was facing extreme difficulties in the field and that his morale had declined markedly. It was difficult to differentiate among the widely differing reports. Additionally, some indicators that should have caused alarm among intelligence analysts got lost in the noise of developments related to more obvious and more widely expected adversary threats. Faced with evidence of increasing enemy activity near urban areas and along the borders of the country, the allies were forced to decide where, when, and how the main blow would fall. They failed in this effort.

As James J. Wirtz, author of *The Tet Offensive: Intelligence Failure in War*, points out, there was an ever-increasing amount of information indicating that the Communists were preparing to attack urban areas. On the other hand, Communist diversionary efforts intended to fix the majority of U.S. units in their normal operating areas increased in intensity. When indications that PAVN units were massing near Khe Sanh were confirmed by ground attacks against the firebase on January 21, reinforcements and the attention of U.S. commanders were directed toward the border area.[15]

Nowhere did General William C. Westmoreland, the MACV commander, predict a countrywide offensive. He thought there would be perhaps a "show of force," but otherwise the enemy's main effort would be directed at Khe Sanh and the northern provinces. His intelligence officer expected a threat in the Khe Sanh–Thua Thien area, but not much in the Saigon area (which conformed to the pattern of recent enemy activity in the battles of 1967). This fit well with the analysts' beliefs about enemy strategy and capabilities. Wirtz describes this situation very well when he observes that "individuals tend to make a decision when they possess information that confirms their preexisting beliefs, even though this information may fail to described adequately the present situation." Wirtz calls this the theory of "unmotivated bias."[16]

When intelligence indicators coincide with preferences, predisposition, and preexisting beliefs, the real message behind the gathering intelligence may be lost. In this case, as Larry Cable writes, the result was "an unwillingness to accept intelligence that runs counter to personal predilections, prejudices, and beliefs such as to constitute a variant of the common psychological occurrence called cognitive dissonance."[17] Thus, Westmoreland and most of his staff evaluated the intelligence in light of what they already believed, discounting most of it because it did not conform to their preconceived notions about the enemy situation and intentions.

The Communists skillfully contributed to the erroneous perceptions held at MACV headquarters. As John Prados writes, "adversary actions created a deception—an alternative interpretation of some plausibility. American commanders chose to believe in that other interpretation."[18] The nature and scope of the intelligence failure is debatable, but it is clear that there was a failure in "strategic conceptualization, which in turn was the product of the polluted policy process."[19]

The impact of surprise in Tet Offensive cannot be overstated. As Wirtz writes, "the Tet offensive represents an extraordinarily successful instance of surprise attack. Surprise itself altered the balance of political will between the combatants."[20] The scope and ferocity of the attacks stunned the American people, and although the offensive was an overwhelming defeat of the Communist forces at the tactical level, the sheer fact that the enemy had pulled off such an offensive and caught the allies by surprise ultimately contributed to the strategic Communist victory and the turning point of the war.

Chapter 10

WHAT HAPPENED AT HUE?

On October 31, 1969, *Time* reported that 2,300 bodies of South Vietnamese men, women, and children had been unearthed in several mass graves around Hue. The magazine article said that Communist cadres had executed the victims during the battle for the city in February 1968. What actually happened at Hue remains a topic of intense debate to this day.

One of the first in-depth assessments of the civilian deaths at Hue was by Douglas Pike, of the U.S. Information Agency. In *The Viet Cong Strategy of Terror*, published by the U.S. Mission in Saigon in 1970, Pike asserts that the Viet Cong (VC) executed many of the 5,800 civilians who were missing after the battle ended on February 24.

Pike reports that 1,200 bodies were discovered in eighteen hastily concealed shallow graves in the months following the end of the battle. The second major group of graves was found in the first seven months of 1969. A third group was discovered in September 1969, when three Communist defectors told intelligence officers of the 101st Airborne Division that they had witnessed the killing of several hundred people at Da Mai Creek, about ten miles south of Hue in February 1968. A subsequent search revealed the remains of about three hundred people in the creekbed. The fourth discovery of bodies was made in Phu Thu Salt Flats in November 1969, near the fishing village of Luong Vien some ten miles east of Hue.

All total, Pike reports that nearly two thousand bodies were recovered from these mass graves. Pike maintains that at least half of the bodies revealed clear evidence of "atrocity killings: to include hands wired behind backs, rags stuffed in mouths, bodies contorted but without wounds (indicating burial alive)."[1]

Pike charges that the killings were deliberately done and were not the result of rage, frustration, or panic during the Communist withdrawal, as others had suggested at the time of the discovery of the bodies. He says that the executions were done by local VC cadres and were the result of "a decision rational and justifiable in the Communist mind. In fact, most killings were, from the Communist calculation, imperative."[2] Pike points out that the Communist line on the Hue killings later at the Paris talks was that it was not the work of Communists but of "dissident local political parties."[3]

Journalist Don Oberdorfer, author of *Tet!*, first published in 1971, writes that while North Vietnamese troops at Hue were locked in combat with the Marines and South Vietnamese soldiers, VC cadres took over control of the city and began to round up government workers, foreigners, and other "reactionaries."[4] Oberdorfer cites a number of examples of what happened after the roundup. Stephen Miller, a twenty-eight-year-old American Foreign Service Officer, was in the home of Vietnamese friends when VC troops captured him. They led him away to a field behind a Catholic seminary, bound his arms, and then executed him. Physicians Raimund Discher, Alois Altekoester, and Horst Gunther Krainick thought they would be safe as foreign aid workers, but they were wrong. The Viet Cong came and took them and Krainick's wife away. Their bodies were later found dumped in a shallow grave in a nearby field. Similarly, two French priests, Father Urbain and Father Guy, were led away. Father Urbain's body was later found, bound hand and foot, where he had been buried alive. Father Guy's body was found in the same grave with Urbain and eighteen other victims; Guy had been shot in the back of the head. A Vietnamese priest met a similar fate. Father Buu Dong, who had tried to minister to both sides and even had a photograph of Ho Chi Minh in his room, was taken away. His body was found twenty-two months later in a shallow grave along with the remains of three hundred other victims.

Pham Van Tuong was on the list of "reactionaries" because he was a part-time janitor at the government information office. When VC troops visited his home, they found him hiding with his family. He emerged with his three-year-old daughter, five-year-old son, and two nephews. The Viet Cong immediately gunned down all five, leaving the bodies in the street for the rest of the family to see when they emerged moments later.

Mrs. Nguyen Thi Lao, a forty-eight-year-old widow who sold cigarettes from a street stand, was led away without any explanation. She was found in a common grave at the local high school, having been buried alive, arms bound behind her. She may have been mistaken for her sister, who was a clerk in one of the local government offices.

On the fifth day of the occupation, VC troops came to Phu Cam Cathedral, where they had gathered some four hundred men and boys. Some had been on the enemies list, some were of military age, and some just looked prosperous. VC cadres led them away to the south. It was apparently this group whose remains were later found in the bed of Da Mai Creek.

Don Oberdorfer believes that the Viet Cong executed 2,800 people in Hue, but he also acknowledges reports that in the last stages of the NLF occupation, Saigon government assassination teams operating in Hue began to systematically round up some of those believed to have aided the Communists. Most of these individuals were never seen again, and there is no record of what actually happened to them. However, the general belief is that they were executed. [5]

While that may be true, there is overwhelming evidence to suggest that the preponderance of the victims were deliberately killed by the Communists during the battle. Both Gunther Lewy, author of *America in Vietnam*, and Peter Macdonald, author of *Giap*, cite a captured enemy document that stated that, during the occupation of the city, the Communists "eliminated 1,892 administrative personnel, 38 policemen, 790 tyrants."[6]

In *A House in Hue*, Omar Eby describes the experience of a group of Mennonite aid workers who were trapped in their house when the Communists took over the city. He reports that the Mennonites in the house observed several Americans, one an agriculturist from the U.S. Agency for International Development, being led away by VC cadres with their arms tied behind their backs. They were later found executed. Eby reports that one of the Mennonites said, "During the first days the North Vietnamese had everything under control. It was only later that the VC began kidnapping and murdering."[7]

Truong Nhu Tang, author of *A Vietcong Memoir*, tells of a conversation with one of his VC colleagues about the situation at Hue that acknowledges that atrocities occurred at Hue, but his account differs in terms of describing the motivation for the killings. He says that a close friend told him that "discipline in Hue had been seriously inadequate. . . . Fanatic young soldiers had indiscriminately shot people, and angry local citizens who supported the revolution had on various occasions taken justice into their own hands. . . . It had simply been one of those terrible spontaneous tragedies that inevitably accompany war."[8]

Not everyone agrees that a massacre occurred at Hue, or at least one as described by Pike, Oberdorfer, and the others. In an article in the June 24, 1974, issue of *Indochina Chronicle* (reprinted in the *Congressional Record* on February 19, 1975), political scientist D. Gareth Porter maintains that the massacre is one of the "enduring myths of the Second Indochina War."[9] He then charges that Douglas Pike, who he calls a "media manipulator par excellence," was in collusion with the ARVN 10th Political Warfare Battalion to manufacture the story of the massacre at the direction of Ambassador Ellsworth Bunker. While acknowledging that some executions occurred, Porter asserts that the killings were not part of any overall plan. Additionally, he charges that Pike overestimated the number of those killed by the VC cadres and that "thousands" of civilians killed in Hue "were in fact victims of American air power and of the ground fighting that raged in the hamlets, rather than NLF execution."[10] Moreover, he agrees with Oberdorfer that teams of Saigon government assassins fanned out through the city with their own list of targets, eliminating NLF sympathizers, but on a much greater scale than Oberdorfer suggests. Porter concludes that "the official story of an indiscriminate slaughter of those who were considered to be unsympathetic to the NLF is a complete fabrication."[11]

The passage of time has not quelled the controversy over what happened in Hue. Writing in 1991, historian Marilyn B. Young, author of *The Vietnam Wars*, disputes the "official" figures of executions at Hue. While acknowledging that there were executions, she cites freelance journalist Len Ackland, who was present and estimated the figure to be somewhere between three hundred and four hundred.[12] Young attempts "to understand" what happened at Hue. She says that the task of the NLF in Hue was to destroy the government administration of the city and to establish, in its place, a "revolutionary administration." How that justifies the execution of any civilians, regardless of the number, is unclear.

The topic of what happened at Hue was revived in 2002. Bui Tin, a former colonel in the North Vietnamese Army, shares his insights into the Vietnam War and its aftermath in his book *From Enemy to Friend*. Once a presidential palace guard for Ho Chi Minh and a participant in the decisive battle of the French-Indochina War at Dien Bien Phu, Tin served as a frontline commander. On April 30, 1975, he rode a tank onto the presidential palace grounds in Saigon to accept the South Vietnamese surrender from General Duong Van "Big" Minh. In his book, Tin deals with a number of issues on the war from the Communist perspective.

With regard to the massacres in Hue, Bui Tin acknowledges that some executions of civilians did occur. However, he explains that the discipline of the troops broke down under the intensity of the American bombardment. According to Tin, the "units from the north" had been "told that Hue was the stronghold of feudalism, a bed of reactionaries, the breeding ground of Can Lao Party loyalists who remained true to the memory of former South Vietnamese president Ngo Dinh Diem and of Nguyen Van Thieu's Democracy Party."[13] He says that more than ten thousand prisoners were taken and the most important sent north. When the Marines launched their counterattack to retake the city, the Communist troops were instructed to hang on to the prisoners and to move them with the retreating troops. However, according to Tin, in the "panic of retreat," some of the company and battalion commanders shot their prisoners "to ensure the safety of the retreat." He cited this breakdown in discipline as the reason for the massacres.`

Perhaps one of the most cogent assessments of the aftermath of what happened at Hue is best expressed by Don Oberdorfer, who writes, "Hardly anyone took the trouble to investigate the full details of what happened; after Tet, America and most of the world was interested in proofs and prophesies, not in history. The President of the United States and others cited the killings in Hue as an object lesson in Communist immorality and a foretaste of the bloodbath ahead should the Communists triumph in South Vietnam. Opponents of the President's policies treated the killings as an aberration of war or denied that any purposeful large-scale slaughter had taken place."[14]

Richard Falk effectively agrees with Oberdorfer: "The subsequent history of Vietnam makes one wonder whether the shadow cast by Tet did not add significantly to the fear and hostility of Southerners towards the North, to the mass exodus after liberation, and to the phenomenon of the boat people, which undercut the basic claim of national liberation and reunification."[15] We may never know what really happened at Hue, but it is clear that mass executions did occur and that reports of a massacre there had a significant impact on South Vietnamese and American attitudes for many years after the Tet Offensive and would ultimately contribute to the panic that seized South Vietnam when the North Vietnamese launched their final offensive in 1975.

Chapter 11

WHY KHE SANH?

Ever since 1968, historians, military leaders, and other observers have argued about what General Vo Nguyen Giap was attempting to accomplish at Khe Sanh. The question has best been phrased by Peter Brush: "Was Khe Sanh a territorial imperative or a bait and switch?"[1] Both sides claimed victory at Khe Sanh, fueling a long-running debate.

The U.S. commander in Vietnam, General William Westmoreland, was clearly convinced that Khe Sanh was the focal point of the Communist plans in 1968. He believed that the attacks by the Viet Cong (VC) and People's Army of Vietnam (PAVN) elsewhere in Vietnam during the Tet Offensive were meant as a diversion "while concentrating on creating something like Dien Bien Phu at Khe Sanh and seizing the two northern provinces [of South Vietnam]."[2] This may have been wishful thinking on Westmoreland's part, since he had always wanted to get the Communists to stand and fight on ground of his choosing in a set-piece battle. Khe Sanh appeared to provide the opportunity he had been seeking.

Those who maintain that overrunning Khe Sanh was Giap's main focus and not merely a diversion cite considerable evidence to make their argument. On January 2, 1968, the Marines killed five PAVN soldiers just outside the defensive perimeter of Khe Sanh; they were apparently reconnoitering the base. It appeared that this reconnaissance was in preparation for an attack—because why, argue those who believe Khe Sanh was not a diversion, would they have had to get so close to the Marine base for a diversionary attack?

Stronger support is provided by the intelligence gleaned from the interrogation of Senior Lieutenant L Thanh Tonc after his surrender at Khe Sanh on January 21. The PAVN officer said that he and his comrades had been told that the fall of Khe Sanh would be the decisive battle of the war. After it fell, according to the lieutenant, PAVN forces would advance eastward to capture all of Route 9 and cut off the northern provinces of South Vietnam. Those who assert that Khe Sanh was a diversion maintain that the intelligence from Tonc's interrogation is not conclusive evidence because Tonc may only have been fed propaganda by his superiors.

Nevertheless, the sheer number of forces in the Khe Sanh area when the first attack began on January 21 suggests strongly that the Communists wanted to take the base. The PAVN force included three infantry divisions, a fourth infantry division nearby in a support role, tanks, and two artillery regiments with antiaircraft support. This was an extremely large force just to tie down six thousand Marines and create a diversion to attract Westmoreland's attention. Those who believe that Khe Sanh was not a diversion maintain that Giap kept this large force at Khe Sanh when they could have perhaps been better used elsewhere during the Tet Offensive; therefore, he hoped to achieve much more than a mere diversion there.[3]

In fact, Giap's forces launched five battalion-size or larger attacks against Khe Sanh and the surrounding outposts. In the interim, they were subjected to continuous shelling and aerial bombardment. Why, ask those who believe Giap planned to take Khe Sanh, would he launch these attacks and leave his forces in the area, where they could be easily targeted by artillery and tactical air support, if he did not intend to make an all-out push to take the base?

Several commentators draw exactly the opposite conclusion about Giap's intentions at Khe Sanh. Neil Sheehan, the author of *A Bright Shining Lie*, agrees with those who assert that Khe Sanh was a diversion: "Khe Sanh was the biggest lure of the war. The Vietnamese Communists had no intention of attempting to stage a second Dien Bien Phu there. The objective of the siege was William Westmoreland, not the Marine garrison. The siege was a ruse to distract Westmoreland while the real blow [the Tet Offensive] was prepared."[4]

William S. Turley, author of *The Second Indochina War: A Short Political and Military History, 1954–1975*, cites a postwar interview with PAVN Colonel Nghiem Tuc, the deputy editor of *Quan Doi Nhan Dan* (People's Army) newspaper, who claimed that Khe Sanh was never intended to be another Dien Bien Phu. In 1968, he said, the Communists knew that the United States was at the peak of its military power. To achieve another Dien Bien Phu at that time was "impossible."[5] Turley concludes that in addition to providing a strategic diversion, the Khe Sanh battle was a test of the U.S. reaction to the PAVN use of the demilitarized zone (DMZ). According to Turley, Giap wanted to determine how the United States would respond if he staged attacks from the DMZ—specifically, whether the United States would send troops into the North.[6]

Cecil Currey, Giap's biographer, who interviewed the general extensively, maintains that Giap's primary intention was indeed to stage a diversion and that any notions of overrunning the base were secondary. Moreover, he asserts that "Giap's target was larger than just Khe Sanh; it was all of the Republic of Vietnam."[7] With the eyes of the world focused on Khe Sanh, he was free to position his soldiers and the Viet Cong to launch the Tet Offensive.

General Philip Davidson, Westmoreland's wartime intelligence chief and author of *Vietnam at War*, calls the notion that Giap intended Khe Sanh to be a strategic diversion to divert American attention away from the cities a "myth . . . with no factual basis."[8] He points out that a diversion could have been achieved with far fewer troops and that Giap clearly meant to "overwhelm Khe Sanh with two, three, or four NVA divisions, ending the war with a stunning military victory."[9] He calls any suggestion that Khe Sanh was a diversion "obvious nonsense," noting that "Giap's alleged diversion consisted of some 32,000 to 40,000 NVA troops (and good ones at that) tying down 6,000 Marines and ARVN Rangers. If Khe Sanh was an NVA diversion, military history provides few examples of one more expensive."[10] Davidson makes a very good point; it is unlikely that a general would use two or three reinforced divisions to divert four Marine battalions, certainly when those forces were badly needed in Quang Tri City and Hue during the Tet offensive. Moreover, Giap paid too costly a butcher's bill around Khe Sanh not to have had some important purpose in mind for putting those forces there in the first place. Otherwise, why would he have continued the attack long after the diversion had been accomplished and the Tet Offensive launched?

Davidson believes that Giap himself was in the Khe Sanh area, proving that the siege was meant to be a major effort by the North Vietnamese. He cites several intelligence reports that indicated that Giap was indeed there. Additionally, radio intercepts revealed that there was a very senior PAVN headquarters in a cave in the Khe Sanh area. Davidson also notes that Giap was not seen in Hanoi between September 2, 1967, and February 5, 1968, and adds, "The best guess is that Giap was in the cave and that he planned a Phase III battle at Khe Sanh."[11]

Peter McDonald, author of *Giap*, disagrees, citing lack of North Vietnamese helicopters or other transportation capable of getting Giap to the combat zone from Hanoi in a timely fashion. Macdonald believes that it was unlikely that the North Vietnamese general would have left the center of military control in Hanoi during a major nationwide offensive in the south.[12]

Robert J. O'Neill, author of *General Giap*, also thinks it highly improbable that Giap was in the Khe Sanh area. Like Macdonald, he asserts that Giap would not have absented himself from the only headquarters from which all the activities of the entire North Vietnamese military offensive could be controlled. Moreover, he thinks it unlikely that Giap would have placed himself in position to suffer a personal defeat at the hands of the Americans at Khe Sanh.[13]

The PAVN committed a large number of troops at Khe Sanh. It is not clear why they decided to call off the struggle after having done so. Perhaps it had never had the significance that Westmoreland attached to it. Still, there are a number of puzzling aspects about the North Vietnamese action at Khe Sanh. For one, after the ammunition dump at Khe Sanh had been blown up, the North Vietnamese made no attempt to follow up their advantage and launch a full-scale attack against the base. If their primary intent had been to capture Khe Sanh, this would have been the opportunity to do so.

In addition, the North Vietnamese made no effort to cut off the water supply to Khe Sanh. Soldiers at the base received their water from a stream that ran about 1,500 feet outside the installation. Cutting off the water source would have made the American soldiers even more heavily dependent on supplies from the air, possibly too dependent for their needs to be met and perhaps even causing them to abandon the base.

During February, while the siege was still under way, the Communists pulled three regiments away from Khe Sanh and sent them to the battle raging in and around Hue. Apparently, the capture of Hue seemed more important to them than Khe Sanh. Some historians have theorized that by early March, Giap had realized that his forces could never overrun the base; thus, it was senseless to stay and take the pounding from allied artillery and air support. Another analysis insists that the abandonment of Khe Sanh was related to the failure of the North Vietnamese to hold Hue and gain control of Quang Tri and Thua Thien provinces. Still another theory is that the Communists never intended to capture Khe Sanh and withdrew because they had achieved their objective of diverting allied forces away from the towns and cities.

Marine Lieutenant General Victor Krulak suggests that Giap's action at Khe Sanh conformed to Westmoreland's hopes of creating a killing ground. Once Giap saw the strength the Americans would commit, he left enough men at the combat base to freeze U.S. forces there and shifted his troops to support other phases of Tet. "In the end," Krulak asserts, "Giap, having milked as much out of the Khe Sanh operation as he could, simply caused his forces to melt away. . . . Their only investment was blood, to which they assigned a low importance."[14]

Yet another explanation is related by William S. Turley, who interviewed the deputy editor of *Quan Doi Nhan Dan* in Hanoi in 1984. The editor said that Khe Sanh was never meant to be another Dien Bien Phu, but the battle, aside from "providing a strategic diversion," was "a test of the U.S. reaction to the PAVN's use of the demilitarized zone." The PAVN command wanted to know what the U.S. government would do if the PAVN staged attacks from that area, specifically whether it would send ground troops into North Vietnam. When that did not happen, Hanoi went ahead with the Tet Offensive.[15]

Giap himself does not help to clear up the mystery. During an interview with Peter Macdonald many years after the war, he said, "Khe Sanh was not important to us. Or it was only to the extent that it was to the Americans. It was the focus of attention in the United States because their prestige was at stake, but to us it was part of the greater battle that would begin after Tet. It was only a diversion, but one to be exploited if we could cause many casualties and win a big victory."[16]

Hanoi's official history of the war clearly states that the Route 9–Quang Tri Front responsible for the battle at Khe Sanh "was a combat battlefield for our main force units that was assigned the missions of annihilating the enemy forces and of drawing in and *tying down* [emphasis added] a significant portion of the mobile reserve forces of the U.S. and puppet armies, there creating favorable conditions for the focal points of our attacks and uprisings, and especially for Tri-Thien and Hue."[17]

Such comments, like many statements by Giap and other Communist military leaders during and after the war, have to be taken with a grain of salt, since they appear to be somewhat self-congratulatory after the fact. They may or may not represent the actual strategic thinking in 1968 that led to the action at Khe Sanh.

Some observers have taken another tack with the issue, looking at the end result of what happened at Khe Sanh. Ronnie E. Ford, author of *Tet 1968: Understanding the Surprise*, maintains that Westmoreland destroyed a large part of the PAVN regulars assembled near Khe Sanh, preventing that force from playing out what Ford believed was its true role—acting as the "second wave" of the overall plan for the offensive and achieving its ultimate objective of seizing Hue and Da Nang, thus paving the way for North Vietnamese regular units to stream into South Vietnam.[18] Harry Summers of the U.S. Army War College, author of *Historical Atlas of the Vietnam War*, agrees with Ford. Citing postwar documents from Hanoi that reveal that much more was at stake than merely a diversion, Summers asserts that Khe Sanh was to be a test of whether to proceed with Phase II of the General Offensive–General Uprising, which began with the "border wars" the previous September.[19]

Ford, Summers, and other observers may or may not be correct in their conclusions about the role of Khe Sanh in the overall Tet Offensive campaign. What is known is that Giap surrounded Khe Sanh with more than twenty thousand soldiers but never made a concerted effort to take the position. The mystery remains why the PAVN failed to do so while leaving their troops at the mercy of the massed firepower of artillery and air strikes. Perhaps, as Peter Brush suggests, Khe Sanh achieved Giap's diversion, and he thought he had nothing to lose by continuing the fight. But in the end, he "stayed too long, fought too hard, and sustained too many casualties."[20]

Khe Sanh proved to be a costly battle for both sides. The Marines were able to hold the base, but U.S. forces abandoned it in June 1968. The meaning of the furious fighting that raged at and around Khe Sanh for seventy-seven days in 1968 remains unknown.

Chapter 12

TET AND THE MEDIA

The role of the media during the Vietnam War remains controversial, and there has been a long-standing argument that the coverage of the war and particularly the Tet Offensive ultimately led to the American defeat in Vietnam. It is true that as the war progressed, televised coverage of the fighting in Vietnam became more and more important to changing public opinion. Vietnam was the first war covered extensively on U.S. television, and by the time of the commitment of American combat troops in 1965 more than half of the American people relied on TV as their principal source of news.[1]

The media coverage of the Tet Offensive had a great influence on the eventual outcome of the fighting and its aftermath. The reporters did not believe the official statements that came out of the Military Assistance Command, Vietnam (MACV) during and after the bloody fighting of the offensive, and the media coverage generally reflected this disbelief.

The journalists were not wholly to blame for this attitude. MACV, the Pentagon, and the president himself all helped to create the credibility gap that ruined press-military relations long before 1968. Army and Marine press officers had reported every in-country operation, regardless of outcome, as a major step forward. Fear of public vilification of its actions forced both the White House and MACV to whitewash or at least play down any reports that would adversely affect support of the war at home. This situation, according to

Clarence Wyatt, author of *Paper Soldiers: The American Press and the Vietnam War*, resulted in "a steadily increasing suspicion and tension between the press and the government."[2]

President Johnson attempted to repair this situation in late 1967 when he ordered a public-relations campaign designed "to present sound evidence of progress in Vietnam."[3] He admonished his top advisers "to sell our product" and "to get a better story to the American people."[4] The "Success Campaign," as it later became known, did indeed achieve some brief, momentary successes, but the Tet Offensive exploded like a bombshell in South Vietnam, leaving many Americans feeling that the president had lied to them about progress in the war.

Images of the bloody Tet fighting, especially in Saigon and Hue, flooded American airwaves. Coverage of the sapper attack on the U.S. Embassy and the infamous photo of South Vietnamese General Nguyen Ngoc Loan's summary execution of a Viet Cong (VC) prisoner were powerful in their impact. As Kathleen Turner, author of *Lyndon Johnson's Dual War*, writes, "With Tet . . . the fighting was suddenly, inescapably, terrifyingly close to the Saigon-based news teams. The proximity of the battle guaranteed extensive coverage by media institutions: it was dramatic, it was easily accessible, and it was for many the first extended view of the enemy."[5]

To viewers back in the United States, Saigon appeared to be a city besieged. According to historian Chester Pach, the correspondents and cameramen "emphasized the unprecedented, astonishing, and frightening sights of Saigon—tanks in the streets, fighter aircraft hitting targets in residential neighborhoods, refugees who had come to the city to escape the war fleeing once again." The television images and news photographs demonstrated only too clearly that normal routines of the city had come to a halt. "Only the coffin makers were open for business," ABC reported.[6]

Such coverage no doubt had an impact on the Americans who watched it every night on the evening news. According to correspondent Don Oberdorfer, the American people were "experiencing the worst of the bloodshed through the new technology of television. The [government's] summaries were not believed. The projected experience was."[7]

A good example of this dynamic at work can be seen in MACV commander William Westmoreland's impromptu press conference on the grounds of the U.S. Embassy on February 1, 1968. Accompanied by the sound of explosions in the background, the general claimed that MACV had foreseen the attacks and that the enemy had lost 5,800 killed in the first days of the offensive. He asserted that the Communists had suffered a great defeat and that the attacks were only diversions from the enemy's main effort, which would come across the demilitarized zone (DMZ) and around Khe Sanh. According to William Hammond,

"To many reporters, Westmoreland seemed to be mouthing platitudes while the wolf was at the gate."[8]

Walter Cronkite, among many others in the media, felt that he had been duped by government assurances that the war in Vietnam was being won. Nine million people viewed his famous February 27 Tet broadcast, in which he declared that the U.S. was "mired in a stalemate" and called for negotiations to end the fighting. This marked the point at which a large segment of middle America came to question the value of continuing the war in Vietnam. Journalist David Halberstam said that when Cronkite made his commentary on the Tet Offensive, "It was the first time in history a war had been declared over by an anchorman."[9]

The lingering question, then, is whether the American media turned the tactical defeat of Communist forces in Tet into a psychological victory for them. There is a lot of disagreement about the answer to the question on the part of commentators and historians. One side of the argument is best represented by the comments of Robert Elegant, who covered Vietnam for several years. Writing some years after the war, he berated his colleagues for distorting Tet and the war, remarking, "Never before Vietnam had the collective policy of the media . . . sought by graphic and unremitting distortion — the victory of the enemies of the correspondents' own side." Elegant charged that the reporting during Tet was "superficial and biased." He further claimed that the ultimate impact of such "skewed reporting" was that "for the first time in modern history, the outcome of a war was determined not on the battlefield but on the printed page and, above all, on the television screen."[10]

Elegant was not alone in this sentiment. Howard K. Smith of ABC News resigned his position, charging that the press was "contributing to the confusion and frustration now damaging the American spirit." He said that press coverage of General Loan's execution of the VC suspect was an example of what he meant. He pointed out that no one had made "even a perfunctory acknowledgment . . . of the fact that such executions, en masse, are the Viet Cong way of war." [11]

Keyes Beech, who served for many years as a journalist in Vietnam, also condemns his colleagues in the press. Echoing Elegant's sentiments, Beech charges that "the media helped lose the war" and that in the end, "the war was lost in the U.S., not in Vietnam."[12]

On the other side of the issue are those who adamantly refuse to accept that the media was at fault for the impact of the Tet Offensive. Charles Mohr, another war correspondent, contends that the American people were shocked into a new level of awareness about the actual situation in Vietnam when they were confronted with the discrepancy between Westmoreland's optimistic reports and the dramatic reality of the enemy's actual military capability.[13] Thus, according to Mohr, the reporters were not making the news, but just reporting what they saw and letting viewers and readers draw their own conclusions. The enduring images from that reporting were not those of victory, but rather those of the sapper raid on the embassy, Loan's execution of the VC suspect, and the bitter and destructive struggle in Hue. These images were testaments to many Americans of a war gone wrong. As Paul Elliott suggests, "the desperate street fighting, the sickening images of civilian suffering and death and the never-ending story of Khe Sanh seemed to provide the government and the people with an opportunity to reassess their commitment to the war."[14]

Perhaps the most in-depth examination of the role of the media in the Tet Offensive is Peter Braestrup's acclaimed two-volume study *Big Story: How the American Press and Television Reported and Interpreted the Crisis of Tet in Vietnam and Washington*.[15] Braestrup, a war correspondent and head of the *Washington Post* Saigon bureau from 1968 to 1973, provides an exhaustive examination of the role of the media during the Tet Offensive and its aftermath. He argues that unfair and biased reporting during the offensive turned the majority of Americans against the war in Vietnam. He cites the adversarial theme in much of the reporting during Tet, saying, that "the collective emanations of the major media were producing a kind of continuous black fog of their own, a vague conventional 'disaster' image."[16]

Braestrup cites the fighting at the U.S. Embassy as a prime example of biased reporting. Reporters and cameramen were sure that VC sappers had penetrated the chancery building and seized the embassy. Erroneous reports from the military police were partly to blame. Uncorrected stories to this effect were filed with news agencies in the United States, resulting in sensationalist headlines gracing the front pages of American newspapers.

Braestrup asserts that even after "the fog of war began to lift" and allied success became apparent, TV executives would not listen. He cites one case in which an NBC producer rejected a proposed late-1968 series depicting Tet as a major American victory because, as the producer said, "Tet was already established in the public's mind as a defeat, and therefore it was an American defeat."[17] Braestrup concludes that at Tet, "the press shouted that the patient was dying, then weeks later began to whisper that he somehow seemed to be recovering—whispers apparently not heard amid the clamorous domestic reactions to the initial shouts."[18]

The network newscasts devoted more attention to Khe Sanh than any other battle during the Tet Offensive. After the bitter fighting at Hue was over, this left the battle on the Laotian border the only remaining combat story in South Vietnam for the reporters to cover. The story was compelling, particularly because of the emphasis the president and other U.S. officials placed on the fight there. Braestrup writes that Khe Sanh was both a symbol of the frustration of the Vietnam War and a potential disaster in the mold of Dien Bien Phu — "a historical ghost" evoked in eleven of thirty-one film reports on the siege.[19]

Reporting at Khe Sanh was very selective, featuring the damage done to the Marines by the North Vietnamese artillery but neglecting the heavy casualties inflicted by American artillery and B-52s. The reporters and commentators kept predicting the attack that never came. They also exaggerated aircraft losses at the base. During the course of the fighting, several C-123 and C-130 aircraft had been shot down or damaged by incoming rounds. Although these losses were expected for an operation this size, the reporters repeatedly used the loss of the same aircraft in their stories, giving an impression that planes were falling out of the sky every day. According to Braestrup, the focus on Khe Sanh, after most of the rest of the fighting was over, gave the impression that the outcome of the offensive was still in doubt into March, long after the fighting had tapered off in most of the rest of the country and the North Vietnamese had begun thinning their forces at Khe Sanh.

Braestrup does not credit the negative reporting as solely the result of bias on the part of reporters. A number of other factors had an impact on the tone and nature of the reporting. Braestrup asserts that many of the less experienced, more naive reporters were influenced by the panic they themselves felt, and this colored their reporting of the events as they occurred. He maintains that the focus on Saigon, Hue, and Khe Sanh drained the limited resources of the American press away from the smaller, less dramatic, less accessible action that, nonetheless, involved the bulk of American troops and casualties. According to Braestrup, these events were left to the daily war summaries provided by MACV briefers and communiqué writers, which were "scanty" and "fragmentary, supplying little context that would have aided a larger understanding of the war."[20]

Braestrup charges that the Johnson administration played a major role in the nature of the reporting and its impact. Although the president tried to reassure the American public, Braestrup believes that Johnson and his advisors did not take a sufficiently aggressive role in trying to explain the offensive and its outcome on the battlefield; this failure "magnified the damage and prolonged the image of a great disaster."[21] Braestrup concludes, "Rarely has contemporary crisis-journalism turned out, in retrospect, to have veered so widely from reality. Essentially, the dominant themes of the words, and film from Vietnam . . . added up to a portrait of defeat for the allies. Historians, on the contrary, have concluded that the Tet Offensive resulted in a severe military-political setback for Hanoi in the South. To have portrayed such a setback for one side as a defeat for the other — in a major crisis abroad — cannot be counted as a triumph for American journalism."[22]

Kathleen Turner agrees with some of Braestrup's conclusions about flaws in the reporting during the Tet Offensive. She asserts that as the offensive continued, the lack of familiarity with the Vietnamese language, culture, and countryside, compounded by lack of mobility, hampered both the ability and the inclination of many reporters to see the wider context of the Tet offensive.[23] She does not believe, however, that biased reporting turned Tet from a victory into a defeat; rather, she maintains that Johnson's long-standing inability to deal with the press exacerbated the situation in 1968 and worsened the impact of the surprise attack and its aftermath.

Others have taken strong exception to Braestrup's charges about the role of the media in the offensive and its aftermath. Paul Elliott disagrees with Braestrup's thesis that Tet reporting increased antiwar sentiment, noting that a poll published within Braestrup's book indicates that there was little relation between the two. He asserts that public resolve did not falter or crumble, as Braestrup insists, but actually strengthened as a strong mood of retaliation against the VC swept through America.[24] Elliott is only partially correct, because after the initial wave, public opinion on Johnson and the war effort fell quickly.

Daniel C. Hallin, author of *The "Uncensored War": The Media and Vietnam*, asserts that public opinion turned against Johnson's handling of the war during 1965–67, when television reporting was most favorable to administration policies in Vietnam. He argues that before Tet, editorial comments by television journalists ran nearly four to one in favor of administration policy; after Tet, it ran two to one against.[25] He concludes that Johnson exaggerated the effects of TV news in shaping public attitudes toward the war.[26]

Hallin, however, acknowledges that Tet caused a major shift in television's image of the war. Nevertheless, Tet "was less a turning point than a crossover point, a moment when trends that had been in motion for some time reached balance and began to tip the other way."[27] He maintains that "journalists seem to have interpreted Tet, without consciously making the distinction, for what it *said* rather than what it *did*—as proof, regardless of who won or lost it, that the war was not under control."[28]

Paul Elliott, author of *Conflict and Controversy*, asserts that the American media did not induce mass pessimism in Washington; rather, the media tended to reflect the mood of the government, which was reacting to the lack of progress in Vietnam and mirroring the concerns and worries that the American people already had about the war. He disagrees with those who maintain that the media reported Tet as an American defeat, citing more than a few examples of where the media correctly reported that Tet was a loss for the Communists. For example, Elliott points out that Walter Cronkite reported on February 14 that "first and simplest, the Viet Cong suffered a military defeat."[29]

Clarence Wyatt, author of *Paper Soldiers: The American Press and the Vietnam War*, challenges Braestrup's assertion about television's impact on the

American public and its perception of the Tet Offensive. In a study that covers the period from 1962 to 1975, Wyatt asserts that, contrary to the charges of Braestrup and others that the press exerted substantive influence in a negative way on home-front opinion, the news coverage of the war reflected, virtually unchallenged, official government information, statements, and views. "The press," he concludes, "was more a paper soldier than an antiwar, anti-government crusader."[30]

In addition, Wyatt maintains that relatively few people even watched the television news in the 1960s. He cites a survey conducted by the Simmons Market Research Bureau in 1969, which found that only 24 percent of the adult population in America watched a television news show. Moreover, according to a 1967 Harris Poll cited by Wyatt, for those who did watch television news, the experience did not necessarily mean that the coverage would make them more likely to oppose the war; only 31 percent who responded said it that it did.[31] Most likely, according to Wyatt, the television coverage probably tended to reinforce what the viewers already believed.

Wyatt acknowledges that skepticism began to influence reporting, particularly during and after the Tet Offensive, but only after official sources "clammed up, lied, or were overtaken by events," such as in the early days of the offensive. Wyatt maintains that the Tet reporting was "the product of characteristics of American journalism and government information policies that had been developing for years."[32] According to Wyatt, attempts by the administration and the military to confront the press or deny information threatened the press's ability to do its job and inspired its anger and suspicion.

With his book *Reporting Vietnam: Media and Military at War*, William Hammond provides a comprehensive study that traces the military's controversial relations with the news media during the Vietnam War from Kennedy through Johnson and Nixon. Hammond, a senior historian with the U.S. Army's Center of Military History, reveals that animosity between the military and the press had not always been the rule. Based on recently declassified government documents and other exhaustive research, Hammond demonstrates that the relations between the military and the media at first shared a common vision of American involvement in Vietnam. However, as the war dragged on, the reporters began to challenge the consistently upbeat reports from the military.

Hammond discusses at length the impact of the photo of General Loan's shooting of the VC suspect in Saigon. Contrary to most conventional wisdom, Hammond asserts that this vivid image probably had little effect on American public opinion, noting that twenty million people watched the Huntley-Brinkley news program on the night the film first played, yet NBC received only ninety letters on the subject, and only fifty-six of those accused the network of bad taste (the rest complained that the film appeared at a time when children

could watch).[33] Interestingly, Hammond concludes that gloomy and sensa-
tional reporting had little effect on American public opinion, but "it nonetheless reinforced doubt already circulating within the Johnson administration."[34]

In the end, part of the blame for the ultimate outcome of the Tet Offensive
may lie in biased and erroneous reporting, but the earlier bursts of optimism
from the highest levels of government that told Americans that the United
States was winning in Vietnam did not square well with the stunning surprise
of the Communists attacks. All the reports, news photos, and film footage, good
or bad, only served to add velocity to a situation made bad by the credibility gap
that had begun to develop well before the Communists launched their offensive
in 1968. Having gained a victory in countering the Tet Offensive, there was no
need to juggle the numbers this time, but the credibility gap had opened up
too far. Journalists in Saigon looked for signs of defeat everywhere, and when
they looked hard enough they seemed to find them. As the *New York Times*
observed, "These are not the deeds of an enemy whose fighting efficiency has
'progressively declined' and whose morale is 'sinking fast,' as United States military officials put it in November."[35] This was the same impression that many
Americans had of the bitter fighting that they saw on their televisions during
the Tet Offensive.

Chapter 13

TET AND AMERICAN MILITARY STRATEGY

The Tet Offensive clearly demonstrated to many observers that American strategy in Vietnam to that point had been seriously flawed. The U.S. had committed tremendous amounts of both manpower (close to 540,000 troops by mid-1968) and money (by mid-1967, government spending for the war was running at a rate of $20 billion annually) to the war, which had a significant impact on the country at home.[1] Yet the Tet Offensive proved that this expenditure provided no guarantee of victory, and this led many Americans in and out of government to question the continued utility of the strategy that was being pursued.

During the early days of U.S. commitment in Vietnam, the American answer to the situation was counterinsurgency, using Special Forces and other advisors in an attempt to deal with the Viet Cong. However, with the decision by North Vietnam to send military forces down the Ho Chi Minh Trail into South Vietnam in 1964, the conflict escalated drastically. Soon the war outstripped the capabilities of the advisors and the South Vietnamese forces, and President Lyndon Johnson turned to the commitment of U.S. combat troops. With the arrival of these regular forces, the focus of U.S. strategy shifted to conventional operations to defeat the Communists; these operations were characterized by "search-and-destroy" tactics that relied heavily on firepower. The strategy quickly become one of attrition, in which the goal was to kill so many of the enemy troops that eventually they would be no longer able to field combat-ready military units and would therefore be willing to negotiate a settlement of the conflict on U.S. terms.

Ultimately, attrition became a numbers game in which American leaders, both civilian and military, became obsessed with body counts. The overall objective of the attrition strategy was to wear down the enemy and find his breaking point—to find that point where the leadership in Hanoi decided that the price of continuing the war in the south was too high.

By the end of 1967, General William Westmoreland, commander of Military Assistance Command, Vietnam (MACV), had nearly 485,000 troops at his disposal, all focused on prosecuting the attrition strategy. In 1966 and 1967, U.S. forces conducted large-scale search-and-destroy operations throughout South Vietnam that were marked by lavish and, some would say, indiscriminate use of firepower. By late 1967, Westmoreland declared that the crossover point was being approached in which U.S. forces were inflicting more losses on the Viet Cong and North Vietnamese than the enemy could replace.

The Tet Offensive in 1968 gave Westmoreland the opportunity he had been seeking. After recovering from the initial surprise of the attack, his forces had the chance to destroy large numbers of enemy troops in pitched battles where U.S. firepower could be brought to bear; this would be attrition at its best. Although large numbers of the enemy troops were killed, the situation did not turn out the way Westmoreland expected. Andrew F. Krepinevich, author of *The Army and Vietnam*, maintains that, for the American people and the Johnson administration, the Tet Offensive "provided the shock that led to their loss of faith in the Army's strategy."[2] Krepinevich is extremely critical of that strategy and asserts that U.S. forces should have focused on counterinsurgency, rather than large-unit operations in search-and-destroy missions. He charges that the Army slavishly adhered to what he called the "Concept," which was marked by conventional tactics that had been perfected during World War II and subsequently refined to counter the Soviets in Europe. According to Krepinevich, the Army failed when it tried to transplant the "Concept" to the different situation that confronted U.S. forces in Vietnam—a Communist insurgency.

Krepinevich maintains that the strength and scope of the Tet Offensive demonstrated the futility of the "Concept" and its reliance on attrition to the neglect of the social and political factors so crucial to winning the war. The stunning nature of the offensive, coupled with Westmoreland's request for additional troops, proved that attrition was not working and "led to a full-blown review of U.S. strategy in Vietnam, ending in the explicit rejection of the Army strategy by the civilian leadership."[3] To Krepinevich, the request for additional troops clearly "reflected the bankruptcy of the Army's strategy."[4]

Unfortunately, according to Krepinevich, the Tet Offensive "brought no reevaluation of the Concept within the Army itself. The Army had convinced itself that it had won the Tet Offensive; therefore, no soul-searching was neces-sary."[5] Thus, he writes, "The military's response to the implications of the Tet Offensive was the same as it had been throughout the war: apply the Concept, but at a higher level of intensity."[6] Accordingly, Westmoreland asked for more men in order to escalate the war horizontally into Laos and Cambodia.

The counter to Krepinevich's argument is provided by Colonel Harry Summers, author of On Strategy, who concludes that U.S. strategy failed in Vietnam because military and civilian leaders failed to apply the timeless prin-ciples of war correctly. Using a framework drawn from Carl von Clausewitz's military classic On War, Summers implies that the North Vietnamese would not have been able to launch a large-scale offensive like that in 1968 had the United States taken the war directly toward the Communist center of gravity, which was, to Summers, clearly Hanoi and North Vietnam. When the U.S. leadership failed to target that center of gravity, the North Vietnamese were able to launch the Tet Offensive. Summers asserts that the offensive was a "resounding tactical failure," but acknowledges that the offensive "struck what was to prove a fatal blow against our center of gravity—the alliance between the United States and South Vietnam."[7]

Historian Herbert Y. Schandler takes exception with those who agree with Summers's conclusions. He asserts that the American failure in Vietnam up to the time of Tet 1968 was not a failure caused by the limitations placed upon military action. Neither was it caused by the press or dissent on the home front. On the contrary, according to Schandler, overwhelming American military power had finally been brought to bear; clearly, the United States enjoyed complete control of the sea and air and had a "striking superiority" in mobil-ity and materiel on land. However, this did not result in an American victory. Schandler writes, "The American failure was caused by the lack of realization in Washington that military power alone could not solve a long-range political problem, that of the competence and political stability of the South Vietnamese government."[8]

The Tet Offensive caused President Johnson to take another look at how the war was being conducted. Stunned by the scope and ferocity of the Communist attacks, he was taken aback by Westmoreland's request for additional troops in the aftermath of the fighting. When he tasked Defense Secretary Clark Clifford to make a recommendation on the additional troop request, they responded by proposing an alternative strategy for MACV, one that focused on traditional counterinsurgency operations and abandoned the strategy of atttrition.[9]

In the course of preparing Clifford's consideration of the additional troop request, a heated debate developed between General Earle Wheeler, chair-man of the Joint Chiefs of Staff, and civilians in the Defense Department over strategy in Vietnam. Wheeler maintained that there was nothing wrong with the current strategy that a more forceful application (and additional troops) would not cure. Clifford asked Wheeler if he could predict when the war might be brought to a conclusion, asking, "What is our plan for military victory in Vietnam?"[10] He was not happy with the answer he got when it appeared that the military planned to continue with the same strategy of attrition. In the end, Clifford, as a newcomer, toned down his report and did not directly challenge the Army's ground strategy. However, he did insert the following passage in the report:

> There can be no assurance that this very substantial additional deploy-ment would leave us a year from today in any favorable military position. All that can be said is that the additional troops would enable us to kill more of the enemy and would provide more security if the enemy does not offset them by lesser [*sic*] reinforcements of his own. There is no indication that they would bring about a quick solution in Vietnam and, in the absence of better performance by the GVN and the ARVN, the increased destruction and increased Americanization of the war could, in fact, be counterproductive.[11]

In the end, President Johnson deployed a much smaller package in response to Westmoreland's request for additional troops. Reeling from the near loss in the New Hampshire presidential primary, the president convened a meeting of the "Wise Men" to advise him on future strategy and policy in Vietnam. They gave him their verdict: believing that continued escalation of the war and increased troop strength in South Vietnam would be fruitless, they recom-mended a concentration on improving the South Vietnamese armed force and phasing out U.S. forces while seeking a negotiated settlement.[12]

Twelve days later, Johnson made his now famous speech, announcing that he would not run for reelection. Within the Defense Department, Clifford began to implement his work group's recommendations, among them the modernization of the South Vietnamese armed forces. General Creighton Abrams replaced Westmoreland on July 1, 1968. He attempted to change Army operations away from their conventional orientation and instituted a "one war" plan in which the pacification and population security got equal billing with the "big war." When Richard Nixon took office in January 1969, he ordered that the process started by Clifford, which the new president described as Vietnamization, be accelerated. Concurrently, he began to withdraw American troops from South Vietnam.

Even with all these factors, the nature of American military strategy did not change overnight. There was still an emphasis on body count and attri-tion. For example, the bloody battle of Hamburger Hill was fought in May

1969. Eventually, however, as more American forces were pulled out of South Vietnam, the focus of U.S. strategy shifted to preparing the South Vietnamese to assume the burden for fighting the war alone.

While the Tet Offensive had not directly affected the nature of U.S. military strategy on the ground in South Vietnam, it led to a complete reevaluation of U.S. strategic policy in Southeast Asia. As Michael Lind, author of *Vietnam: The Necessary War*, concludes, the United States may have won tactically in the Tet Offensive, but "the excessive costs of winning badly by means of an ill-conceived attrition strategy in South Vietnam made a U.S. withdrawal as a result of domestic pressure inevitable."[13]

NOTES

INTRODUCTION

1. Marc Jason Gilbert and William Head, eds., *The Tet Offensive* (Westport, CT: Praeger, 1996), 2.

2. Richard Falk, *Appropriating Tet* (Princeton, NJ: Princeton University Center of International Studies, 1988), 11.

3. Although the main attack commenced during the early morning hours of January 31, several PAVN and VC units launched premature attacks on January 30, as will be discussed later in the book.

4. Don Oberdorfer, *Tet! The Turning Point in the Vietnam War* (Baltimore, MD: Johns Hopkins University Press, 2001), xi.

1. PRELUDE

1. The government of the Republic of Vietnam in Saigon called the insurgents "Viet Cong," an abbreviation of *Viet Nam Cong Sam,* meaning Vietnamese Communist. The National Liberation Front, established in 1960 as the leader of the insurgent movement in South Vietnam, denied that it was Communist, but the organization, which included noncommunist nationalists, was dominated and controlled by the Communists.

2. The People's Army of Vietnam was more popularly known during the war as the North Vietnamese Army (NVA), but the more correct term is PAVN, which will be used in this book.

3. William J. Duiker, *The Communist Road to Power in Vietnam* (Boulder, CO: Westview, 1981), 262.

4. Hoang Ngoc Lung, *Indochina Monographs: The General Offensives of 1968–69* (Washington, DC: U.S. Army Center of Military History, 1981), 7.

5. *The Pentagon Papers: The Defense Department History of United States Decisionmaking on Vietnam—The Senator Gravel Edition* (Boston: Beacon Press, 1971), 2:507.

6. Duiker, *Communist Road to Power*, 263.

7. George C. Herring, *LBJ and Vietnam: A Different Kind of War* (Austin: University of Texas Press, 1994), 141.

8. Quoted in Don Oberdorfer, *Tet! The Turning Point in the Vietnam War* (Baltimore, MD: Johns Hopkins University Press, 2001), 104.

9. Quoted in Spencer Tucker, *Vietnam* (London: UCL Press, 1999), 136.

10. Richard A. Hunt, *Pacification: The American Struggle for Vietnam's Hearts and Minds* (Boulder, CO: Westview, 1995), 133.

11. Thomas C. Thayer, *War Without Fronts: The American Experience in Vietnam* (Boulder, CO: Westview, 1985), 31.

12. Ibid., 31–33. These intelligence estimates would be the subject of a huge controversy, which is explained in more detail in chapter 13 of this book.

13. Duiker, *Communist Road to Power*, 263.

14. Quoted in James R. Arnold, *Tet Offensive 1968: Turning Point in Vietnam* (London: Osprey, 1990), 9.

15. Timothy J. Lomperis, "Giap's Dream, Westmoreland's Nightmare," *Parameters* 18 (June 1988), 18. Lomperis, a political scientist, defined Giap's "dream" as the achievement of a Dien Bien Phu–like victory over the Americans.

16. On September 14, 1967, Giap published in Hanoi his now-famous "The Big Victory, the Great Task," which was a plea for return to the protracted war of guerrilla-type actions. His efforts to resist the general offensive failed, and he became its chief architect. Patrick J. McGarvey, ed., *Visions of Victory: Selected Vietnamese Communist Military Writings, 1964–1968* (Stanford, CA: Hoover Institution, 1969), 223.

17. Quoted in Cecil Currey, *Victory at Any Cost: The Genius of Viet Nam's Gen. Vo Nguyen Giap* (Dulles, VA: Brassey's, 1999), 262–263.

18. Cecil Currey, "Giap and Tet Mau Than 1968: The Year of the Monkey," in Marc Jason Gilbert and William Head, eds., *The Tet Offensive* (Westport, CT: Praeger, 1996), 82.

19. Currey, *Victory at Any Cost*, 264.

20. William S. Turley, *The Second Indochina War: A Short Political and Military History, 1954–1975* (New York: Westview, 1986), 100; Currey, "Giap and Tet Mau Than 1968," 73.

21. Duiker, *The Communist Road to Power in Vietnam*, 265.

22. According to Ngo Vinh Long, the Central Committee issued the final order for the offensive in the form of Resolution 14 on October 25, 1967. Ngo Vinh Long, "The Tet Offensive and Its Aftermath," in Gilbert and Head, *The Tet Offensive*, 99.

23. Phillip B. Davidson, *Vietnam at War* (Novato, CA: Presidio, 1988), 396–397. *Dau tranh*, the Vietnamese communist military and political strategy adopted in the 1930s, combined Marxist, Leninist, Maoist, and Vietnamese doctrines. According to

this strategy, all political and military actions against the enemy were intertwined and were ultimately focused on exhausting the enemy's will to continue the war. For a detailed discussion of *dau tranh*, see Douglas Pike, *Viet Cong: The Organization and Techniques of the National Liberation Front of South Vietnam* (Cambridge, MA: MIT Press, 1966), 85–92.

24. Stanley Karnow, *Vietnam: A History*, 2d ed. (New York: Penguin Books, 1997), 548.

25. Tran Van Tra, "Tet: The 1968 General Offensive and General Uprising," in Jayne S. Werner and Luu Doan Huynh, eds., *The Vietnam War: Vietnamese and American Perspectives* (Armonk, NY: M. E. Sharpe, 1993), 40.

26. Ngo Vinh Long, "The Tet Offensive and Its Aftermath," 89. For a more detailed discussion of Communist motivations and objectives of the Tet Offensive, see Part II.

27. Tran Van Tra, "Tet," 45–51.

28. Davidson, *Vietnam at War*, 398.

29. Duiker, *Communist Road to Power*, 264.

30. Tran Van Tra, "Tet," 48–51.

31. Hoang Ngoc Lung, *The General Offensives of 1968–69*, 30.

32. Ibid., 27.

33. "Directive from Province Party Standing Committee to District and Local Organs on Forthcoming Offensive and Uprisings, 1 November 1967," Vietnam Documents and Research Notes, April 1968, reprinted in Steven Cohen, ed., *Vietnam: Anthology and Guide to a Television History* (New York: Knopf, 1983), 201–203.

2. BORDER BATTLES, HILL FIGHTS, AND KHE SANH

1. John Carland, "An NVA General Looks Back," *Vietnam* (December 2002), 35.

2. For military purposes, South Vietnam was divided into four Corps Tactical Zones (CTZ). The I Corps Tactical Zone included the northern portion of the country just south of the Demilitarized Zone (DMZ). II Corps Tactical Zone included the Central Highlands and the adjacent coastal plain. III Corps Tactical Zone included the eleven provinces that surrounded Saigon and abutted the Cambodian border. IV Corps Tactical Zone included the Mekong Delta. These designations were later changed to "military regions."

3. Con Thien was also the western anchor of the so-called McNamara Line of electronic sensors under construction at the time.

4. Official reports put VC and PAVN losses at some nine hundred killed in action. Such numbers were often estimates and were thus subject to question. The allied forces sustained about sixty dead during the battle for Loc Ninh.

5. Hoang Ngoc Lung, *Indochina Monographs: The General Offensives of 1968–69* (Washington, DC: U.S. Army Center of Military History, 1981), 28.

6. Quote cited in Phillip B. Davidson, *Vietnam at War* (Novato, CA: Presidio, 1988), 469.

7. Cecil B. Currey, *Victory at Any Cost: The Genius of Viet Nam's Gen. Vo Nguyen Giap* (Dulles, VA: Brassey's, 1997), 267.

8. Giap's remarks stating new strategy appeared in North Vietnam's armed forces newspaper, *Quang Doi Nhan Dan*, quoted in Edwin H. Simmons, "Marine Corps Operations in Vietnam, 1967," *The Marines in Vietnam*, 1954–1973 (Washington, DC: History and Museums Division, Headquarters, U.S. Marine Corps, 1985), 97.

9. The senior Marine commander, Lieutenant General Robert Cushman, disagreed that holding Khe Sanh was critical. He, like his predecessor, thought that his Marines should be conducting combat operations to act as a barrier closer to the coastline to protect the Combined Action Companies, which was a program to win the hearts and minds of the South Vietnamese people in the hamlets and villages in the populated areas of I Corps.

10. William C. Westmoreland, *A Soldier Reports* (Garden City, NY: Doubleday, 1976), 272. There was an actual plan for this operation, called El Paso.

11. The Combined Action Program (CAP) was a Marine initiative that focused on counterinsurgency. It assigned Marine squads and platoons to live and work with the Vietnamese Regional and Popular Forces. The theory was that the presence of the Marines in the villages would be far more effective in excluding Communist forces from the countryside than periodic sweeps by large units. Marine generals supported the approach, but Westmoreland thought that the Marines would be more effective as part of large-unit operations.

12. The low-altitude parachute extraction system (LAPES) is used to deliver heavier cargo when the combat situation does not permit aircraft to land. When the aircraft makes an extremely low-level pass just over the runway, the rear cargo ramp is lowered and a parachute attached to the cargo is released that extracts the vehicle or other heavy cargo, strapped to a pallet, from the rear of the aircraft. As the aircraft gains altitude, the pallet slides down the runway until it stops.

13. Phillip B. Davidson, *Vietnam at War: The History, 1946–1975* (Novato, CA: Presidio, 1988), 496.

14. Quoted in Clark Dougan and Stephen Weiss, *The Vietnam Experience: Nineteen Sixty-Eight* (Boston: Boston Publishing, 1983), 10.

15. Westmoreland, *A Soldier Reports*, 314.

16. This contingency plan was never executed, but there were some adjustments made to Marine deployments in the Quang Tri area just south of the Demilitarized Zone.

17. Westmoreland, *A Soldier Reports*, 339.

18. The 26th Marine Regiment was reinforced by 1st Battalion, 9th Marines, the 37th ARVN Ranger Battalion, and the 1st Battalion, 13th Marine Artillery.

19. Robert Pisor, *The End of the Line: The Siege of Khe Sanh* (New York: Norton, 1982), 108–112.

20. Quoted in Dougan and Weiss, *Nineteen Sixty-Eight*, 42.

21. Frank E. Vandiver, *Shadows of Vietnam* (College Station: Texas A&M University Press, 1997), 271; Westmoreland, *A Soldier Reports*, 316–317.

3. THE TET OFFENSIVE

1. Don Oberdorfer, *Tet! The Turning Point in the Vietnam War* (Baltimore, MD: Johns Hopkins University Press, 2001), 120.

2. Sam Adams, a CIA analyst, later charged that MACV had falsified enemy strength figures in order to show progress in the war. These charges led to a CBS News TV documentary entitled "The Uncounted Enemy: A Vietnam Deception." General Westmoreland subsequently sued the television network for $120 million for defaming his honor, naming Adams as one of the co-defendants. Westmoreland withdrew his suit before it went to trial. See Adams, *War of Numbers: An Intelligence Memoir* (South Royalton, VT: Steerforth, 1994) and Don Kowet, *A Matter of Honor* (New York: Macmillan, 1984).

3. Quoted in James R. Arnold, *Tet Offensive 1968* (London: Osprey, 1990), 35.

4. Oberdorfer, *Tet!*, 121.

5. Maneuver battalions include units that can be maneuvered against the enemy in combat operations, such as infantry, mechanized infantry, armor, and armored cavalry. The number of maneuver battalions was a measure of U.S. combat capability in the Vietnam War.

6. Tran Van Tra, "Tet: The 1968 General Offensive and General Uprising," in Jayne S. Werner and Luu Doan Huynh, eds., *The Vietnam War: Vietnamese and American Perspectives* (Armonk, NY: M. E. Sharpe, 1993), 45.

7. Quoted in Clark Dougan and Stephen Weiss, *The Vietnam Experience: Nineteen Sixty-Eight* (Boston: Boston Publishing, 1983), 12.

8. Duiker, *The Communist Road to Power in Vietnam* (Boulder, CO: Westview, 1981), 267. Estimates of Communist troops involved in the offensive vary, but most authorities accept the figure of approximately eighty thousand.

9. Stanley Karnow, *Vietnam: A History*, 2d ed. (New York: Penguin Books, 1997), 536.

10. William C. Westmoreland, *A Soldier Reports* (Garden City, NY: Doubleday, 1976), 421.

11. Karnow, *Vietnam*, 556.

12. The sappers were promised instant promotion after the objectives were secured; this motivation was necessary, no doubt, because of the suicidal nature of their missions.

13. The chief of the transmitter station used a standby studio equipped with tape recorders; thus, he was able to broadcast without interruption, using primarily pre-recorded programs. Nobody ever detected anything abnormal over the air.

14. Quoted in Clarence R. Wyatt, *Paper Soldiers: The American Press and the Vietnam War* (New York: Norton, 1993), 168.

15. Quoted in Oberdorfer, *Tet!*, 34.

16. Quoted in Arnold, *Tet Offensive 1968*, 57.

17. Original quote found in Spencer Tucker, *Vietnam* (London: UCL Press, 1999), 136.

18. Dougan and Weiss, *Vietnam Experience*, 19.

19. Loan had been responsible for crushing the dissident Buddhist movement in Hue two years earlier.

20. Oberdorfer, *Tet!*, 161–171.

21. Bui Diem, *In the Jaws of History* (Bloomington: Indiana University Press, 1999), 220.

22. Quoted in Karnow, *Vietnam*, 561.

23. Quoted in Arnold, *Tet Offensive 1968*, 50.

24. Peter Braestrup, *Big Story: How the American Press and Television Reported and Interpreted the Crisis of Tet in Vietnam and Washington* (Boulder, CO: Westview, 1977), 1:254. Peter Arnett reported the major's comment. B.G. Burkett, *Stolen Valor: How the Vietnam Generation Was Robbed of Its Heroes and Its History* (Dallas, TX: Verity Press, 1998), 120–121, says that he ran down the "unidentified" major who was the senior U.S. advisor in Ben Tre and that the major told him that he had told Arnett that in defending the town it was a shame that some of it was destroyed. Thus, Arnett misquoted the American officer. Nevertheless, the quote became one of the most memorable of the war.

25. William H. Hammond, *Reporting Vietnam: Media & Military at War* (Lawrence: University Press of Kansas, 1998), 115.

4. THE BATTLE FOR HUE

1. Edward F. Murphy, *Semper Fi Vietnam: From Da Nang to the DMZ, Marine Corps Campaigns, 1965–1975* (Novato, CA: Presidio, 1997), 189.

2. Other estimates of the number of NVA troops involved in the capture of Hue range as high as twelve thousand. See William J. Duiker, *The Communist Road to Power in Vietnam* (Boulder, CO: Westview, 1981), 267.

3. Pham Van Son, *Tet—1968* (Salisbury, NC: Documentary Publications, 1980), 2:459.

4. Don Oberdorfer, *Tet! The Turning Point in the Vietnam War* (Baltimore, MD: Johns Hopkins University Press, 2001), 225.

5. George W. Smith, *The Siege at Hue* (New York: Ballantine Books, 2000), 225.

6. James J. Wirtz, *The Tet Offensive: Intelligence Failure in War* (Ithaca, NY: Cornell University Press, 1991), 98.

7. Pham Van Son, *The Viet-Cong Tet Offensive 1968* (Saigon: RVNAF Printing and Publications Center, 1969), 272–276.

8. Quoted in Jack Shulimson et al., *U.S. Marines in Vietnam: The Defining Year 1968* (Washington, DC: History and Museums Division, Headquarters U.S. Marine Corps, 1997), 171.

9. Ibid., 174.

10. Ibid.

11. Ibid.

12. Westmoreland message to Wheeler, dated 31 January 68, Westmoreland Papers, Center of Military History, quoted in Shulimson et al., *U.S. Marines in Vietnam*, 176.

13. Ibid.

14. Ibid.

15. Ibid., 179–180.

16. Ibid., 204–205.

17. Ibid., 211.

18. Quoted in Harry Summers, *Historical Atlas of the Vietnam War* (New York: Houghton Mifflin, 1995), 134.

19. Quoted in George Donelson Moss, *A Vietnam Reader: Sources and Essays* (Englewood Cliffs, NJ: Prentice-Hall, 1991), 279.

5. THE SIEGE OF KHE SANH

1. Samuel Zaffiri, *Westmoreland* (New York: William Morrow, 1994), 283.

2. Quoted in Peter Brush, "The Battle of Khe Sanh, 1968," in Marc Jason Gilbert and William Head, eds., *The Tet Offensive* (Westport, CT: Praeger, 1996), 196.

3. Moyers S. Shore, *The Battle of Khe Sanh* (Washington, DC: History and Museums Division, Headquarters U.S. Marine Corps, 1969), 63. Shore reports that one battalion that held the rock quarry 1,500 meters southwest of the airfield conducted patrols from its perimeter out to a distance of nine-tenths of a mile (1,500 meters).

4. Clark Dougan and Stephen Weiss, *The Vietnam Experience: Nineteen Sixty-Eight* (Boston: Boston Publishing, 1983), 40.

5. Robert Pisor, *The End of the Line: The Siege of Khe Sanh* (New York: Norton, 1983), 86.

6. Quoted in Brush, "The Battle of Khe Sanh, 1968," 196.

7. Lyndon Baines Johnson, *Public Papers of the Presidents of the United States: Lyndon B. Johnson, 1968–69* (Washington, DC: U.S. Government Printing Office, 1970), 155–163; see also Lyndon Baines Johnson, The *Vantage Point: Perspectives of the Presidency, 1963–1969* (New York: Holt, Rinehart, and Winston, 1971), 383.

8. Quoted in Dougan and Weiss, *Vietnam Experience*, 45.

9. Quoted in Larry Berman, *Lyndon Johnson's War: The Road to Stalemate in Vietnam* (New York: Norton, 1989), 149.

10. Shore, *The Battle of Khe Sanh*, 64.

11. Lt. Gen. Willard Pearson, *The War in the Northern Province, 1966–1968* (Washington, DC: Department of the Army, 1975), 72.

12. Text of Cronkite report found in Peter Braestrup, *Big Story: How the American Press and Television Reported and Interpreted the Crisis of Tet in Vietnam and Washington* (Boulder, CO: Westview, 1977), 2:180–189.

13. Shore, *The Battle of Khe Sanh*, 92.

14. Brush, "The Battle of Khe Sanh, 1968," 209.

15. Pisor, *The End of the Line*, 235.

16. Mark W. Woodruff, *Unheralded Victory: The Defeat of the Viet Cong and the North Vietnamese Army, 1961–1973* (Arlington, VA: Vandemere Press, 1999), 115.

17. Karnow, *Vietnam*, 553.

18. Quoted in Dougan and Weiss, *Vietnam Experience*, 51.

19. Ibid.

20. Quoted in Shore, *The Battle of Khe Sanh*, 151.

21. Brush, "The Battle of Khe Sanh, 1968," 209.

22. Quoted in Ronald H. Spector, *After Tet: The Bloodiest Year in Vietnam* (New York: Free Press, 1993), 71.

6. THE IMPACT OF THE TET OFFENSIVE

1. Tran Van Tra, "Tet: The 1968 General Offensive and General Uprising," in Jayne S. Werner and Luu Doan Huynh, eds., *The Vietnam War: Vietnamese and American Perspectives* (Armonk, NY: M. E. Sharpe, 1993), 48.

2. Ibid.

3. Edwin E. Moise, *Historical Dictionary of the Vietnam War* (Lanham, MD: Scarecrow Press, 2001), 392.

4. Larry H. Addington, *America's War in Vietnam: A Short Narrative History* (Bloomington: Indiana University Press, 2000), 124.

5. Bui Tinh, *From Enemy to Friend: A North Vietnamese Perspective on the War* (Annapolis, MD: Naval Institute Press, 2002), 64.

6. Richard Falk, *Appropriating Tet* (Princeton, NJ: Princeton University Center of International Studies, 1988), 7.

7. Text by Walter Cronkite found in Peter Braestrup, *Big Story: How the American Press and Television Reported and Interpreted the Crisis of Tet in Vietnam and Washington* (Boulder, CO: Westview, 1977) 2:180–189.

8. Quoted in Robert Buzzanco, "The Myth of Tet," in Marc Jason Gilbert and William Head, eds., *The Tet Offensive* (Westport, CT.: Greenwood, 1996), 231 and Phillip B. Davidson, *Vietnam at War: The History, 1946-1975* (Novato, CA: Presidio, 1988), 436.

9. Quoted in Don Oberdorfer, *Tet! The Turning Point in the Vietnam War* (Baltimore, MD: Johns Hopkins University Press, 2001)160.

10. Ibid., 176.

11. Stanley Karnow, *Vietnam: A History*, 2d ed. (New York: Penguin Books, 1997), 558.

12. William C. Westmoreland, *A Soldier Reports* (Garden City, NY: Doubleday, 1976), 350–359.

13. Quoted in Clark Dougan and Stephen Weiss, *The Vietnam Experience: Nineteen Sixty-Eight* (Boston: Boston Publishing, 1983), 70.

14. Wheeler Report, 27 February 1968, declassified document reprinted in Robert J. McMahon, ed., *Major Problems in the History of the Vietnam War* (New York: Houghton Mifflin, 2003), 321–324.

15. George Herring, *America's Longest War, The United States and Vietnam, 1950–1975*, 4th ed. (New York: McGraw-Hill, 2002), 235.

16. Westmoreland, *A Soldier Reports*, 356–357.

17. Falk, *Appropriating Tet*, 19.

18. Lyndon Baines Johnson, *The Vantage Point: Perspectives of the Presidency, 1963–1969* (New York: Holt, Rinehart, and Winston, 1971), 392.

19. Clark M. Clifford, *Counsel to the President: A Memoir* (New York: Random House, 1991), 475.

20. Quoted in James S. Olson and Randy Roberts, *Where the Domino Fell: America and Vietnam, 1945 to 1990* (New York: St. Martin's, 1991), 189.

21. Clifford, *Counsel to the President*, 493–494.

22. Oberdorfer, *Tet!*, 241.

23. All quotes found in Olson and Roberts, *Where the Domino Fell*, 186.

24. Ibid., 191.

25. Herring, *America's Longest War*, 243.

26. Quoted in Herbert Y. Schandler, *The Unmaking of a President: Lyndon Johnson and Vietnam* (Princeton, NJ: Princeton University Press, 1972), 202.

27. Quoted in Oberdorfer, *Tet!*, 174.

28. Karnow, *Vietnam*, 572.

29. Johnson, *The Vantage Point*, 418.

30. Quoted in Herring, *America's Longest War*, 251.

31. Johnson, *The Vantage Point*, 418.

32. Lyndon B. Johnson, *Public Papers of the Presidents of the United States: Lyndon B. Johnson, 1968–69* (Washington, DC: U.S. Government Printing Office, 1970), 1:469–476.

7. ASSESSING THE TET OFFENSIVE

1. David F. Schmitz, *The Tet Offensive: Politics, War, and Public Opinion* (Lanham, MD: Rowman & Littlefield, 2005), xiv–xv.

2. William J. Duiker, *The Communist Road to Power in Vietnam* (Boulder, CO: Westview, 1981), 270–271.

3. Dave Palmer, *Summons of the Trumpet* (San Rafael, CA: Presidio, 1978), 186.

4. William C. Westmoreland, *A Soldier Reports* (Garden City, NY: Doubleday, 1976), 404; George C. Herring, *America's Longest War: The United States and Vietnam, 1950–1975* (New York: McGraw-Hill, 2002), 232; Gunther Lewy, *America in Vietnam* (New York: Oxford University Press, 1980), 127, 134, 146–147; Jeffrey J. Clarke, *Advice and Support: The Final Years, 1965–1973* (Washington, DC: U.S. Army Center of Military History, 1988), 327–328. Ngo Vinh Long, "The Tet

Offensive and Its Aftermath," in Marc Jason Gilbert and William Head, eds., *The Tet Offensive* (Westport, CT: Praeger, 1996), 105, disputes these figures, maintaining that they were greatly inflated. Cecil Currey, "Giap and Tet Mau Than 1968: The Year of the Monkey," in Marc Jason Gilbert and William Head, eds., *The Tet Offensive* (Westport, CT: Praeger, 1996), 84, states that 40,000 battlefield deaths for the VC and PAVN was probably closer to the truth than the official U.S. estimates.

5. Richard A. Hunt, *Pacification: The American Struggle for Vietnamese Hearts and Minds* (Boulder, CO: Westview, 1995), 139.

6. Ibid., 143. Not all historians agree that the Viet Cong was severely crippled during the 1968 Tet Offensive. See Ngo Vinh Long, "The Tet Offensive and Its Aftermath," in Gilbert and Head, *The Tet Offensive*, 89–123. Long argues that the Viet Cong recovered from its losses and played an important role in the eventual Communist victory.

7. Quoted in Stanley Karnow, *Vietnam: A History*, 2d ed. (New York: Penguin Books, 1997), 547.

8. Don Oberdorfer, *Tet! The Turning Point in the Vietnam War* (Baltimore, MD: Johns Hopkins University Press, 2001), 329–330.

9. Tran Van Tra, *Vietnam: History of the Bulwark B2 Theater, Volume 5: Concluding the 30-Years War, Southeast Asia Report No.* 1247 (Washington, DC: Foreign Broadcast Information Service, February 2, 1983), 35.

10. Quoted in Peter Macdonald, *Giap: The Victor in Vietnam* (New York: Norton, 1993), 268. Not everyone agrees that the National Liberation Front was seriously crippled by the outcome of the Tet Offensive. Ngo Vinh Long, "The Tet Offensive and Its Aftermath," in Jayne Werner and David Hunt, eds., *The American War in Vietnam* (Ithaca, NY: Southeast Asia Program, Cornell University, 1993), 23–45, writes, "because of its popular support, the NLF was not destroyed but managed to rebuild itself . . . and it was only with this recovery that military successes in 1971 and 1972 were possible and forces from the North could begin to operate in the South again without suffering prohibitive losses."

11. Casualty figures for the Tet Offensive vary drastically depending on the exact time frame covered, but these figures, which cover January–March 1968, come from Harry G. Summers Jr., *Historical Atlas of the Vietnam War* (New York: Houghton Mifflin, 1995), 130.

12. Hunt, *Pacification*, 137.

13. Ibid., 141.

14. Virginia Pohle, *The Viet Cong in Saigon: Tactics and Objectives During the Tet Offensive* (Santa Monica, CA: Rand Corporation, 1969), viii.

15. Duiker, *Communist Road to Power*, 270.

16. Leslie Gelb and Richard Betts, *The Irony of Vietnam: The System Worked* (Washington, DC: Brookings Institution, 1979), 171.

17. Ibid., 269.

18. Bui Tin, *From Enemy to Friend: A North Vietnamese Perspective on the War* (Annapolis, MD: Naval Institute Press, 2002), 64.

19. Quoted in Karnow, *Vietnam*, 536.

20. James R. Arnold, *Tet Offensive 1968: Turning Point in Vietnam* (London: Osprey, 1990), 87.

21. Gilbert and Head, *The Tet Offensive*, 1. In their book, the editors provide a collection of excellent essays that attempt to address what they describe as "wishful thinking, analytical dogmas, and political agendas" that they believe influence any consideration of the Tet Offensive.

22. Tran Van Tra, "Tet: The 1968 General Offensive and General Uprising," in Jayne S. Werner and Luu Doan Huynh, eds., *The Vietnam War: Vietnamese and American Perspectives* (Armonk, NY: M. E. Sharpe, 1993), 57–58.

23. Ibid., 60.

24. Quoted in Macdonald, *Giap*, 269.

25. Oberdorfer, *Tet!*, 20.

26. Townsend Hoopes, *The Limits of Intervention: An Inside Account of How the Johnson Policy of Escalation in Vietnam Was Reversed* (New York: McKay, 1969), 145.

27. Bernard Brodie, "Tet Offensive," in Noble Frankland and Christopher Dowling, eds., *Decisive Battles of the Twentieth Century: Land-Sea-Air* (New York: David McKay, 1976), 321.

28. Ibid.

29. Schmitz, *The Tet Offensive*, xv.

30. Tran Van Tra, "Tet: The 1968 General Offensive and General Uprising," 61.

31. Oberdorfer, *Tet!*, 329.

8. MOTIVATIONS AND OBJECTIVES OF THE TET OFFENSIVE

1. Edwin E. Moise, *Historical Dictionary of the Vietnam War* (Lanham, MD: Scarecrow Press, 2001), 391.

2. George C. Herring, *America's Longest War America's Longest War: The United States and Vietnam, 1950–1975* (New York: McGraw-Hill, 2002), 227.

3. James S. Olson and Randy Roberts, *Where the Domino Fell: America and Vietnam, 1945 to 1990* (New York: St. Martin's, 1991), 182.

4. Quoted in Marc Jason Gilbert, ed., *Why the North Won the Vietnam War* (New York: Palgrave, 2002), 67.

5. Ngo Vinh Long, "The Tet Offensive and Its Aftermath," in Marc Jason Gilbert and William Head, eds., *The Tet Offensive* (Westport, CT: Praeger, 1996), 119.

6. Marilyn B. Young, *The Vietnam Wars: 1945–1990* (New York: HarperCollins, 1991), 216.

7. Military History Institute of Vietnam, *Victory in Vietnam: The Official History of the People's Army of Vietnam, 1954–1975*, trans. Merle L. Pribbenow (Lawrence: University Press of Kansas, 2002), 214–215.

8. Jon M. Van Dyke, *North Vietnam's Strategy for Survival* (Palo Alto, CA: Pacific Books, 1972), 32.

9. Patrick J. McGarvey, ed., *Visions of Victory: Selected Vietnamese Communist Military Writings, 1964–1968* (Stanford, CA: Hoover Institution, 1969), 222.

10. For similar interpretations of the objectives of the Tet Offensive, see Hoang Ngoc Lung, *The General Offensives of 1968–69* (Washington, DC: U.S. Army Center of Military History, 1981), 26; Dave Palmer, *Summons of the Trumpet* (San Rafael, CA: Presidio, 1978), 176; and U. S. Grant Sharp, *Strategy for Defeat* (San Rafael, CA: Presidio, 1978), 214.

11. William J. Duiker, *The Communist Road to Power in Vietnam* (Boulder, CO: Westview, 1981), 264.

12. Norman Podhoretz, *Why We Were in Vietnam* (New York: Simon & Schuster, 1982), 175; Harry Summers, *On Strategy: A Critical Analysis of the Vietnam War* (Novato, CA: Presidio, 1982), 96.

13. Quoted in James R. Arnold, *Tet Offensive 1968: Turning Point in Vietnam* (London: Osprey, 1990), 86.

14. The translation of Tran Van Tra's article is reprinted in Jayne S. Werner and Luu Doan Huynh, eds., *The Vietnam War: Vietnamese and American Perspectives* (Armonk, NY: M. E. Sharpe, 1993), 52–53.

9. MILITARY INTELLIGENCE AND SURPRISE AT TET

1. John Prados, "The Warning That Left Something to Chance: Intelligence at Tet," in Marc Jason Gilbert and William Head, eds., *The Tet Offensive* (Westport, CT: Praeger, 1996), 143.

2. Vo Nguyen Giap, *Big Victory, Great Task* (New York: Praeger, 1968), 90.

3. Hoang Ngoc Lung, *The General Offensives of 1968–1969*, 19–20; Dave Palmer, *Summons of the Trumpet* (San Rafael, CA: Presidio, 1978), 169.

4. Hoang Ngoc Lung, *The General Offensives of 1968–69* (Washington, DC: U.S. Army Center of Military History, 1981), 33.

5. Quoted in Prados, "The Warning That Left Something to Chance," 146–147.

6. Ibid., 153.

7. Quoted in David F. Schmitz, *The Tet Offensive: Politics, War, and Public Opinion* (Lanham, MD: Rowman & Littlefield, 2005), 84.

8. Phillip B. Davidson, *Vietnam at War* (Novato, CA: Presidio, 1988), 429–430.

9. Sam Adams, "Vietnam Cover-up: Playing War with Numbers," *Harper's*, May 1975; Sam Adams, *War of Numbers: An Intelligence Memoir* (South Royalton, VT: Steerforth, 1994). Adams, a CIA analyst, charged that MACV deliberately downplayed the number of guerrillas in South Vietnam and that this deception played a major role in the surprise of the Tet Offensive. Adams became the source for a CBS television documentary about American intelligence failures in Vietnam, "The Uncounted Enemy: A Vietnam Deception," that was the subject of a lawsuit brought by William Westmoreland, former MACV commander against CBS. Ultimately, the lawsuit was settled out of court.

10. Thomas C. Thayer, *War Without Fronts: The American Experience in Vietnam* (Boulder, CO: Westview Press, 1985), 27–33.

11. Hoang Ngoc Lung, *The General Offensives of 1968–69*, 38.

12. Marilyn B. Young, *The Vietnam Wars, 1945–1990* (New York: HarperCollins, 1991), 221.

13. Hoang Ngoc Lung, *The General Offensives of 1968–69*, 39. U.S. and ARVN forces conducted Operation Cedar Falls in January 1967 in the "Iron Triangle," an area northwest of Saigon. It was a large-scale search and destroy operation. Cedar Falls was followed by Operation Junction City (February–March 1967), the largest U.S. military operation of the war, which was conducted in War Zone C, the area adjacent to the Cambodian border west of Saigon.

14. Ronnie E. Ford, *Tet 1968: Understanding the Surprise* (London: Frank Cass, 1995), 167.

15. James J. Wirtz, *The Tet Offensive: Intelligence Failure in War* (Ithaca, NY: Cornell University Press, 1994), 180.

16. Ibid., 10.

17. Larry Cable, "Don't Bother Me with the Facts; I've Made Up My Mind: The Tet Offensive in the Context of Intelligence and U.S. Strategy," in Gilbert and Head, *The Tet Offensive*, 167.

18. Prados, "The Warning That Left Something to Chance," 162.

19. Ibid, 179.

20. Wirtz, *The Tet Offensive*, 275.

10. WHAT HAPPENED AT HUE?

1. Douglas Pike, *The Viet Cong Strategy of Terror* (Saigon: U.S. Mission, 1970), 25.

2. Ibid., 27.

3. Ibid., 29.

4. Don Oberdorfer, *Tet! The Turning Point in the Vietnam War* (Baltimore, MD: Johns Hopkins University Press, 2001), 225.

5. Ibid., 232–233.

6. Gunther Lewy, *America in Vietnam* (New York: Oxford University Press, 1980), 274; Peter Macdonald, *Giap: The Victor in Vietnam* (New York: Norton, 1993), 267.

7. Omar Eby, *A House in Hue* (Scottsdale, PA: Herald Press, 1968), 103.

8. Truong Nhu Tang, *A Vietcong Memoir* (New York: Harcourt Brace Jovanovich, 1985), 154.

9. D. Gareth Porter, "U.S. Political Warfare in Vietnam—The 1968 'Hue Massacre,'" *Indochina Chronicle* 33 (June 24, 1974): 1.

10. Ibid., 4.

11. Ibid., 5.

12. Marilyn B. Young, *The Vietnam Wars: 1945–1990* (New York: HarperCollins, 1991), 217.

13. Bui Tin, *From Enemy to Friend: A North Vietnamese Perspective on the War* (Annapolis, MD: Naval Institute Press, 2002), 67. The Can Lao Party (Personalist

Labor Revolutionary Party) had been established by former South Vietnamese President Ngo Dinh Diem and his brother No Dinh Nhu. It was a secret organization based on a combination of reform ideas and respect for personality. It had members all through Diem's administration and the armed forces.

14. Oberdorfer, *Tet!*, 202.

15. Richard Falk, *Appropriating Tet* (Princeton, NJ: Princeton University Center of International Studies, 1988), 30.

11. WHY KHE SANH?

1. Peter Brush, "The Battle of Khe Sanh, 1968," in Marc Jason Gilbert and William Head, eds., *The Tet Offensive* (Westport, CT: Praeger, 1996), 191.

2. William C. Westmoreland, *A Soldier Reports* (Garden City, NY: Doubleday, 1976), 316.

3. Brush, "The Battle of Khe Sanh, 1968," 198.

4. Neil Sheehan, *A Bright Shining Lie* (New York: Random House, 1988), 710.

5. Interview in William S. Turley, *The Second Indochina War: A Short Political and Military History, 1954–1975* (New York: Westview, 1986), 108.

6. Ibid., 105.

7. Cecil B. Currey, *Victory at Any Cost: The Genius of Viet Nam's Gen. Vo Nguyen Giap* (Dulles, VA: Brassey's, 1997), 266.

8. Phillip B. Davidson, *Vietnam at War* (Novato, CA: Presidio, 1988), 495.

9. Ibid., 497.

10. Ibid., 495.

11. Ibid, 505.

12. Peter Macdonald, *Giap: The Victor in Vietnam* (New York: Norton, 1993), 285.

13. Robert J. O'Neill, *General Giap* (North Melbourne, Australia: Cassell, 1969), 195–196.

14. Victor H. Krulak, *First to Fight: An Inside View of the U.S. Marine Corps* (Annapolis, MD: Naval Institute Press, 1984), 217–219.

15. William S. Turley, *The Second Indochina War: A Short Political and Military History, 1954–1975* (Boulder, CO: Westview, 1986), 105.

16. Macdonald, *Giap*, 269.

17. Military History Institute of Vietnam, *Victory in Vietnam: The Official History of the People's Army of Vietnam, 1954–1975* (Lawrence: University Press of Kansas, 2002), 216.

18. Ronnie E. Ford, *Tet 1968: Understanding the Surprise* (London: Frank Cass, 1995), 111; Macdonald, *Giap*, 291.

19. Harry G. Summers Jr., *Historical Atlas of the Vietnam War* (New York: Houghton Mifflin, 1995), 138.

20. Brush, "The Battle of Khe Sanh, 1968," 208.

12. TET AND THE MEDIA

1. Chester J. Pach Jr., "The War on Television: TV News, the Johnson Administration, and Vietnam," in Marilyn B. Young and Robert Buzzanco, eds., *A Companion to the Vietnam War* (Malden, MA: Blackwell, 2002), 451.

2. Clarence Wyatt, *Paper Soldiers: The American Press and the Vietnam War* (New York: Norton, 1993), 168.

3. Larry Berman, *Lyndon Johnson's War: The Road to Stalemate in Vietnam* (New York: Norton, 1989), 84–85.

4. Pach, "The War on Television," 458.

5. Kathleen J. Turner, *Lyndon Johnson's Dual War: Vietnam and the Press* (Chicago: University of Chicago Press, 1985), 217–218.

6. Pach, "The War on Television," 461.

7. Don Oberdorfer, *Tet! The Turning Point in the Vietnam War* (Baltimore, MD: Johns Hopkins University Press, 2001), 159.

8. William Hammond, *Reporting Vietnam: Media and Military at War* (Lawrence: University Press of Kansas, 1998), 111.

9. David Halberstam, *The Powers That Be* (New York: Knopf, 1979), 514.

10. Robert Elegant, "How to Lose a War: Reflections of a Foreign Correspondent," *Encounter* 57 (August 1981), 73–77.

11. Quoted in Hammond, *Reporting Vietnam*, 121.

12. Keyes Beech, "How to Lose a War: A Response from an 'Old Asia Hand,'" in Harrison Salisbury, ed., *Vietnam Reconsidered: Lessons From a War* (New York: Harper & Row, 1984), 152.

13. Charles Mohr, "Once Again—Did the Press Lose Vietnam?" in Grace Sevy, ed., *The American Experience in Vietnam* (Norman: University of Oklahoma Press, 1989), 145–147.

14. Paul Elliott, *Vietnam: Conflict & Controversy* (London: Arms & Armour, 1996), 146.

15. Peter Braestrup, *Big Story: How the American Press and Television Reported and Interpreted the Crisis of Tet in Vietnam and Washington*, 2 vols. (Boulder, CO: Westview, 1977). *Big Story* was republished by Anchor Books as a one-volume paperback in 1978, by Yale University Press in 1983, and in an unabridged and updated version by Presidio in 1994.

16. Peter Braestrup, *Big Story: How the American Press and Television Reported and Interpreted the Crisis of Tet in Vietnam and Washington*, abridged edition (New Haven, CT: Yale University Press, 1983), 509.

17. Ibid.

18. Ibid., 517.

19. Ibid., 303–306.

20. Ibid., 219.

21. Interview with Peter Braestrup in Kim Willenson, *The Bad War: An Oral History of the Vietnam War* (New York: New American Library, 1987), 190; Braestrup, *Big Story*, 468–461.

22. Braestrup, *Big Story*, 508.

23. Kathleen J. Turner, *Lyndon Johnson's Dual War: Vietnam and the Press* (Chicago: University of Chicago Press, 1985), 218.

24. Elliott, *Vietnam: Conflict & Controversy*, 140.

25. Daniel C. Hallin, *The "Uncensored War": The Media and Vietnam* (Berkeley: University of California Press, 1989), 161.

26. Ibid., 211–215.

27. Ibid., 168.

28. Ibid., 173.

29. Elliott, *Vietnam: Conflict & Controversy*, 141.

30. Wyatt, *Paper Soldiers*, 218.

31. Ibid., 148.

32. Ibid., 188.

33. Hammond, *Reporting Vietnam*, 115.

34. Ibid., 122.

35. Quoted in Hammond, *Reporting Vietnam*, 112.

13. TET AND AMERICAN MILITARY STRATEGY

1. Don Oberdorfer, *Tet! The Turning Point in the Vietnam War* (Baltimore, MD: Johns Hopkins University Press, 2001), 81.

2. Andrew F. Krepinevich Jr., *The Army and Vietnam* (Baltimore, MD: Johns Hopkins University Press, 1986), 237.

3. Ibid., 240.

4. Ibid., 241.

5. Ibid., 250.

6. Ibid.

7. Harry G. Summers Jr., *On Strategy: A Critical Analysis of the Vietnam War* (Novato, CA: Presidio, 1982), 120–121.

8. Herbert Y. Schandler, "America and Vietnam: The Failure of Strategy, 1964–1967," in Peter Braestrup, ed., *Vietnam as History* (Washington, DC: Woodrow Wilson International Center for Scholars, 1984), 32.

9. Krepinevich, *The Army and Vietnam*, 243; *The Pentagon Papers: The Defense Department History of United States Decisionmaking on Vietnam—The Senator Gravel Edition* (Boston: Beacon Press, 1971), 4:564–565.

10. Clark Clifford, "A Vietnam Reappraisal," *Foreign Affairs* 47 (July 1969): 601–623.

11. *Pentagon Papers*, 4:580.

12. Maxwell D. Taylor, *Swords and Plowshares* (New York: Norton, 1972), 386–388.

13. Michael Lind, *Vietnam, the Necessary War: A Reinterpretation of America's Most Disastrous Military Conflict* (New York: Free Press, 1999), 78.

PART III

Chronology, 1967–68

8–26 January 1967

Operation Cedar Falls conducted in area near Saigon known as the Iron Triangle.

22 February–14 May 1967

Operation Junction City, the largest U.S. operation to date with more than twenty-two allied battalions participating, takes place in War Zone C near the Cambodian border

10 March 1967

The Republic of Vietnam Council of Ministers approves a new constitution for South Vietnam

20 March 1967

President Johnson meets with Nguyen Cao Ky and Nguyen Van Thieu in Guam

April 1967

The Central Committee of the Lao Dong (Workers') Party passes Resolution 13 at its Thirteenth Plenum in Hanoi, calling for a "spontaneous uprising [in the South] in order to win a decisive victory in the shortest possible time"

April–October 1967
U.S. Marine units fight a series of sharp battles for control of the hills surrounding Khe Sanh base in the I Corps area

4 April 1967
Martin Luther King Jr. delivers his antiwar speech "A Time to Break Silence" in New York City

15 April 1967
Large antiwar demonstrations occur across the United States, including an estimated 300,000 protestors at a peace rally in New York City

10 May 1967
The Johnson administration establishes the Civilian Operations and Revolutionary Development Support (CORDS) organization to coordinate the pacification effort in South Vietnam

7 July 1967
The Central Committee of the Lao Dong (Workers') Party in Hanoi decides to go ahead with the General Offensive–General Uprising in South Vietnam; funeral held in Hanoi for General Nguyen Chi Thanh

7–11 July 1967
Secretary of Defense Robert McNamara, accompanied by General Earle Wheeler, chairman of the Joint Chiefs of Staff, travels to Vietnam for a firsthand assessment of the situation

9 July
Presidential assistant Walt W. Rostow, on *Meet the Press*, states that North Vietnam's strategy has "shifted from a posture of trying to win the war to keeping the war going"

13 July 1967
President Johnson declares in a press conference that "we are very sure we are on the right track" militarily in Vietnam but acknowledges that more troops will be needed

19 July 1967
A Hanoi delegation led by Deputy Premier Le Thanh Nghi leaves for Beijing, China, on the first leg of a trip to secure additional weapons and other aid from Communist countries; in Washington, Secretary of State Dean Rusk

tells a news conference that the enemy is "hurting badly," but sees a "still tough, long job ahead"

Late July 1967
Viet Cong commanders meet in Cambodia to begin planning for the General Offensive–General Uprising

3 August 1967
President Johnson announces that he will raise U.S. troop ceiling to 525,000 and calls for 10 percent surtax on individual and corporate income; Viet Cong internal document describes "new situation and mission" that will lead to the climax of the war that will "split the sky and shake the earth"

5 August 1967
The People's Republic of China signs a new aid pact with North Vietnam in a ceremony in Peking; Johnson advisor Clark Clifford and retired General Maxwell Taylor return from trip to capitals of America's Asian allies; Clifford reports that allies unanimously agree that bombing of North Vietnam should be continued at present or even higher levels

7 August 1967
Army Chief of Staff General Harold K. Johnson reports the "smell of success" in the Allied war effort, marking the beginning of the president's "success" media campaign

8 August 1967
House Republican Leader Gerald Ford attacks Johnson administration for "pulling punches" in bombing of North Vietnam while sending more Americans to die in the ground war

11 August 1967
North Korea signs military pact with North Vietnam in ceremony in Pyongyang

15 August 1967
An article by Robert Pisor of the *Detroit News* reports concern in Saigon about "a massive, countrywide military strike" by Communists to improve position prior to commencement of peace talks

20 August 1967
An Associated Press survey reports that U.S. Senate support for president's war

policy has drastically eroded; of senators replying to survey, forty-four generally support war politics, but forty disapprove

22 August 1967
Richard M. Nixon, in an interview with the *Christian Science Monitor*, calls
for "massive pressure" short of nuclear weapons to shorten the war

25 August 1967
Secretary of Defense Robert S. McNamara, testifying before Senate
Preparedness Subcommittee, says that the war cannot be won by bomb-
ing, the most pessimistic appraisal of the bombing campaign to date;
several senators reply that the United States may as well "get out" if
McNamara is correct

1 September 1967
President Johnson, at a news conference, says there is no "deep division"
in his administration's leadership concerning the bombing of North
Vietnam

3 September 1967
Nguyen Van Thieu is elected president and Nguyen Cao Ky elected vice
|president of the Republic of Vietnam with 27 percent of the total
vote; peace candidate Truong Dinh Dzu wins second-highest presidential vote

4 September 1967
Governor George Romney, in a Detroit television interview, says "brainwash-
ing" in Saigon by U.S. generals and diplomats brought about his previous
support of the war

11 September–31 Oct 1967
PAVN forces besiege U.S. Marines at Con Thien, two miles south of the
DMZ; the fighting exacts an extremely heavy toll on both sides

14–16 September 1967
Defense Minister Vo Nguyen Giap, in several Hanoi radio broadcasts,
endorses a strategy of protracted war but declares that "our fight will be
more violent in the days ahead"

21 September 1967
U.S. Ambassador to the United Nations Arthur Goldberg asks in a major
speech what the Hanoi regime would do if the bombing stopped

23 September 1967

The Soviet Union signs a new aid agreement with North Vietnam in a Moscow ceremony

26 September 1967

The *Christian Science Monitor* reports that support for the Johnson administration's Vietnam policy was eroding in the U.S. House of Representatives; of 205 House members responding, 43 said they had recently shifted positions from support for the administration policies on the war to more emphasis on finding a way out

28 September 1967

Viet Cong Military Region 4 directive secretly orders intensification of political and military action in the Saigon area

29 September 1967

President Johnson declares in a Texas speech that the United States will stop the bombing of North Vietnam if Hanoi will agree to start negotiations, which becomes known as the "San Antonio Formula"; in Saigon, a new United States Embassy chancery is dedicated

Late September

Hue City Committee of National Liberation Front orders development of grassroots organization and plans for occupation of the city

8 October 1967

A *New York Times* survey reports that U.S. political and congressional support for Vietnam War is waning

12 October 1967

Secretary of State Dean Rusk calls the Vietnam War a testing ground for Asia's ability to withstand the threat of "a billion Chinese . . . armed with nuclear weapons"

16–21 October 1967

Antiwar activists hold demonstrations against the draft throughout the United States; the largest occurs outside the Army Induction Center in Oakland, California

20 October 1967

Life magazine, in an editorial shift, calls for a pause in the bombing of North Vietnam and declares that "homefront support for the war is eroding"

21–23 October 1967

Three Army battalions backed by tear gas repulse a stone- and bottle-throwing assault by some antiwar protesters at the Pentagon; in London, antiwar protesters try to storm the U.S. Embassy

25 October 1967

Resolution 14 is passed by the Lao Dong (Workers') Party Central Committee in Hanoi, ordering a "general offensive–general uprising" (*tong cong kich–tong khoi nghia*).

27 October 1967

PAVN forces attack the South Vietnamese base at Song Be in Phuoc Long Province, near the Cambodian border

29 October–3 Nov 1967

PAVN troops attempt to take and hold an ARVN outpost at Loch Ninh, a district capital in Binh Long Province

30 October 1967

The National Assembly standing committee of the Democratic Republic of Vietnam (North Vietnam) approves a decree on punishment for counter-revolutionary activity

31 October 1967

Nguyen Van Thieu is inaugurated as president of Republic of Vietnam

1 November 1967

Defense Secretary McNamara secretly recommends termination of United States bombing of North Vietnam and limitation of ground involvement in South Vietnam

2 November 1967

Senior unofficial advisers, known as the "Wise Men," give broad approval of Johnson administration war policies in a Washington meeting

3 November–1 December 1967

PAVN regiments mass in the Dak To area, resulting in a series of bloody battles with elements of the U.S. 4th Infantry Division and the 173rd Airborne Brigade that lasts twenty-two days

6 November 1967

A document captured by U.S. forces near Dak To says that battles in that area were meant to divert U.S. forces to the mountainous areas while improving techniques of coordinated attacks

10 November 1967

President Ho Chi Minh signs decree on counterrevolutionary crimes

11 November 1967

President Johnson begins a Veterans Day tour of eight military installations to shore up support for the war

13 November 1967

Ellsworth Bunker, U.S. Ambassador to South Vietnam, on a trip to Washington, reports "steady progress" in the war zone

16 November 1967

MACV commander General William C. Westmoreland tells the House Armed Services Committee in Washington that U.S. military withdrawal from Vietnam can begin within two years if progress continues

17 November 1967

The National Liberation Front, the political wing of the Viet Cong, proclaims a three-day cease-fire for both Christmas and New Year's and a seven-day cease-fire for the upcoming Tet (Vietnamese New Year) holiday

19 November 1967

U.S. forces in Quang Tin Province capture a Communist Party document ordering the General Offensive and General Uprising

21 November 1967

At a speech at the National Press Club, Westmoreland reports that progress is being made in the war and that the war has entered the final phase "when the end begins to come into view"; he predicts that U.S. troop withdrawals can begin in two years

24 November 1967

MACV officially reduces its estimate of Communist strength in South Vietnam from 294,000 to 223,000–248,000 troops

26 November 1967

Senator Robert F. Kennedy says President Johnson has shifted war aims set out by President John Kennedy and seriously undermined the moral position of the United States

29 November 1967

President Johnson announces that Robert McNamara will step down as secretary of defense to become president of the World Bank

30 November 1967

Antiwar Democrat Eugene McCarthy announces that he will enter primaries to challenge President Lyndon Johnson for the Democratic presidential nomination in 1968

4 December 1967

Four days of antiwar protests begin in New York; among the 585 protesters arrested is renowned pediatrician Dr. Benjamin Spock; in Saigon, General Westmoreland and General Cao Van Vien (chief of the Republic of Vietnam Joint General Staff) begin discussion of Christmas, New Year's, and Tet cease-fires

5 December 1967

Republican leaders Senator Everett Dirksen and Representative Gerald Ford say that the Johnson administration has not done all it could to negotiate settlement of the war

15 December 1967

MACV turns over responsibility for Saigon's defense to South Vietnamese armed forces

18 December 1967

General Earle Wheeler, chairman of the Joint Chiefs of Staff, tells the Detroit Economic Club "we are winning the war," but warns that the Communists may try a last desperate effort similar to the Battle of the Bulge in World War II; President Johnson rejects McNamara's plan to halt South Vietnam bombing and limit U.S. participation in the war

19 December 1967

In a television interview, President Johnson says talks between Saigon government and members of the National Liberation Front "could bring good results"

20 December 1967
General Westmoreland cables Washington that Communists have decided on
an intensified countrywide effort to win the war

21 December 1967
President Johnson, in Canberra for the state funeral for Prime Minister Har-
old Holt, tells the Australian Cabinet that "kamikaze" attacks are coming in
South Vietnam

23 December 1967
North Vietnam President Ho Chi Minh addresses a national rally in Hanoi,
calling for greater feats of battle in both North and South Vietnam to win
the war; in Rome, President Johnson meets with Pope Paul and agrees to a
twelve-hour extension of the New Year's cease-fire in Vietnam

25 December 1967
Viet Cong commanders reconnoiter assigned objectives in Saigon during
Christmas cease-fire

30 December 1967
Messengers deliver Ho Chi Minh's Tet poem to officials and diplomats in
Hanoi; Foreign Minister Nguyen Duy Trinh announces that North Vietnam would begin negotiations with the United States if bombing and other
acts of war against the North were stopped

31 December 1967
U.S. troop levels reach 485,600, with 16,021 American combat deaths to date

1 January 1968
President Johnson imposes mandatory curbs on most direct U.S. investment
abroad, asks for restrictions on overseas travel of U.S. citizens and other
moves to cut sharply growing balance of payments deficit and gold drain

3 January 1968
Senator Eugene McCarthy enters the New Hampshire primary in his quest
for the Democratic presidential nomination

5 January 1968
Operation Niagara begins with an intensive intelligence and surveillance
effort in the area around Khe Sanh; U.S. press release in Saigon reports
Communist order that troops should flood lowlands, attack Saigon, and

launch the General Offensive and General Uprising; in the United States, Dr. Benjamin Spock and three others are indicted for counseling draft resistance

9 January 1968

Brigadier General William R. Desobry, retiring as senior U.S. advisor in the Mekong Delta, says that the Viet Cong in region are "poorly motivated and poorly trained" and that "ARVN now has the upper hand completely"

10 January 1968

General Westmoreland, after consultation with Lt. Gen. Frederick Weyand of II Field Force, orders redeployment of U.S. forces from border areas to positions closer to Saigon

15 January 1968

General Westmoreland warns of Communist attacks before or after Tet at a U.S. Mission Council meeting in Saigon

15-17 January 1968

The National Liberation Front presidium meets, hears reports on impending military action

18 January 1968

Singer Eartha Kitt, at a White House luncheon, blames crime and race riots on the Vietnam War

19 January 1968

President Johnson names Clark Clifford to succeed Robert McNamara as secretary of defense, effective 1 March 1968

20 January 1968

A Marine battalion and PAVN forces fight a battle on the hills northwest of Khe Sanh

21 January 1968

PAVN forces overrun the village of Khe Sanh and begin to shell Khe Sanh Combat Base, initiating a seventy-seven-day siege; in Seoul, South Korea, North Korean infiltrators unsuccessfully attempt a raid on the presidential mansion in the most dramatic military action since the Korean War

23 January 1968

North Koreans seize the U.S. intelligence ship *Pueblo*

24 January 1968

Ambassador Bunker and General Westmoreland cable Washington that Communists may break the Tet truce and urge South Vietnamese government to cancel the truce in I Corps Tactical Zone

25 January 1968

General Westmoreland reports that the situation at Khe Sanh is critical and may represent the turning point of the Vietnam War; in Washington, President Johnson calls 14,787 reservists to active duty in the Korea crisis and orders the nuclear carrier *Enterprise* toward Korea

26 January 1968

Viet Cong units move to villages on the outskirts of Can Tho and Vinh Long in the Mekong Delta

27 January 1968

The Communist seven-day cease-fire for Tet begins; troops are restricted to their posts and all leaves are canceled under last-minute orders

29 January 1968

The Tet Lunar New Year celebration begins in North Vietnam; the Tet cease-fire for allies is canceled in I Corps Tactical Zone, but cease-fire takes effect in the rest of South Vietnam at 6:00 p.m.

30 January 1968

Communists launch surprise attacks on Nha Trang, followed by attack on two cities in I Corps and five cities in II Corps; allied commanders cancel Tet cease-fire throughout all of South Vietnam, and MACV orders all U.S. units on "maximum alert"; in Washington, the Senate confirms Clark Clifford to be secretary of state

31 January 1968

Communists launch simultaneous attacks on major cities, towns, and military bases throughout South Vietnam, including an assault on the U.S. Embassy in Saigon; President Thieu declares martial law; in the United States, the American news media are dominated by accounts of the heaviest fighting of the Vietnam War—CBS and NBC present thirty-minute special reports on the Tet Offensive; in Hanoi, children and old people are evacuated to the countryside in preparation for the anticipated U.S. bombing attacks

1 February 1968

Richard Nixon formally announces his candidacy for the presidency

2 February 1968

Heavy fighting continues in South Vietnam, although the number and intensity of attacks begin to ebb; President Johnson, in a White House press conference, says that the Tet Offensive is a "complete failure"; MACV reports 12,704 Communist troops killed in action since the Tet Offensive began—U.S. battle deaths are listed as 318 and those of the South Vietnamese forces as 661 in the same period

3 February 1968

Heavy fighting continues in Saigon, Hue, Kontum, Pleiku, Dalat, Phan Thiet, and other cities; MACV lists enemy losses at 15,595 killed in action with 415 U.S. and 905 ARVN killed in the fighting since the offensive started; the Central Committee of the National Liberation Front calls for the Viet Cong and the people to strike "even harder, deeper, and on a wider front"; in the United States, Senator Eugene McCarthy accuses the Johnson administration of deceiving itself and the American people about the progress of the war

4 February 1968

Administration officials appear on television interview programs to defend war policy

5 February 1968

Nhan Dan, the official newspaper of Lao Dong Party in Hanoi, declares, "The once-in-a-thousand year opportunity has come. The bugle has sounded victory"

6 February 1968

MACV reports that fighting has diminished throughout South Vietnam, but heavy fighting continues in Cholon and Hue; a U.S. spokesman in Saigon reports 21,330 enemy troops killed since Tet began; the Communist Party Current Affairs Committee in Can Tho Province in the Mekong Delta declares that the General Offensive is a long-term project that may last three or four months, not just a few days; in Washington, Martin Luther King Jr. leads two thousand marchers through Arlington National Cemetery to protest the "cruel and senseless" war

7 February 1968

Lang Vei Special Forces camp near Khe Sanh falls to PAVN troops using Russian-made tanks; Westmoreland flies to Da Nang and orders military redeployments and study of troop needs beyond the 525,000-man ceiling

8 February 1968

Joint Chiefs of Staff Chairman Wheeler offers Westmoreland additional men
from 82nd Airborne Division and a U.S. Marine division; Westmoreland
asks plans be made for redeployment of the units to Vietnam; Senator
Robert F. Kennedy, speaking in Chicago, says Tet Offensive has shattered
official illusions about Vietnam

9 February 1968

U.S. forces from the 199th Light Infantry Brigade land by helicopter to clear
Communist troops in the area around the Saigon racetrack; President
Thieu announces partial mobilization of South Vietnam; Secretary
of State Dean Rusk, in a background briefing, demands of journalists,
"Whose side are you on?"

10 February 1968

U.S. planes raid the Haiphong area for the first time in a month; a Communist Party committee in Bien Hoa Province near Saigon says in a secret
report that "the people's spirit for uprising is still very weak"

11 February 1968

The Saigon government announces the call-up of 65,000 more men

12 February 1968

President Johnson approves dispatch of 10,500 additional troops from the 82nd
Airborne Division and 27th Marine Regimental Landing Team; in Hue,
U.S. Marines move north of the Perfume River to take control of the fight
for the Citadel; a Louis Harris poll reports that U.S. public support for the
war increases in the wake of the Tet attacks

13 February 1968

A Gallup Poll reports that 50 percent of Americans disapprove of President
Johnson's handling of the war

14 February 1968

Senator Stuart Symington reports that the cost of Vietnam War for the fiscal
year is $32 billion

15 February 1968

A U.S. Air Force F-4 Phantom shot down over Hanoi becomes the eight hun-
dredth U.S. aircraft lost in the three-year air war over North Vietnam

16 February 1968

President Johnson, in a surprise press conference, says that rumors that General Westmoreland may be relieved of command are false and may have originated abroad; he also announces that additional troops will be approved for Vietnam as needed

17 February 1968

A record weekly total of U.S. casualties is set during the preceding seven days, with 543 killed and 2,547 wounded; President Johnson flies to Fort Bragg, North Carolina, to visit reinforcements departing for Vietnam, and then flies to the USS *Constellation* at sea in the Pacific to visit with the crew

18 February 1968

Communist gunners shell forty-five cities and bases, including Tan Son Nhut airbase and Saigon; ground attacks are launched against four cities

20 February 1968

The Senate Foreign Relations Committee begins hearings on the 1964 Gulf of Tonkin incident

21 February 1968

COSVN orders a pullback and return to harassing tactics; fresh Marine reinforcements are sent to Hue; General Wheeler leaves for Saigon to hold consultations with General Westmoreland

23 February 1968

The Department of Defense announces a Selective Service call for 48,000 men—the second-highest number of the Vietnam War; at Khe Sanh, Marines are bombarded by 1,307 incoming artillery rounds

24 February 1968

South Vietnamese troops storm the former Imperial Palace in the Citadel of Hue, tearing down the National Liberation Front flag and replacing it with the Republic of Vietnam flag

25 February 1968

General Wheeler departs Saigon for Washington after mapping out a request for 206,000 additional U.S. troops; General Westmoreland tells the Associated Press that additional U.S. forces will probably be needed

27 February 1968

CBS News anchorman Walter Cronkite, who has just returned from Saigon and Hue, tells Americans during his evening broadcast that he is certain "the bloody experience of Vietnam is to end in a stalemate"

28 February 1968

In a White House meeting, General Wheeler, on behalf of General Westmoreland, asks President Johnson for an additional 206,000 soldiers and mobilization of reserve units in the United States; President Johnson orders Clark Clifford to form a task force to study the troop request

29 February 1968

PAVN forces launch three attacks against the 37th ARVN Ranger Battalion at Khe Sanh but are turned back each time

1 March 1968

Clark Clifford is sworn in as the new secretary of defense

2 March 1968

The last enemy troops are driven from Hue by three U.S. Marine battalions and South Vietnamese troops after a month of the heaviest fighting of the entire Tet Offensive; the Clifford task force begins its troop-request study

4 March 1968

The Clifford task force recommends the immediate dispatch of 22,000 more U.S. troops to Vietnam, a reserve call-up of 250,000 men, increased draft calls, and further study of the developing situation

7 March 1968

Chairman J. W. Fulbright of the Senate Foreign Relations Committee and other senators publicly ask Johnson administration to consult Congress before any new troop buildup in Vietnam.

9 March 1968

A Gallup poll reports a new wave of pessimism among Americans about the war in Vietnam

10 March 1968

The *New York Times* breaks the news of General Westmoreland's request for 206,000 troops, saying that it has stirred controversy within administration ranks

12 March 1968

President Johnson narrowly defeats antiwar Democrat Eugene McCarthy
by three hundred votes in the New Hampshire Democratic primary, but
McCarthy wins 42 percent of the vote

14 March 1968

Senator Robert Kennedy and Theodore Sorenson meet Secretary of Defense
Clifford to discuss possible a U.S. commission to reverse the government's
Vietnam policy, but Johnson rejects plan

15 March 1968

Former Secretary of State Dean Acheson, in a private report to President
Johnson, says that U.S. victory in Vietnam is not feasible within the limits
of public tolerance

16 March 1968

Senator Robert F. Kennedy announces his candidacy for the presidency; polls
indicate that Kennedy is now more popular than President Johnson

16 March 1968

More than three hundred Vietnamese civilians are massacred in My Lai hamlet by members of Charlie Company, 1st Battalion, 20th Infantry, while
participating in an assault against suspected Viet Cong encampments in
Quang Ngai Province; the massacre will not come to light until early 1969;
the number of total U.S. combat deaths since January 1961 reaches 20,096

20 March 1968

Pressure on Khe Sanh lessens; Bru tribesmen report that PAVN artillery has
withdrawn into Laos; the 304th North Vietnamese Division is relieved of its
tunneling mission near Khe Sanh base and ordered to withdraw to the east

22 March 1968

President Johnson announces that General Westmoreland will become
Army Chief of Staff in mid-1968 and that General Creighton Abrams will
become commander of Military Assistance Command, Vietnam; Khe
Sanh Combat Base receives 1,100 rounds of rocket and mortar fire

23 March 1968

Wheeler flies secretly to meet with Westmoreland at Clark Field in the
Philippines and tells him that President Johnson will approve only 13,500
additional soldiers out of the original 206,000 requested; Wheeler also

instructs Westmoreland to urge the South Vietnamese to expand their own war effort

25 March 1968

A Harris poll reports that 60 percent of a public opinion sample believes that the Tet Offensive was a standoff or defeat for the U.S. cause in Vietnam

25–26 March 1968

President Johnson convenes the "Wise Men," who advise against additional troop increases and recommend a negotiated peace in Vietnam

30 March 1968

U.S. Marines and PAVN troops engage in a three-hour battle near Khe Sanh, the last major ground battle of the seventy-seven-day siege; a Gallup poll reports that 63 percent of those polled disapprove of President Johnson's handling of the war, an all-time low in public approval of his performance

31 March 1968

President Johnson announces in a nationally televised speech that he will order a unilateral halt to all U.S. bombing north of the 20th parallel and seek negotiations with Hanoi; he also announces his decision not to seek reelection

1 April 1968

The U.S. 1st Cavalry Division (Airmobile) begins Operation Pegasus to reopen Route 9 to the Marine base at Khe Sanh; President Thieu declares that the Tet Offensive has "completely failed"

4 April 1968

Martin Luther King Jr. is assassinated in Memphis

23–30 April 1968

Student protestors occupy several buildings at Columbia University until forcibly removed by police

26 April 1968

200,000 demonstrate against the war in New York City

3 May 1968

Johnson announces that formal peace talks will take place in Paris

12 May 1968

Peace negotiations begin between the United States and North Vietnam in Paris

May 1968

In what becomes known as Mini-Tet, Communist forces attack South Vietnam at various places but are turned back by U.S. and ARVN forces

4 June 1968

Robert F. Kennedy wins the Democratic presidential primary in California and is assassinated in Los Angeles that evening

17 June 1968

American forces abandon Khe Sanh

1 July 1968

General Abrams formally succeeds General Westmoreland as MACV commander

3 July 1968

Westmoreland replaces General Harold K. Johnson as Army Chief of Staff; MACV releases figures showing that more Americans were killed during the first six months of 1968 than in all of 1967

4 July 1968

U.S. infantrymen repulse a combined PAVN–VC attack on their base at Dau Tieng, forty miles northwest of Saigon

12–13 August 1968

Heavy fighting erupts again in the Mekong Delta between VC and allied troops

18 August 1968

In the heaviest fighting in three months, PAVN and VC forces conduct nineteen separate attacks on allied positions throughout South Vietnam

22–23 August 1968

VC forces conduct numerous rocket and mortar attacks on Saigon and numerous other cities

26–29 August 1968

The Democratic National Convention in Chicago nominates Vice President Hubert Humphrey for president; riots occur between Chicago police and antiwar demonstrators

11–16 September 1968

About 1,500 VC and PAVN troops launch a major attack on Tay Ninh in III Corps Tactical Zone

31 October1968

President Johnson announces a complete halt to bombing over North Vietnam, ending Operation Rolling Thunder

5 November 1968

Richard Nixon narrowly defeats Hubert Humphrey in the 1968 presidential election

31 December 1968

U.S. military personnel in Vietnam number 536,000; to date, 30,610 U.S. smilitary personnel have been killed in action

PART IV

The Tet Offensive A to Z

I Corps. Designation for the senior South Vietnamese Army (ARVN) head-quarters in northern South Vietnam, located at Da Nang. The corps headquarters controlled the ARVN 1st, 2nd, and 3rd Divisions. The counterpart U.S. command to I Corps was the III Marine Amphibious Force (III MAF), also located at Da Nang.

I Corps Tactical Zone (I CTZ). Term used to designate the tactical area of responsibility of the South Vietnamese Army's (ARVN) I Corps. It encompassed the five northernmost provinces in South Vietnam.

II Corps. Designation for the senior ARVN headquarters in the Central Highlands, which was located at Pleiku. The corps headquarters controlled the ARVN 22nd and 23rd Divisions. The counterpart U.S. headquarters was I Field Force Vietnam (I FFV) located at Nha Trang.

II Corps Tactical Zone (II CTZ). Term used to designate the tactical area of responsibility for the South Vietnamese Army's (ARVN) II Corps. It encompassed twelve provinces the Central Highlands and the adjoining coastal lowlands.

III Corps. Designation for the senior South Vietnamese (ARVN) headquarters in central South Vietnam. III Corps headquarters was located in Bien Hoa, northeast of Saigon, and controlled the ARVN 5th, 18th, and 25th Divisions. The U.S. counterpart headquarters to III Corps was II Field Force Vietnam (II FFV) located at Long Binh.

III Corps Tactical Zone (III CTZ). Term used to designate the tactical area of responsibility for the South Vietnamese Army's (ARVN) III Corps. It encompassed the eleven provinces that surrounded Saigon and included an area that ran from the northern Mekong Delta to southern Central Highlands, which contained 38 percent of the country's population and about 90 percent of its industry. It also contained a number of Communist base areas, such as the Iron Triangle, Ho Bo Woods, and War Zones C and D.

IV Corps. Designation for the senior South Vietnamese Army (ARVN) headquarters in the Mekong Delta, located at Can Tho. The corps headquarters controlled the ARVN 7th, 9th, and 21st Divisions. A senior adviser to the South Vietnamese corps commander represented the U.S. command.

IV Corps Tactical Zone (IV CTZ). Term used to designate the tactical area of responsibility for the South Vietnamese Army (ARVN) IV Corps in the Mekong Delta. There was no corresponding U.S. corps-level headquarters.

Abrams, Creighton W. Jr. (1914–74). Commander of U.S. Military Assistance Command, Vietnam (MACV) (1968–72) and U.S. Army chief of staff (1972–74). In 1967, General William C. Westmoreland, the commander of MACV, gave Abrams the responsibility for improving and modernizing the Army of the Republic of Vietnam (ARVN) and, along with Robert W. Komer, for managing pacification programs in South Vietnam. During the 1968 Tet Offensive, Westmoreland sent Abrams to I Corps Tactical Zone to take direct control of the fighting in the northernmost two provinces just south of the DMZ. In July 1968, he succeeded Westmoreland as MACV commander. His assignment was to oversee the Vietnamization of the war and, beginning in 1969, to draw down the number of U.S. troops in South Vietnam. In 1972, Abrams left Vietnam to assume the duties as U.S. Army chief of staff. His primary task was to revitalize the U.S. Army in the aftermath of the Vietnam War. During his tenure, the draft was ended and the army became an all-volunteer force. Held in the highest regard by his officers and men, Abrams died of lung cancer in 1974 while chief of staff.

Adams, Eddie (1933–2004). Associated Press photographer who, on February 1, 1968, at the height of the Tet Offensive, took what is perhaps the most infamous photograph of the Vietnam War. With his camera, he captured the instant that General Nguyen Ngoc Loan, chief of the South Vietnamese national police, shot a cringing Viet Cong suspect in the head outside the Au Quang Pagoda in Saigon. The photograph, which won Adams the Pulitzer Prize, demonstrated to many Americans the brutality of the Vietnam War.

Arc Light, Operation. Code name for the use of high-altitude B-52 bombing missions in support of U.S. and Army of Republic of Vietnam (ARVN) ground operations in South Vietnam, Cambodia, and Laos. Deployed to Andersen Air Force Base in Guam and later to bases in Okinawa and U-Tapao, Thailand, the first Arc Light strike occurred on June 18, 1965, marking the debut of the big bombers in Vietnam; the last mission was flown on August 19, 1973. These strikes were particularly effective in breaking up enemy concentrations surrounding Khe Sanh during the seventy-seven-day siege in 1968.

Army of the Republic of Vietnam (ARVN). The land-forces component of the Republic of Vietnam Armed Forces (RVNAF). Created in 1955, the ARVN was organized along the lines of U.S. Army forces, emphasizing conventional methods of warfare that included large-scale infantry formations supported by tanks and artillery. In 1968, in terms of sheer numbers, the ARVN appeared to be a strong military force, but in reality it suffered serious deficiencies in command and control, tactics, and the use of resources. The heavy fighting during the Tet Offensive sorely tested the ARVN. The focus of the Vietnamization program implemented in 1969 was to increase the combat capability of the ARVN and other services within the RVNAF. Some progress was made, but ultimately the South Vietnamese forces were defeated in 1975 after U.S. military aid and assistance was withdrawn.

Arnett, Peter (1934–). New Zealander who was a war correspondent in Vietnam for the Associated Press from 1962 to 1975. During the Tet Offensive, he reported that a major at Ben Tre in the Mekong Delta said, "It became necessary to destroy the town to save it." It has been charged that Arnett misquoted the major, but the statement became one of the most remembered of the war.

attrition strategy. The primary U.S. military strategy that guided the American war effort in Vietnam from start to finish. The objective of this strategy was to kill the enemy's soldiers and destroy their equipment faster than the People's Army of Vietnam (PAVN) and Viet Cong (VC) could replace them. The assumption was that eventually losses would grow to an unacceptable level and Hanoi would withdraw support for the insurgency in South Vietnam and abandon its quest to reunify Vietnam. This strategy was built around America's materiel and technological strengths and focused on the use of massive fire-power. Ultimately, the strategy failed because the VC and PAVN controlled the pace and intensity of battle. They could seek sanctuary across South Vietnam's borders, which allied forces were prohibited from crossing. More important, the Communists were willing to pay a high price for eventual victory, and no matter how many casualties the allies inflicted on them, they continued to fight on.

Australia. In April 1965, Australia deployed its first combat troops to Vietnam. By 1968, there were about seven thousand Australian troops in country, fight-ing as part of the First Australian Task Force. Australian forces occupied a base camp in Phuoc Tuy province and conducted combat operations throughout the province and adjoining areas. A small contingent of soldiers from New Zealand fought with the Australians. The ANZAC troops were part of the Free World Military Forces, which also included troops from South Korea, Thailand, and the Philippines. In addition to ground forces, Australia also provided a guided missile destroyer and a squadron of B-57 Canberra bombers. The last Australian troops departed Vietnam in January 1973.

B-52. Large, eight-engine, high-altitude bomber, originally designed to deliver nuclear weapons against targets in the Soviet Union. In Vietnam, B-52s were used in the conventional role, bombing in support of U.S. and South Vietnamese ground operations in South Vietnam, along the Ho Chi Minh Trail in Cambodia and Laos, and in the 1972 "Christmas bombing" of North Vietnam. First used in South Vietnam on June 18, 1965, the bombers could carry an enormous load of 500-, 750-, and 1,000-pound high-explosive, general-purpose bombs and operated at altitudes of well over 30,000 feet. The B-52s played a major role in the support of besieged U.S. Marines at Khe Sanh in 1968.

Ban Me Thuot. Capital of Darlac province in the Central Highlands and headquarters for the South Vietnamese 23rd Division. Ban Me Thuot was one of the places attacked before dawn on January 30, 1968, twenty-four hours ahead of schedule in the Tet Offensive. It was to become the initial target of the PAVN final offensive in March 1975.

Ben Tre. A town in the eastern part of the Mekong Delta, southwest of Saigon. It was the capital of Kien Hoa province and became famous when Associated Press reporter Peter Arnett reported that an unnamed U.S. adviser had said of it during the Tet Offensive, "It became necessary to destroy the town to save it."

Bien Hoa. The capital of Bien Hoa province, twenty miles northeast of Saigon, Bien Hoa was the site of a U.S.-South Vietnamese airbase that was the largest in Vietnam and one of the busiest airfields in the world. It was also the site of the headquarters for the South Vietnamese Army III Corps. There was significant fighting in Bien Hoa during the 1968 Tet Offensive.

body count. Measure employed by the U.S. military to assess progress in the war of attrition against the Communists in Vietnam by keeping track of enemy casualties. Body counts were regularly announced to the media to indicate how the conflict was progressing. Some argue that the focus on body count desensitized U.S. troops and officers and contributed to tensions between Vietnamese civilians and the U.S. military. As the war continued, pressure from both military and civilian officials, who wanted to show the American public that the war was being won, led to routine inflation of body counts and a widening credibility gap between the military and the American public. Ironically, the reported body count proved more accurate than at first believed. In an interview in 1969, General Vo Nguyen Giap admitted that the People's Army of Vietnam had lost more than 500,000 soldiers killed on the battlefield, which was roughly the number that total body counts had indicated.

Bunker, Ellsworth (1894–1984). U.S. ambassador to the Republic of Vietnam (1967–73). Bunker became a strong proponent of the American war effort and of General William C. Westmoreland's methods of fighting it. He also advocated extending military operations into Laos and Cambodia and supported the Cambodian incursion by U.S. and South Vietnamese troops in 1970. Graham Martin replaced him as ambassador in March 1973.

Calley, William (1943–). Commander of a platoon from C Company, 1st Battalion, 20th Infantry, Americal Division, that murdered several hundred South Vietnamese villagers on March 16, 1968, in what became known as the My Lai massacre. After an initial cover-up by the Army, thirteen officers and enlisted men were charged with war crimes. Only Lieutenant Calley was found guilty, specifically for the murder of twenty-two unarmed civilians, and sentenced to life imprisonment. The Court of Military Appeals upheld the conviction, but the Secretary of the Army eventually reduced Calley's sentence to ten years. On March 19, 1974, President Richard Nixon paroled him.

Cedar Falls, Operation. A seventeen-day search-and-destroy operation conducted in January 1967 by some thirty thousand U.S. and South Vietnamese troops, which was aimed at destroying the Viet Cong (VC) tunnels in the sixty-square-mile Iron Triangle, thirty miles from Saigon in Binh Duong province.

During the operation, the VC-controlled village of Ben Suc was destroyed and its six thousand inhabitants relocated. Although many tunnels were destroyed, VC troops returned to the area six months later.

Central Highlands. Located in II Corps Tactical Zone, the Central Highlands were the southern end of the Truong Son Mountains in west-central South Vietnam. An area of approximately 5,400 square miles, it was sparsely populated, primarily by Montagnard tribesman. The principal towns in the region are Kontum, Pleiku, Ban Me Thuot, and Dalat. There were several large attacks in the Central Highlands during the Tet Offensive. North Vietnam's final offensive in 1975 began at Ban Me Thuot. South Vietnamese forces crumbled rapidly after they withdrew from the Central Highlands.

Central Office for South Vietnam (COSVN). Formed in 1961 when the southern and central branches of the Lao Dong Party (Vietnam Workers) merged. The original purpose of COSVN was to direct the Viet Cong (VC) guerrillas in the South. Nguyen Chi Thanh, a northerner, assumed command of COSVN in 1964, and eventually it controlled both VC and People's Army of Vietnam (PAVN) forces in South Vietnam. The headquarters was the target of a number of allied operations because U.S. strategists, who believed COSVN was located in Laos and later in Cambodia, thought that locating and destroying the headquarters would cripple the Communist war effort. Unlike the elaborate fixed U.S. and South Vietnamese headquarters, COSVN was more what the U.S. military would term a forward command post, consisting of a few senior commanders and key staff officers. The allies never succeeded in locating or destroying it.

Chairman, Joint Chiefs of Staff. By law, the senior officer of the U.S. armed services, who presides over the Joint Chiefs of Staff. Army General Earle G. Wheeler was the chairman of the Joint Chiefs of Staff for most of the Vietnam War (1964–70).

Cholon. An ethnically Chinese area, Cholon was a section of metropolitan Saigon on the southwest side of the city. It was the scene of bitter fighting during the 1968 Tet Offensive.

Civil Operations and Revolutionary Development Support (CORDS). Agency established in 1967 to exercise control over the American pacification efforts, military and civilian, in South Vietnam. It was later renamed Civil Operations and Rural Development Support. The CORDS program deployed unified civil-military advisory teams in all of South Vietnam's 250 districts and

44 provinces. The province senior adviser controlled the pacification activities in each province; about half the province senior advisers were military personnel, and half civilians. With the heavy casualties sustained by the Viet Cong during the 1968 Tet Offensive, the CORDS program achieved some success from 1969 to 1971 in spreading the influence and control of the Saigon government over the countryside.

Civilian Irregular Defense Group (CIDG). A CIA/Special Forces program that involved training indigenous mountain tribes to provide intelligence and interdict Communist infiltration into South Vietnam from Cambodia and Laos. The tribesmen received salaries, medical care, and development aid in exchange for fighting for the Saigon government. A CIDG camp at Lang Vei was overrun by North Vietnamese troops during the fighting at Khe Sanh in February 1968. In 1970, CIDG units were converted to South Vietnamese Ranger units.

Clifford, Clark M. (1906–98). A longtime adviser to Lyndon Johnson, Clark Clifford became secretary of defense in 1968 after the departure of Robert S. McNamara. When the military requested 206,000 additional troops after the Tet Offensive in 1968, Clifford, who had initially supported the war effort, advised the president to refuse the request, halt the bombing of North Vietnam, and de-escalate American participation in the war. After Johnson announced in March that he would not seek a second term, Clifford spent the last months of the president's term laying the groundwork for U.S. withdrawal and what would become known as Vietnamization during the Nixon administration.

Combined Action Program (CAP). A program of the U.S. Marines in Vietnam whereby small Marine units were located in villages to help promote the security and pacification of the surrounding area. The Marines assigned to a village would live in the village and make it their base of operations for extended periods. The objective was for the Marine unit to provide security while getting to know the villagers, helping in civic and health projects, and teaching the villagers to protect themselves and their homes. When the battle for Khe Sanh began in 1968, a Marine combined action company located in Khe Sanh village became one of the early targets of the PAVN in the battle.

Con Thien. A village in Quang Tri province, just south of the demilitarized zone (DMZ), and the site of a U.S. Marine outpost that was attacked by People's Army of Vietnam (PAVN) forces in September 1967. In this battle, which lasted almost a month, the PAVN bombarded the Marines nearly continuously, but the Marines, with the aid of U.S. air, naval, and artillery support, successfully defended the base. This battle was part of the PAVN strategy to divert attention away from the South Vietnamese towns and cities as the Communists prepared to launch the Tet Offensive.

Corps Tactical Zone (CTZ). South Vietnam was divided for military command purposes into four tactical zones numbered from north to south. An ARVN corps commander was responsible for South Vietnamese operations in each corps tactical zone.

Cronkite, Walter L., Jr. (1916–). A widely respected CBS Evening News anchor (1954–81), Cronkite was cautiously optimistic about the Vietnam War until the 1968 Tet Offensive, when, shocked by the discrepancy between the shock and intensity of the Tet Offensive and the U.S. military's claims during the preceding months that the Communist forces were weakening, he traveled to Vietnam to see for himself what was happening. Upon his return to the United States, he reported that the war was a "bloody stalemate" in which there was little likelihood that there would be a clear winner. He did not, as has sometimes been claimed, describe the Tet Offensive as a Communist military victory, but he left no doubt that he thought the administration's war policies were not working. Sensing that Cronkite accurately reflected public opinion, President Lyndon Johnson reportedly remarked, "If I have lost Walter Cronkite, I have lost middle America."

Dak To. A town located in the western Central Highlands near the Laotian and Cambodian borders. The area around Dak To was the scene of a series of bitter battles from October to November 1967, when North Vietnamese forces attacked elements of the U.S. 4th Infantry Division and 173rd Airborne Brigade. This action was part of the pre-Tet deception plan meant to draw American attention and resources away from South Vietnamese cities in the coastal lowlands.

Dalat. The capital of Tuyen Duc province in the Central Highlands, Dalat was the home of the South Vietnamese Military Academy, the Political Warfare College, and a university. Dalat was the site of a battle during the 1968 Tet Offensive.

Da Nang. South Vietnam's second-largest city, located in Quang Nam Province in northern I Corps Tactical Zone, Da Nang included a major port and jet-capable airfield and was the headquarters for the South Vietnamese Army's I Corps and its 3rd Division. The city was also the site of several major U.S. installations, including, in 1968, the headquarters of the III Marine Amphibious Force.

dau tranh. Literally translated as "the struggle," *Dau tranh* was the overarching Vietnamese Communist military and political strategy. Adopted in the 1930s, it combined Marxist, Leninist, Maoist, and Vietnamese ideologies and doctrines. This strategy included not only political but also military measures working together toward the final goal, which was reunification of North and South Vietnam.

Demilitarized Zone (DMZ). A 6.25-mile (10 km)-wide buffer zone created by the 1954 Geneva Conference that became the de facto border between North Vietnam and South Vietnam. The DMZ ran five kilometers on either side of the Ben Hai River, generally along the 17th parallel. Although both sides agreed to withhold military forces from the zone, People's Army of Vietnam (PAVN) and Viet Cong units often took refuge inside it from U.S. planes and artillery. In response, the United States constructed a series of fire support bases along Route 9 just south of the DMZ in 1966–67. The PAVN attacked across the DMZ during the 1972 Easter Offensive.

Dien Bien Phu. Site of a decisive battle between the Viet Minh and French forces during the First Indochina War. Located near the Laotian border, Dien Bien Phu was a French outpost manned by fifteen thousand troops. The French commanders hoped to draw the Viet Minh into a set-piece battle in which it was supposed that superior French firepower would destroy them. The French grossly underestimated their enemy. Viet Minh General Nguyen Giap entrenched artillery in the surrounding hills and massed five divisions totaling about sixty thousand troops around the French positions. The Viet Minh began shelling the French and ultimately overran the French garrison on May 7, 1954, after a two-month siege. The Viet Minh victory ended the eight-year Indochina War and brought about France's withdrawal from Indochina in July 1954. Both the Johnson administration officials and the American news media drew strong parallels between Dien Bien Phu and the siege of Khe Sanh in 1968.

dust off. The evacuation of wounded soldiers by helicopter; also called "Medevac." Helicopters would pick up the wounded troops on the battlefield and fly them to the nearest field hospital. Getting the injured to hospitals quickly meant that many men survived wounds that would have been fatal in previous wars.

Fire Support Base (FSB). A self-contained base that was established to provide artillery fire support to patrolling units operating within the range of the guns on the base. Hundreds of fire support bases were established throughout South Vietnam during the war.

Free World Military Forces (FWMF). The designation of allied units deployed to Vietnam to support the South Vietnamese. These forces included troops from South Korea, Thailand, Australia, New Zealand, and the Philippines, who took part in combat operations in South Vietnam.

friendly fire. Term used to describe combat deaths or wounds caused by the guns, bombs, or artillery of one's own side in a war.

Grunt. Popular nickname for U.S. Army and Marine Corps ground combat forces in South Vietnam.

Hanoi. The administrative capital of the Democratic Republic of Vietnam (North Vietnam). Located in the Red River Delta, Hanoi experienced periodic bombing during the war with the United States. President Lyndon Johnson announced a halt to the bombing in the aftermath of the Tet Offensive, but Richard Nixon resumed the bombing after he assumed office as president.

Harriman, W. Averell (1891–1986). Diplomat who served as one of the "Wise Men" in 1968 and advised President Lyndon B. Johnson to de-escalate the war in Vietnam. The president subsequently named Harriman to head the U.S. delegation at the Paris peace talks when they began in May 1968. He urged compromise with the North Vietnamese, but Johnson rejected his proposal and replaced him in January 1969 with Henry Cabot Lodge.

Ho Chi Minh (1890–1969). Founder of the Vietnamese Communist Party (1930) and the first president of the Democratic Republic of Vietnam (1945–69). Born Nguyen Tat Thanh, he was the father of the Vietnamese revolution and the most influential figure in modern Vietnam. After the 1954 defeat of the French, he played a key role in the formulation of policy in the DRV. He remained a major voice on diplomacy and strategy in the struggle for South Vietnam until the mid-1960s, when his role in decision making became largely ceremonial due to failing health. He died in September 1969.

Ho Chi Minh Trail. The People's Army of Vietnam (PAVN) infiltration and supply route into South Vietnam by land though Laos and Cambodia. A network of trails rather than a single path, the Ho Chi Minh Trail ran through the Truong Son mountain range along the border between Vietnam and Laos. By 1967, an estimated twenty thousand PAVN troops moved into South Vietnam via the trail each month. The allies tried many times to stop the movement of soldiers and supplies down the trail, but were unable to do so. The PAVN troops who played a key role in the fighting during the 1968 Tet Offensive came down the trail from the north.

Hue. South Vietnam's third largest city, forty-five miles south of the demilitarized zone (DMZ) on the Perfume River in Thua Thien province. An old imperial capital, considered Vietnam's most beautiful city, Hue was the scene of widespread protests against President Diem in May 1963 and against President Ky in March 1966. During the 1968 Tet Offensive, the People's Army of Vietnam and the Viet Cong captured the city and held it for twenty-five days. In the fight by U.S. Marines and South Vietnamese troops to retake Hue, much of the city was destroyed. After the battle, bodies were found in several mass graves; it was reported that the Communists had massacred them during the occupation of the city. By late 1969, nearly three thousand bodies had been exhumed, although there is a claim that some of these were killed by South Vietnamese teams seeking to eliminate suspected Communists and their sympathizers.

Humphrey, Hubert H. (1911–78). U.S. senator (1948–65) and vice president (1965–69). He was a strong advocate of the Vietnam War and President Lyndon B. Johnson's policies. When Johnson announced in March 1968 that he would not run for reelection, Humphrey won the Democratic nomination. The nominating convention in Chicago proved a disaster for him when conflict broke out both inside and outside the convention hall. Humphrey repudiated some of Johnson's war policies during the election campaign, but Richard Nixon narrowly defeated him all the same. Humphrey was elected to the Senate again in 1970 and served until his death in 1978.

Iron Triangle. The nickname for a Communist base area lying mostly in Binh Duong province, less than twenty miles northwest of Saigon. Its borders were approximately defined on the southwest by the Saigon River, on the east by the Thi Tinh River, and on the north by a line running from Ben Suc east to Ben Cat. Heavily forested and sparsely populated, the 125-square-mile area was laced with tunnels and fortifications. Operation Cedar Falls was launched by U.S. and South Vietnamese forces in January 1968 to destroy Viet Cong forces and facilities in and around the Iron Triangle, but the operation was only partially successful, and Communist troops eventually reoccupied the area.

Johnson, Lyndon Baines (1908–73). President of the United States (1963–69). Formerly a U.S. Representative (1937–48) and U.S. Senator (1949–61), Johnson became vice president and succeeded President John F. Kennedy when Kennedy was assassinated in Dallas, Texas, on November 22, 1963. Believing he was following Kennedy's intentions, the new president pledged not to "lose" South Vietnam. In August 1964, armed with the Gulf of Tonkin Resolution, Johnson began an escalation of the war that resulted in the arrival of more than 400,000 U.S. troops in South Vietnam by the end of 1967. He came under increasing criticism at home for his handling of the war. Stunned by the scope and violence of the Tet Offensive, he announced on March 31, 1968, that he would reduce the bombing of North Vietnam, that the United States was ready for peace talks, and that he would not run again for president. After defeating Vice President Hubert H. Humphrey in the 1968 presidential election, Republican Richard M. Nixon succeeded Johnson, who died in 1973 at his home in Texas.

Joint Chiefs of Staff (JCS). The highest military body in the United States. It consists of the Army chief of staff, the Air Force chief of staff, the commandant of the Marine Corps, and the chief of naval operations, along with the chairman. During the Vietnam War, the JCS advised the president on the war, strongly endorsing the domino theory (which held that if one nation fell to Communists, adjacent nations would soon fall) and urging Johnson to escalate the war. Additionally, the chiefs were responsible for strategic planning and logistical and administrative matters for their respective services. They had no direct operational control over troops, but reported directly to the secretary of defense and issued orders in his name.

Joint General Staff (JGS). South Vietnam's counterpart to the U.S. Joint Chiefs of Staff, which included the component commanders of the Republic of Vietnam Armed Forces: the Army of the Republic of Vietnam (ARVN), the Republic of Vietnam Air Force (VNAF), and the Vietnamese Navy (VNN), which included the Vietnamese Marine Corps (VNMC). Unlike the JCS, the JGS had direct operational control over South Vietnam's military forces.

Junction City, Operation. A large joint U.S.-South Vietnamese operation in the Iron Triangle area of Tay Ninh province February to May 1967. The purpose of the operation, which involved twenty-two battalions, about 25,000 allied troops, was to find and destroy the Viet Cong (VC) Central Office for South Vietnam (COSVN). Although the operation achieved tactical success by destroying VC forces and capturing large amounts of war materiel, it failed to achieve any long-term strategic advantage. The operation, however, did convince the Communists that their operating and supply bases were vulnerable to allied attack and they subsequently relocated many of these facilities across the border into Cambodia.

Kennedy, Robert F. (1925–68). U.S. attorney general (1961–64) and U.S. senator (1964–68). After the Tet Offensive of 1968, Kennedy entered the race for the democratic nomination for president and made the war the central issue of his campaign, advocating a negotiated solution. He was assassinated on June 5, 1968, in Los Angeles after winning the California primary.

Khe Sanh. A Marine Corps base in northwestern South Vietnam, about six miles from the Laotian border and about fourteen miles south of the demilitarized zone (DMZ). The area was first occupied by U.S. Special Forces troops in 1962. In the summer of 1966, General Westmoreland ordered the Marines to set up a base to counter infiltration by the People's Army of Vietnam (PAVN) into South Vietnam from Laos. The garrison was reinforced to regimental strength in the spring of 1967 and fought a series of battles for control of the strategic hills surrounding the base. By the end of 1967, U.S. intelligence indicated that elements of three PAVN divisions were in the Khe Sanh area. In January 1968, the garrison was further reinforced, raising the number of defenders to more than six thousand Marines and ARVN Rangers. The PAVN launched an attack on January 21, laying siege to the Marine base for the next seventy-seven days. The battle received much attention because of the parallels between the situation and that at Dien Bien Phu in 1954. On April 15, in Operation Pegasus, a relief force under the 1st Cavalry Division broke through and lifted the siege. On July 5, the Marines abandoned the base. Khe Sanh was reoccupied in January 1971 and served as the base for the South Vietnamese incursion into Laos.

Kontum. The capital of Kontum Province, located in the northern portion of the Central Highlands in II Corps Tactical Zone, Kontum was one of the towns attacked prematurely by the Communist forces on January 30, 1968, to launch the Tet Offensive.

Korea, Republic of. South Korea first sent soldiers to Vietnam in 1965. By the end of the war, the Republic of Korea had sent large numbers of combat troops, a level second only to that of the United States. Korean troop deployment reached a high of fifty thousand in 1968. These troops were part of the Free World Military Forces, which also included forces from Thailand, Australia, New Zealand, and the Philippines. The last Korean troops departed Vietnam in 1973.

LaHue, Foster C. (1917–66). Marine general who commanded Task Force X-Ray, responsible for control of U.S. Marines in the battle for Hue during the Tet Offensive in 1968.

Lang Vei. Site of a U.S. Special Forces camp near the border of South Vietnam and Laos, about nine miles southwest of Khe Sanh base. On February 7, 1968, a North Vietnamese division equipped with Soviet-made tanks overran the camp, which was defended by some four hundred Montagnard tribesmen and twenty-four U.S. advisers. Almost three hundred of the Lang Vei garrison were killed, wounded, or missing, including ten U.S. Special Forces soldiers killed and thirteen wounded.

Lao Dong Party. The Vietnamese Workers' Party created in February 1951, which became the leading political party in the Democratic Republic of Vietnam (North Vietnam) and the guiding force in the struggle for reunification of North and South Vietnam. A separate Communist Party for South Vietnam was established in 1962, but this was a propaganda ploy; the Lao Dong Party remained in reality the Communist party for all Vietnam, North and South.

Le Duan (1908–86). Founding member of the Indochinese Communist Party and general secretary of the Lao Dong Party (1957–86). In 1968, Le Duan was instrumental in Hanoi's decision to launch the general offensive. After the death of Ho Chi Minh in 1969, Le Duan emerged as one of the leading members of the government of North Vietnam.

Le Duc Tho (1911–90). Influential member of the Lao Dong Party who became principal negotiator for the Democratic Republic of Vietnam at Paris when the peace talks opened on May 13, 1968. Ultimately, he would meet secretly with Henry Kissinger in clandestine negotiations that would result in the signing of the Paris Peace Accords in 1973.

Loc Ninh. South Vietnamese district town in Binh Long province, seventy miles north of Saigon along the Cambodian border. In one of the border battles preceding the Tet Offensive, Viet Cong forces attacked the U.S. outpost at Loc Ninh on October 29, 1967, and held it for a sort period of time. During intense fighting, U.S. forces recaptured the town, inflicting heavy casualties on the Viet Cong and driving them back.

Long Binh. Large U.S. military logistical and headquarters complex located just outside the city of Bien Hoa, about twenty miles north of Saigon. The base, housing more than forty thousand U.S. personnel at one point, contained several senior U.S. headquarters, hospitals, logistical units, several large ammunition dumps, and the infamous Long Binh Jail, the military's largest confinement facility in South Vietnam. Long Binh was the target of a major Viet Cong attack during the 1968 Tet Offensive.

McCarthy, Eugene J. (1916–2005). U.S. Senator from Minnesota (1959–71), McCarthy ran for the Democratic nomination for president in 1968 on a peace platform, winning 42 percent of the vote in the New Hampshire primary, thus clearly demonstrating the political vulnerability of President Johnson, who subsequently announced that he would not seek another term. However,

McCarthy lost the nomination to Hubert H. Humphrey at the tumultuous Democratic National Convention. Humphrey was subsequently defeated the following November by Richard M. Nixon.

McNamara, Robert S. (1916–). U.S. secretary of defense (1961–68). McNamara headed the Defense Department under presidents Kennedy and Johnson. He presided over the escalation of the war until 1967 when he proposed limiting the bombing of the North, capping U.S. troop deployments, lowering political objectives, and shifting war-fighting responsibility back to the South Vietnamese. President Johnson was not pleased with these recommendations and began to lose confidence in his secretary of defense. Increasingly at odds with the president, McNamara tendered his resignation and left the Pentagon in 1968 to become head of the World Bank. Clark Clifford replaced McNamara as secretary of defense.

McNamara Line. A proposed interdiction zone along the DMZ covered by air-laid mine and bombing attacks pinpointed by air-laid acoustic sensors. The objective of the line was to interdict the flow of personnel and supplies into South Vietnam from the north. Construction of the line began in April 1967, but the effort was abandoned in 1968 when the concept proved unpractical in terms of both resources required and potential effectiveness.

Mekong Delta. The lowland, marshy geographical area of southern South Vietnam formed by the Mekong River and its tributaries. A fertile region laced with canals and irrigation ditches, the Delta was the scene of much fighting during the 1968 Tet Offensive. The Communists had expected the people of the Delta to rise up against the Saigon government when the offensive began, but because the guerrilla-initiated fighting caused further disruption and suffering for the people, they did not rally to the Communists, and their support for the South Vietnamese government increased.

Military Assistance Command, Vietnam (MACV). The senior U.S. military command for South Vietnam, established on February 8, 1962, with General Paul Harkins as its first commander. Harkins was succeeded by General William C. Westmoreland, who commanded MACV from June 1964 to July 1968. The headquarters was housed in several buildings in the city of Saigon until the summer of 1967, when it was moved to a large facility at Tan Son Nhut Air Base, on the northwest edge of the city, where it was attacked during the 1968 Tet Offensive.

Mobile Riverine Force (MRF). A U.S. Army-Navy task force involving the 2nd Brigade of the 9th Infantry Division and the Navy's Task Force 117, which operated in the Mekong Delta. The Navy provided a wide variety of specialized vessels such as gunboats, armored troop carriers, and barracks ships. Combining these vessels with the brigade of Army troops and its associated artillery and other support units resulted in the formation of a floating task force that had the capability to move afloat for up to 150 miles in twenty-four hours and launch combat operations within thirty minutes of anchoring. The MRF played a significant role in turning back the Communist attacks in the Delta during the Tet Offensive and was later awarded a Presidential Unit Citation for its performance during that fighting.

Montagnard. Name meaning "mountain people" given by the French to thirty-three tribes, estimated at 800,000 to 1,000,000 people, living primarily in the Central Highlands. During the 1960s, the Montagnards made up much of the Civilian Irregular Defense Groups (CIDG), organized by the CIA and the U.S. Special Forces to interdict Communist infiltration into South Vietnam. On February 7, 1968, North Vietnamese troops overran four hundred Montagnard tribesmen and their Special Forces advisers at Lang Vei, near Khe Sanh.

My Lai Incident. A massacre of South Vietnamese civilians by a rifle company from the Americal Division on March 16, 1968. A platoon led by Lieutenant William L. Calley Jr. rounded up civilians in the hamlet of My Lai in Son My village, Quang Ngai province, in I Corps. The American soldiers then gunned down approximately three hundred and fifty women, children, and old men, whom they had herded into a ditch. Throughout the day, Calley's platoon and other members of C Company, 1st Battalion, 20th Infantry, under the command of Captain Ernest L. Medina, committed murder, rape, and other atrocities. The chain of command at the time did not investigate these atrocities, but the Army ordered an inquiry after the crimes were brought to light by former infantryman Ron Ridenhour on March 29, 1969. A formal board of inquiry was convened, headed by Lieutenant General William R. Peers. Eventually, court-martial charges were prepared against twelve officers for dereliction of duty. Thirteen officers and enlisted men were charged with war crimes. Only Lieutenant Calley was found guilty, specifically for the murder of twenty-two unarmed civilians, and sentenced to life imprisonment. A cry went up that Calley had been railroaded and that he was a scapegoat. The Court of Military Appeals upheld the conviction, but the Secretary of the Army eventually reduced Calley's sentence to ten years. On March 19, 1974, President Richard Nixon paroled him.

National Liberation Front (NLF). The political organization of the Communist-dominated insurgent movement in South Vietnam, created on December 31, 1960. It was originally formed as a broad national front organization to overthrow the government of Ngo Dinh Diem. The NLF originally claimed that it was a popular front aimed at liberating South Vietnam and not dominated by the Communists. The military arm of the NLF was the People's Liberation Armed Forces, popularly known as the Viet Cong to its enemies. The National Liberation Front was superseded by the Provisional Revolutionary Government in 1969. After the war, the North Vietnamese freely admitted that the NLF was their own creation, totally controlled and directed from Hanoi.

New Zealand. In 1965, New Zealand, which the year before had sent a small contingent of medical personnel and engineers to Vietnam, replaced the original contingent with combat troops, who worked with the Australian Task Force in Phuoc Tuy province. These troops were part of the Free World Military Forces, which also included troops from South Korea, Thailand, and the Philippines. New Zealand began to withdraw its troops in 1970, and most of its combat troops had departed Vietnam by 1971.

Ngo Quang Truong (1929–). South Vietnamese general who commanded the South Vietnamese Army's (ARVN) 1st Division in Hue during the 1968 Tet Offensive. Widely regarded as one of the most competent commanders in the ARVN, Truong led his troops in the bitter fighting to retake the Citadel. In May 1972, he was sent to replace General Hoang Xuan Lam as commander of ARVN I Corps. Under his leadership, the South Vietnamese retook Quang Tri, which North Vietnamese forces had captured during the Eastertide Offensive.

Nguyen Cao Ky (1930–). Prime minister (1965–67) and vice president (1967–71) of the Republic of Vietnam. Relations between Ky and President Nguyen Van Thieu deteriorated after the 1968 Tet Offensive, and he retired from politics in 1971, declining to run as an opposition candidate against Thieu.

Nguyen Chi Thanh (1914–67). People's Army of Vietnam (PAVN) general; commander of operations in South Vietnam (1965–67). In 1967, he advocated a quick victory using conventional tactics and played a major role in the decision to launch the Tet Offensive in 1968. He died in July 1967 as the campaign was being planned, but the offensive was launched anyway under the direction of General Vo Nguyen Giap.

Nguyen Ngoc Loan (1932–98). Army of the Republic of Vietnam (ARVN) general and chief of South Vietnam's national police. During the 1968 Tet Offensive, he summarily executed a Viet Cong (VC) suspect on the streets of Saigon. Eddie Adams of the Associated Press photographed the act; his photograph was widely circulated in the United States and became a symbol of the violence and brutality of the war.

Nguyen Van Thieu (1923–2001). President of the Republic of Vietnam (1967–75). After the Tet Offensive of 1968, he took steps to increase the size and capability of South Vietnam's armed forces. With the election of Richard Nixon as president, Thieu became increasingly concerned as U.S. forces were gradually withdrawn from Vietnam. His forces, with the aid of U.S. airpower, defeated the 1972 North Vietnamese Easter Offensive, but he was coerced by Nixon to accede to the Paris Peace Accords. The fighting continued after the cease-fire and with Nixon's resignation, the U.S. Congress drastically cut military aid to South Vietnam. When the communists launched a new general offensive in 1975, Thieu's forces collapsed in fifty-five days.

Niagara, Operation. Code name for the 18 January–31 March 1968 bombing of People's Army of Vietnam (PAVN) forces besieging the U.S. Marine base at Khe Sanh. After the first phase, which included reconnaissance flights to pinpoint enemy forces, some 24,000 tactical fighter-bomber sorties and some 2,700 B-52 strategic bomber sorties were flown, averaging more than three hundred strikes per day. The PAVN divisions were decimated by more than 110,000 tons of bombs dropped from Navy, Marine, and Air Force aircraft. This airpower played a major role in the successful defense of Khe Sanh.

Nixon, Richard M. (1913–94). President of the United States (1969–74). Nixon defeated Hubert H. Humphrey in the 1968 presidential election, partly by promising to achieve "peace with honor" in Vietnam. After his inauguration, Nixon ordered the gradual reduction of U.S. ground troops and pressed forward with Vietnamization, a policy initiated by the Johnson administration to begin turning the war over to the South Vietnamese. At the same time, he stepped up the air war and ordered U.S. troops into Cambodia in 1970. When the North Vietnamese launched a full-scale offensive on Good Friday in 1972, he responded with massive airpower, including intensive bombing of North Vietnam. By October 1972, the offensive had been blunted, and secret negotiations in Paris had produced a settlement to end the war. President Thieu of South Vietnam balked at the terms, and the North Vietnamese walked out of the negotiations. Nixon responded by bombing North Vietnam with B-52s and other aircraft for twelve days. The North Vietnamese returned to the negotiations; the South Vietnamese, at Nixon's urging, dropped their objections; and the Paris Peace Accords were signed on January 27, 1973. While all this took place, White House officials created a special unit to plug leaks of government documents. This unit played an important role in the subsequent Watergate scandal, which led to Nixon's resignation in August 1974. With Nixon, who had promised continued support to the South Vietnamese, out of office, Congress slashed military aid to Saigon. The fighting continued for two more years until the South Vietnamese, abandoned by its American allies, succumbed to the North Vietnamese on April 30, 1975.

North Vietnamese Army (NVA). See People's Army of Vietnam.

Ontos. A lightly armored tracked vehicle armed with six 106mm recoilless rifles, originally designed as a tank killer. The Marines used the Ontos very effectively in Hue in 1968 to support their infantry troops in house-to-house fighting.

pacification. Unofficial term given to various programs of the South Vietnamese and U.S. governments designed to spread the influence of the Saigon government, destroy enemy influence in the villages, and establish or reestablish local government responsive to the needs of the people. The pacification effort was damaged by the heavy fighting during the 1968 Tet Offensive. The ferocity of the offensive convinced the South Vietnamese government that pacification needed to be made a top priority. The increased resources, coupled with the weakness of the Viet Cong military forces following the heavy fighting of 1968, led to some success between 1969 and 1971, during which the government spread its influence and control over the countryside.

Pegasus, Operation. Code name for the operation of April 1–15, 1968, in which a combined U.S. Army-Marine and South Vietnamese task force, under the 1st Cavalry Division, broke through PAVN lines and lifted the siege of Khe Sanh.

Pentagon Papers. A 7,000-page set of documents chronicling U.S. actions in Vietnam from 1945 to 1968 written between 1967 and 1969 at the instruction of Secretary of Defense Robert McNamara. The documents were secretly copied at the Pentagon by Daniel Ellsberg, a former Marine officer and researcher at the Massachusetts Institute of Technology's Center for International Studies who had been working on the project. In February 1971, he turned them over to the *New York Times*, which began to publish them in June 1971. The last section of the papers deals with the Tet Offensive.

People's Army of Vietnam (PAVN). More popularly known during the war as the North Vietnamese Army (NVA), the PAVN was made up of a main force of regular troops, a regional force of full-time troops responsible for territorial security and support of the main force, and a self-defense force of part-time militia in the villages. In 1964, PAVN regular-force units began to move down the Ho Chi Minh Trail to enter the fighting in South Vietnam. The PAVN played a major role in the 1968 Tet Offensive by drawing U.S. forces out of the lowlands and populated areas with diversionary attacks at Khe Sanh and other points along the borders with Laos and Cambodia. The PAVN also played the key role in the capture of Hue during the offensive. After the heavy Viet Cong losses in the Tet Offensive, the war in the South was fought primarily by PAVN regulars.

People's Liberation Armed Forces (PLAF). See Viet Cong.

Philippines, Republic of the. The Philippines sent two thousand engineer troops to South Vietnam in 1966. These troops were part of the Free World Military Forces, which also included soldiers from South Korea, Thailand, Australia, and New Zealand.

Pleiku. The provincial capital of Pleiku Province in the Central Highlands, Pleiku was the site of the South Vietnamese Army's II Corps headquarters. During the Tet Offensive, the South Vietnamese and American forces in Pleiku were forewarned when troops from the U.S. 4th Infantry Division captured "Urgent Combat Order Number One," which set forth the enemy's plans for the attack on the province capital. Alerted by this document, the allied forces in Pleiku were prepared when the attack came on January 30, 1968.

Republic of Vietnam Armed Forces (RVNAF). The armed forces of South Vietnam, comprising the Army of the Republic of Vietnam (ARVN), the Republic of Vietnam Air Force (VNAF), and the Vietnamese Navy (VNN), which included the Vietnamese Marine Corps (VNMC).

Resolution 13. This resolution, passed by the Central Committee of the Lao Dong Party's Thirteenth Plenum in Hanoi in April 1967, called for a "spontaneous uprising [in the South] in order to win a decisive victory in the shortest possible time." This resolution effectively changed the protracted war approach and led eventually to the decision to launch the Tet Offensive in 1968.

Resolution 14. This resolution passed by the North Vietnamese Lao Dong Party's Central Committee on October 25, 1967, ordering a "general offensive–general uprising" (*Tong Cong Kich–Tong Khoi Nghia*). This order launched preparations for the 1968 Tet Offensive.

Rolling Thunder. Code name for President Lyndon Johnson's bombing campaign against North Vietnam from March 2, 1965, to October 31, 1968 (interrupted by occasional bombing halts). The campaign was designed to induce North Vietnam to come to the negotiating table while also attempting to interdict Communist supply lines to their troops in South Vietnam. The campaign was largely ineffective and resulted in the loss of 922 aircraft to enemy action. Johnson halted it in 1969 in the aftermath of the Tet Offensive.

Rusk, Dean (1909–94). U.S. secretary of state (1961–69). As a leading foreign policy adviser to presidents Kennedy and Johnson, Rusk fully supported and helped implement Kennedy's and then Johnson's decisions to escalate the U.S. commitment in Vietnam.

Saigon. The capital city of South Vietnam, Saigon had a wartime population of over two million. Saigon and adjoining urban areas were in what was called the Capital Military Region, Gia Dinh Province. It was the seat of the South Vietnamese government and the headquarters of U.S. Military Assistance Command, Vietnam. Saigon was the scene of extensive fighting during the 1968 Tet Offensive. After it fell to the Communists on April 30, 1975, Saigon was renamed Ho Chi Minh City.

San Antonio Formula. An August 1967 U.S. offer to stop bombing North Vietnam if Hanoi agreed to enter productive peace negotiations immediately and not take advantage of the cessation. President Lyndon B. Johnson publicly announced the offer in San Antonio, Texas, on September 29, but the North Vietnamese rejected it as they secretly made preparations to launch the 1968 Tet Offensive.

sappers. Viet Cong and North Vietnamese commandos who were adept at penetrating allied defenses. Sappers usually led Communist attacks by breaching defenses with satchel charges and other weapons.

Sharp, U.S. Grant (1906–2001). Commander in Chief of the U.S. Pacific Command (1964–68). As CINCPAC, Admiral Sharp oversaw the U.S. buildup in Vietnam and was in command of all Pacific forces during the 1968 Tet Offensive.

Song Be. The capital of Phuoc Long province, Song Be lies about fifty miles north of Saigon, near the Cambodian border. On October 27, 1967, North Vietnamese and Viet Cong troops attacked a South Vietnamese outpost in

Song Be as part of the diversionary effort to draw allied forces away from South Vietnamese cities before the Communists launched the 1968 Tet Offensive.

Special Forces (SF). Popularly known as the Green Berets, the U.S. Special Forces were organized in 1952 to wage guerrilla war and organize resistance behind enemy lines. Beginning in 1963, they took over a CIA operation that organized Civilian Irregular Defense Groups (CIDGs) among the Montagnard tribesmen of the Central Highlands to conduct interdiction missions and long-range reconnaissance against the Communists in Laos. An SF CIDG camp at Lang Vei was overrun by North Vietnamese troops on February 7, 1968, during the intense fighting around Khe Sanh.

Tan Son Nhut. Large airport on the outskirts of Saigon. It served as head-quarters for MACV and included a huge allied airbase. Tan Son Nhut was the scene of intense fighting during the 1968 Tet Offensive.

Tet. The Vietnamese New Year, the most important holiday of the year. Tet is celebrated in Vietnam during the first week of the first month of the lunar calendar, falling between January 19 and February 20. The holiday is marked by feasting, setting off fireworks, decorating homes, spending time with family, and paying reverence to ancestors. During the Vietnam War, there was normally a cease-fire at Tet, but in 1968, the Communists violated the truce and launched a massive offensive against South Vietnamese cities and towns. The scope of the offensive stunned both the White House and the American public and played a major role in the president's decision not to run for reelection.

Thailand. Thailand was the first Asian country to send troops to Vietnam in 1964. By 1967, there were 11,000 Thai combat troops in Vietnam and at the peak of Thai participation the number reached 16,500. Thai troops conducted com-bat operations from a base near Long Thanh in III Corps Tactical Zone. The Thai soldiers were part of the Free World Military Forces, which also included forces from South Korea, Australia, New Zealand, and the Philippines.

Tran Van Tra (1918–96). Military leader of the National Liberation Front and general in the People's Army of Vietnam (PAVN). As chairman of the Central Office for South Vietnam (COSVN), he coordinated the war in the south, including the attack during the 1968 Tet Offensive. He also played a criti-cal role in the 1972 PAVN invasion and the final offensive in 1975 that resulted in the fall of South Vietnam.

Truong Chinh (1907–88). President of the National Assembly of the Democratic Republic of Vietnam (1960–76) who counseled against launching the Tet Offensive. He wanted Hanoi to focus on the socialist reconstruction of the North, while Le Duan and his faction advocated new measures to win the war in the South. Le Duan won the argument, and the offensive was launched in January 1968.

Viet Cong (VC). South Vietnamese slang (a contraction of *Viet Nam Cong San*, meaning "Vietnamese Communist") for the guerrilla movement in South Vietnam supported by North Vietnam; known officially as the People's Liberation Armed Forces (PLAF). Formerly established in early 1961, the PLAF was the military arm of the National Liberation Front and consisted of regular forces, full-time guerrillas, and self-defense militia. The PLAF assumed the primary role in the 1968 Tet Offensive and suffered more than 40,000 casualties; it subsequently declined as a major factor on the battlefield for the remainder of the war, although it remained strong in several areas, including the Mekong Delta.

Viet Minh. Contraction of *Viet Nam Doc Lap Dong Minh Hoi* (League for the Independence of Vietnam) founded by Ho Chi Minh in 1941; it provided the leadership and troops in the struggle against Japanese and French rule in Vietnam. Viet Minh forces under General Vo Nguyen Giap defeated the French forces at Dien Bien Phu in 1954, which led to the French departure from Indochina.

Vietnamization. Term coined to describe the effort to build up the South Vietnamese armed forces and gradually turn over the war as U.S. forces were withdrawn. Although Vietnamization became the focus of U.S. efforts in Vietnam under President Richard Nixon, the initial steps in the process were taken in the last months of the Johnson administration in the aftermath of the 1968 Tet Offensive.

Vo Nguyen Giap (1911–). General and commander of People's Army of Vietnam (1946–72); North Vietnamese minister of defense (1946–80). Giap was the architect of the Viet Minh victory over the French at Dien Bien Phu. As a major land war erupted in the 1960s, Giap advocated guerrilla warfare and the advancement of a Communist political base in the South. In 1967, though disagreeing with the timing of a general offensive, he designed and directed the Tet Offensive in 1968. Although the Communists sustained a tactical defeat and suffered horrendous casualties, in the end they achieved a great psychological victory that led to a protracted U.S. withdrawal. Giap planned the 1972 Easter

Offensive, which failed, and he was eased from power in 1973 in favor of his protégé, PAVN Chief of Staff Senior General Van Tien Dung, who planned and commanded the final PAVN offensive that conquered South Vietnam in 1975. In 1980, Dung formally replaced Giap as Minister of Defense.

War Zones C and D. Communist base areas located to the north of Saigon in III Corps Tactical Zone. War Zone C was bordered on the west by Cambodia and included the northern half of Tay Ninh Province, the western half of Binh Long Province, and the northwestern Quarter of Binh Duong Province. War Zone D was located to the east of War Zone C and included the northwestern portion of Binh Duong Province, a northeastern portion of Bien Hoa Province, and the northern portion of Long Khanh Province. War Zone C was the site of one of the largest allied search-and-destroy missions of the war, Operation Junction City, in 1967.

Westmoreland, William C. (1914–2005). Commander of U.S. Military Assistance Command, Vietnam (1964–68). From 1965 to 1967, Westmoreland was instrumental in raising the level of U.S. forces in South Vietnam and developing the strategy of attrition for the ground war. During the 1968 Tet Offensive, Westmoreland's forces, though initially taken by surprise by the scope of the offensive, reacted quickly and decisively defeated the attackers. After the offensive was contained, he requested an additional 206,000 troops, which was rejected by President Johnson. Westmoreland was subsequently recalled and made Army chief of staff until he retired in 1972. He died at his home in South Carolina in July 2005.

Weyand, Frederick C. (1916–). U.S. Army general who played a key role in turning back the Communists attackers in the fighting in and around Saigon during the 1968 Tet Offensive. Before the offensive, Weyand, then commander of II Field Force, suspecting that the Communists were preparing to launch a major attack on Saigon, repositioned his forces closer to the capital city. When the Viet Cong attacked, his forces were able to react quickly and saved Saigon. He replaced General Creighton Abrams as commander of the Military Assistance Command, Vietnam (MACV) in 1972 and supervised the final withdrawal of U.S. forces.

Wheeler, Earle G. (1908–75). U.S. Army chief of staff (1962–64) and chairman of the Joint Chiefs of Staff (1964–70). As a key advisor to both presidents Kennedy and Johnson, Wheeler presided over the escalation of the U.S. troop commitment in Vietnam. He advocated the full use of U.S. power against North Vietnam. After the Tet Offensive, Wheeler advised Johnson to call up the reserves and send 206,000 additional troops to Vietnam. Johnson declined the recommendation and began de-escalating the U.S. effort. Wheeler retired in 1970 and died five years later.

"Wise Men." Nickname given to a group of elder statesmen who met periodically from 1965 to 1968 to advise President Lyndon Johnson. They first met in July 1965 and endorsed Secretary of Defense Robert McNamara's proposal for escalating the war. In a meeting in November 1967, most of them continued to back Johnson's Vietnam policies. However, in a meeting held in March 1968 after the Tet Offensive, the Wise Men, stunned by the scope of the offensive, advised the president to begin disengaging from Vietnam. This change of opinion had a profound effect on Johnson and influenced his decision not to run for reelection.

PART V

Documents

PRESIDENT JOHNSON'S "SAN ANTONIO FORMULA" SPEECH OF SEPTEMBER 29, 1967

This evening I came here to speak to you about Vietnam. . . .

Doubt and debate are enlarged because the problems of Vietnam are quite complex. They are a mixture of political turmoil—of poverty—of religious and factional strife—of ancient servitude and modern longing for freedom. Vietnam is all of those things.

Vietnam is also the scene of a powerful aggression that is spurred by an appetite for conquest. . . .

I want to turn now to the struggle in Vietnam itself.

There are questions about this difficult war that must trouble every really thoughtful person. . . .

First, are the Vietnamese—with our help, and that of their other allies— really making any progress? Is there a forward movement? The reports I see make it clear that there is. Certainly there is a positive movement toward constitutional government. Thus far the Vietnamese have met the political schedule that they laid down in January 1966.

The people wanted an elected, responsive government. They wanted it strongly enough to brave a vicious campaign of Communist terror and assassination to vote for it. It has been said that they killed more civilians in four weeks trying to keep them from voting before the election than our American bombers have killed in the big cities of North Vietnam in bombing military targets.

On November 1, subject to the action, of course, of the Constituent Assembly, an elected government will be inaugurated and an elected Senate and Legislature will be installed. . . .

There is progress in the war itself, steady progress considering the war that we are fighting; rather dramatic progress considering the situation that actually prevailed when we sent our troops there in 1965; when we intervened to prevent the dismemberment of the country by the Vietcong and the North Vietnamese.

The campaigns of the last year drove the enemy from many of their major interior bases. The military victory almost within Hanoi's grasp in 1965 has now been denied them. The grip of the Vietcong on the people is broken.

Since our commitment of major forces in July 1965, the proportion of the population living under Communist control has been reduced to well under 20 percent. Tonight the secure proportion of the population has grown from about 45 percent to 65 percent — and in the contested areas, the tide continues to run with us.

But the struggle remains hard. The South Vietnamese have suffered severely, as have we — particularly in the First Corps area in the north, where the enemy has mounted his heaviest attacks, and where his lines of communication to North Vietnam are shortest. Our casualties in the war have reached about 13,500 killed in action, and about 85,000 wounded. Of those 85,000 wounded, we thank God that 79,000 of the 85,000 have been returned, or will return to duty shortly. Thanks to our great American medical science and the helicopter. . . .

As we have told Hanoi time and time and time again, the heart of the matter is really this: The Unite States is willing to stop all aerial and naval bombardment of North Vietnam when this will lead promptly to productive discussions. We, of course, assume that while discussions proceed, North Vietnam would not take advantage of the bombing cessation or limitation.

But Hanoi has not accepted any of these proposals. . . .

Why, in the face of military and political progress in the South, and the burden of our bombing in the North, do they insist and persist with the war?

From many sources the answer is the same. They still hope that the people of the United States will not see this struggle through to the very end. As one Western diplomat reported to me only this week — he had just been in Hanoi — "They believe their staying power is greater than outs and that they can't lose." A visitor from a Communist capital had this to say: "They expect the war to be long, and that the Americans in the end will be defeated by a breakdown in morale, fatigue, and psychological factors." The Premier of North Vietnam said as far back as 1962. "Americans do not like long, inconclusive war. . . . Thus we are sure to win in the end."

Are the North Vietnamese right about us?

I think not. No. I think they are wrong. . . .

source: *Public Papers of the Presidents of the United States: Lyndon B. Johnson, 1967* (Washington, DC: U.S. Government Printing Office, 1970), 876–881.

DIRECTIVE ON FORTHCOMING OFFENSIVE AND UPRISINGS

Provincial Party Standing Committee, 1 November 1967

Local communist cadres received this directive explaining the goals and strategy for the offensive, the plan for the beginning of the general uprising, and the strategy for success. These instructions were sent to the local cadres.

1. Following is information on the new situation. Out troops are continuously attacking the enemy everywhere, especially in the district seats and province capitals. We have started a partial uprising in the city. Several province capitals and district seats have changed hands three or four times. The enemy troops in several districts and provinces have been confused and disorganized.

In the rural, delta and mountain areas, an uprising movement to gain full control of the rural areas has started. The rural people, together with town people, are rising up to fight the U.S., overthrow the puppet government, and seize power. In the face of this situation, the enemy has shifted to the defensive and has been thrown into utmost confusion. A new era, a real revolutionary period, an offensive and uprising period has begun. The victorious day of the people and the trying hours are coming. This is the encouraging factor of the situation. This is what the entire party, entire army, and entire population have been expecting. The people often say: "It is wise to carry through to the end, no matter what the cost in lives and money may be." Now it is time to apply this motto to complete our work as soon as possible without delay. . . .

Upon receipt of this letter, you are required to formulate a plan to prepare the minds of the Party, Group, agencies, and the people by convening a Party Branch meeting (one night) to:

Report the new situation in towns and rural areas. The time is now more favorable [for an offensive] than ever before. This is to notify you that an offensive and uprising will take place in the very near future and we will mount stronger attacks on towns and cities, in coordination with the wide-spread movement in the rural areas. The enemy will be thrown into utmost confusion. No matter how violently the enemy may react, he cannot avoid collapse. This is not only a golden opportunity to liberate hamlets and villages but also an opportunity to liberate district seats, province capitals, and South Viet-Nam as a whole.

Our victory is close at hand. The conditions are ripe. Our Party has carefully judged the situation. We must act and act fast. This is an opportunity to fulfill the aspirations of the entire people, of cadre, of each comrade and of our families. We have long suffered hardships, death, and pain. We are looking for an opportunity to avenge evil done our families, to pay our debt to the Fatherland, to display our loyalty to the country, affection for the people and love for our families. We cannot afford to miss this rare opportunity. All Party members and cadre must be willing to sacrifice their lives for the survival of the Fatherland.

The opportunity is like an attack on an enemy post in which we have reached the last fence and the enemy puts up a fierce resistance. We only need to make a swift assault to secure the target and gain total victory.

If we are hesitant and fearful of hardships and misery, we will suffer heavy losses, fail to accomplish the mission and feel guilty for failing our nation, our people, our families, and our comrades who have already sacrificed themselves. It is time for us to take the initiative in penetrating into enemy bases in provinces, districts, and villages, attacking him five or ten times more violently to score brilliant achievements.

Make all comrades realize that the purpose of the revolutionary activities conducted for many years is mainly to support this phase, in this decisive hour. Even though we make sacrifices, we will gain glorious victory, not only for the people, but also for our Fatherland and families. If we adopt a hesitant attitude, we will not only belittle the value of human beings but also lower the prestige of revolutionary party members. This means we will lose self-respect and we will not be worthy of enjoying the rights of man.

As Party members, we should not think and act in an inferior manner. For this reason all comrades must get together and speak their minds in order to become better acquainted and to transform the whole Party Branch into a determined-to-die unit. All comrades must write a heart-felt letter expressing their decision to the Central Party Committee, to Chairman Ho as well as to the Province Party Committee. . . .

3. How will the uprising be conducted?

There are two fundamental steps:

First, annihilate the enemy's political power. It is fundamental that we capture all tyrants from the village and hamlet administrative machinery and a number of spies. If we are not successful in this area the uprising will not be able to take place.

Second, organize our political power, specifically our district, village, and hamlet administrative machinery.

To conduct an uprising, you must have a roster of all the tyrants and spies and be familiar with the way they live and where they live. Then use suicide cells to annihilate them by any means. The following tasks should also be achieved on the same night:

Conduct meetings and give information of the current situation (about 10 to 15 minutes). Make use of the populace immediately in sabotage and support activities and in raid operations against the spies. The masses should be encouraged to go on strike. Dig trenches and make spikes all night long, and contribute to the transformation of the terrain. All people in each family, regardless of their ages, should be encouraged to take part. This is the best way of motivating the populace and of elevating their pride. We must alter the terrain features at night to secure positions to oppress and strike the enemy in the morning. The cadre, together with the population, will be required to swear that they will stay close to their rice fields, defend their villages, and do their utmost to wrest back control of the entire area, including district seats and towns. A number of old men, women and children should be made available the following morning and ordered to report to enemy district seats or post to inform them [GVN officials] that their [the demonstrators'] village has been occupied by the revolutionary army and that the personnel of the [village] administrative committee as well as their [own] husbands and children have been captured. This demonstration will be aimed at preventing the enemy from battering their village. Young men and healthy farmers will be retained for use in defense work construction, altering terrain, guard duty, and combat. This is done to restrict escapees and limit our casualties. Place emphasis on encouraging enemy soldiers' dependents to struggle for the return of their husbands and children. Make appeals to enemy personnel from the Popular, Regional, and Special forces to surrender. Once the task is achieved, make use of a number of agents under legal cover to organize insurrection committees in white [GVN-controlled] hamlets and villages. At the same time, transfer the determined-to-die cells to the next hamlet or village to push the revolutionary movement forward quickly, observing the same principles applied recently in Tuy Phuoc and other areas of the province. Women and children must be recruited immediately to serve in the self-defense corps and guerrilla force.

A number of loyal farmers, youths, and women will be selected for indoctrination. Upon termination of the course, and after the students have been acquainted with the regulations, an official selection of members for organization and recruitment of personnel for hamlets will take place. This will facilitate the organization of people's cells, such as those for the youths, farmers, and women.

Instructions on carrying out such policies as that for land will be disseminated in the future. If all Party Branches, hamlets, and villages display a strong determination and unanimously carry out the aforementioned tasks, we will surely create various levels of supremacy and will continue to brighten our supremacy. . . .

SOURCE: "Directive from Province Party Standing Committee to District and Local Party Organs on Forthcoming Offensive and Uprisings, 1 November 1967," Vietnam Archive (Larry Berman Collection), Texas Tech University, Lubbock, Texas

CAPABILITIES OF THE VIETNAMESE COMMUNISTS FOR FIGHTING IN SOUTH VIETNAM, NOVEMBER 13, 1967 (EXTRACT)

Conclusions

A. During the past year, Hanoi's direct control and share of the burden of the war in South Vietnam has grown substantially. This trend will continue.

B. Manpower is a major problem confronting the Communists. Losses have been increasing and recruitment in South Vietnam is becoming more difficult. Despite heavy infiltration from North Vietnam, the strength of the Communist military forces and political organizations in South Vietnam declined in the last year.

C. The major portion of this decline has probably been felt at the lower levels, reflecting a deliberate policy of sacrificing these levels to maintain the structure of political cadres and the strength of the Regular military forces. In particular the guerrillas, now estimated to total some 70,000–90,000, have suffered a substantial reduction since the estimated peak of about early 1966. Regular force strength, no estimated at 118,000, has declined slightly, but Viet Cong (VC) units are increasingly dependent upon North Vietnamese replacements.

D. Given current Communist strategy, and levels of operations, a major effort will be necessary if the Regular forces and the guerrillas are to be maintained at or near present levels. To do so will require both a level of infiltration much higher than that observed in 1967 and intensive VC recruitment as well. Considering all the relevant factors, however, we believe there is a fairly good chance that the overall strength and effectiveness of the military forces and the political infrastructure will continue to decline.

E. The Communist leadership is already having problems in maintaining morale and quality. These problems have not yet impaired overall military effectiveness, but they are likely to become more difficult.

F. Difficulties in internal distribution will continue to cause local shortages and interfere with Communist operations from time to time. But we believe that the Communists will be able to continue to meet at least their essential supply requirements for the level of forces and activities in South Vietnam described in this estimate.

G. Communist strategy is to sustain a protracted war of attrition and to persuade the US that it must pull out or settle on Hanoi's terms. Our judgment is that the Communists still retain adequate capabilities to support this strategy for at least another year. Whether or not Hanoi does in fact persist with this strategy depends not only on its capabilities to do so, but on a number of political and international considerations not treated in this estimate.

source: Document declassified by the CIA, December 1, 1975; Vietnam Archive (Douglas Pike Collection), Texas Tech University, Lubbock, Texas

ADDRESS BY COMMANDER OF U.S. FORCES IN VIETNAM, GENERAL WILLIAM C. WESTMORELAND, NOVEMBER 21, 1967 (EXTRACT)

Improving Vietnamese Effectiveness

With 1968, a new phase is now starting. We have reached an important point when the end begins to come into view. What is this third phase we are about to enter?

In Phase III, in 1968, we intend to do the following:

Help the Vietnamese Armed Forces to continue improving their effectiveness.

Decrease our advisers in training centers and other places where the professional competence of Vietnamese officers makes this possible.

Increase our advisory effort with the younger brothers of the Vietnamese Army: the Regional Forces and Popular Forces.

Use U.S. and free-world forces to destroy North Vietnamese forays while we assist the Vietnamese to reorganize for territorial security.

Provide the new military equipment to revitalize the Vietnamese Army and prepare it to take on an ever-increasing share of the war.

Continue pressure on North to prevent rebuilding and to make infiltration more costly.

Turn a major share of frontline DMZ defense over to the Vietnamese Army.

Increase U.S. support in the rich and populated delta.

Help the Government of Viet-Nam single out and destroy the Communist shadow government.

Continue to isolate the guerrilla from the people.

Help the new Vietnamese government to respond to popular aspirations and to reduce and eliminate corruption.

Help the Vietnamese strengthen their policy forces to enhance law and order.

Open more roads and canals.

Continue to improve the Vietnamese economy and standard of living.

THE FINAL PHASE

Now for Phase IV—the final phase. That period will see the conclusion of our plan to weaken the enemy and strengthen our friends until we become progressively superfluous. The object will be to show the world that guerrilla warfare and invasion do not pay as a new means of Communist aggression.

I see phase IV happening as follows:

Infiltration will slow.

The Communist infrastructure will be cut up and near collapse.

The Vietnamese Government will prove its stability, and the Vietnamese Army will show that it can handle the Viet Cong.

The Regional Forces and Popular Forces will reach a higher level of professional performance.

U.S. units can begin to phase down as the Vietnamese Army is modernized and develops its capacity to the fullest.

The military physical assets, bases and ports, will be progressively turned over to the Vietnamese.

The Vietnamese will take charge of the final mopping up of the Viet Cong (which will probably last several years). The U.S., at the same time, will continue the development help envisaged by the President for the community of Southeast Asia.

You may ask how long phase III will take, before we reach the final phase. We have already entered part of phase III. Looking back on phases I and II, we can conclude that we have come a long way.

I see progress as I travel all over Viet Nam.

I see it in the attitudes of the Vietnamese.

I see it in the open roads and canals.

I see it in the new crops and the new purchasing power of the farmer.

I see it in the increasing willingness of the Vietnamese Army to fight North Vietnamese units and in the victories they ware winning.

Parenthetically, I might say that the U.S. press tends to report U.S. actions, so you may not be as aware as I am of the victories won by South Vietnamese forces.

The enemy has many problems.

He is losing control of the scattered population under his influence.

He is losing credibility with the population he still controls.

He is alienating the people by his increased demands and taxes, where he can impose them.

He sees the strength of his forces steadily declining.

He can no longer recruit in the South to any meaningful extent; he must plug the gap with North Vietnamese.

His monsoon offensives have been failures.

He was dealt a mortal blow by the installation of a freely elected representative government.

And he failed in his desperate effort to take the world's headlines from the inauguration by a military victory.

Lastly, the Vietnamese Army is on the road to becoming a competent force. Korean troops in Viet Nam provide a good example for the Vietnamese. Fifteen years ago the Koreans themselves had problems now ascribed to the Vietnamese. The Koreans surmounted these problems, and so can and will the Vietnamese.

We are making progress. We know you want an honorable and early transition to the fourth and last phase. So do your sons and so do I.

It lies within our grasp—the enemy's hopes are bankrupt. With your support we will give you a success that will impact not only on South Viet Nam but on every emerging nation in the world.

SOURCE: Department of State *Bulletin*, December 11, 1967, 785–788, Vietnam Archive (Larry Berman Collection), Texas Tech University, Lubbock, Texas

"SAIGON UNDER FIRE"

CBS News Special Report, January 31, 1968

This is a transcript of the fifteen-minute CBS News Special Report "Saigon Under Fire," hosted by Mike Wallace. It was telecast from 11:15 to 11:30 p.m., following "The Jonathan Winters Show."

WALLACE: Good evening. I'm Mike Wallace.

With a bold series of raids during the last three days the enemy in Vietnam has demolished the myth that Allied military strength controls that country. The Communists hit the very heart of Saigon, the capital of South Vietnam, and at least ten cities which correspond to state capitals here in the United States.

And then, as if to demonstrate that no place in that war-torn nation is secure they struck at least nine American strongholds and unnumbered field positions. Tonight the magnitude of those raids became apparent in the U.S. Command's report on casualties. The Communists paid a heavy toll for their strikes, almost 5,000 dead, including 660 in Saigon alone, and almost 2,000 captured. But Allied casualties also are high: 232 Americans killed, 929 wounded; 300 South Vietnamese killed, 747 wounded, and that toll is expected to climb.

The enemy's well-coordinated attacks occurred throughout South Vietnam, but the most dramatic demonstration of the boldness and capability came at the every symbol of America's presence in Vietnam, the brand new U.S. Embassy building there. CBS News Correspondent Robert Schakne reports:

SCHAKNE: The American Embassy is under siege; only the besiegers are Americans. Inside, in part of the building, are the Vietcong terror squads that charged in during the night. Military Police got back into the compound of the $2.5 million Embassy complex at dawn. Before that a platoon of Vietcong were in control. The Communist raiders never got into the main chancery building; a handful of Marines had it blocked and kept them out. But the raiders were everywhere else. By daylight (voice drowned out by gunfire) No one, unless identified, was allowed in the street. An Australian military policeman was standing guard, firing warning shots to keep the street clear.

Outside the building knots of military policemen held positions. There were bursts of wild shooting in the streets, perhaps snipers in other building and there had been casualties. The bodies of two military policemen who died as they tried to assault the compound lay near their jeep across the boulevard. But even after the military police fought their way back inside, there was more fighting. The raiders were still about the compound. They may have been a suicide cadre. In the end none of them were to surrender.

This is where the Vietcong raiders broke in. They sneaked up and blasted a hole in the reinforced concrete fence surrounding the compound. They were inside before anyone knew it. They had the big Embassy wall to protect them. But none of the raiders lived to tell of their exploit. By 8:00 o'clock, five hours after they first broke in, almost all of them were dead. Nineteen bodies were counted. All in civilian clothes, they had been armed with American—sixteen rifles and also rocket-launchers and rockets. They had explosives, their purpose apparently to destroy the Embassy. In that purpose they did not succeed.

The fighting went on for a total of six hours before the last known Vietcong raider was killed. They were rooted out of bushes, from outlying buildings, and then the last one, the 19th, from the small residence of the Embassy's Mission Coordinator, George Jacobson, who had been hiding all alone, all morning.

What could you see from the window? Were the—were the VC in the buildings?

JACOBSON: No, I did not see any VC in the building except that I knew that there was at least one VC in my house. I knew that he was on the bottom floor of my house.

SCHAKNE: You had quite an escape at the very end. How did that happen?

JACOBSON: Well, they [U.S. troops] put riot gas into the bottom floors of my house, which of course would drive whoever was down below up top where I was. They had thrown me a pistol about ten minutes before this occurred, and with all of the luck that I've had all of my life, I got him before he got me.

SCHAKNE: With the pistol. And he had what?

JACOBSON: An M-16.

SCHAKNE: And you got him.

Then the job of sweeping through the Embassy building and compound, trying to make sure no Vietcong were still hiding. The job of finding unexploded rockets, grenades, and satchel charges. And the casualties. The two American military policemen at one gate, a handful of Marines inside. There wasn't anyone to stop the Vietcong when they came. General Westmoreland came by soon after. His version was that this represented a Vietcong defeat.

WESTMORELAND: In some way, the enemy's well-laid plans went afoul. Some superficial damage was done to the building. All of the enemy that entered the compound as far as I can determine were killed. Nineteen bodies have been found on the premises—enemy bodies. Nineteen enemy bodies have been found on the premises.

SCHAKNE: General, how would you assess yesterday's activities and today's? What is the enemy doing? Are these major attacks?

(sound of explosions)

WESTMORELAND: The enemy very deceitfully has take advantage of the Tet truce in order to create maximum consternation within South Vietnam, particularly in the populated areas. In my opinion this is diversionary to his main effort, which he had planned to take place in Quang Tri Province, from Laos, toward Khesanh and across the Demilitarized Zone. This attack has not yet materialized; his schedule has probably been thrown off balance because of our very effective air strikes.

Now yesterday the enemy exposed himself by virtue of this strategy and he suffered great casualties. When I left my office late yesterday, approximately 8:00 o'clock, we—we had accounted for almost seven hundred enemy killed in action. Now we had suffered some casualties ourselves, but they were small by comparison. My guess is, based on my conversations with my field commanders, that there were probably—there were probably far more than seven hundred that were killed. Now by virtue of this audacious action by the enemy, he has exposed himself, he has become more vulnerable. As soon as President

Thieu, with our agreement, called off the truce, U.S. and American troops went on the offensive and pursued the enemy aggressively.

SCHAKNE: When they built this Embassy it was first to be a secure building. This Embassy was designed as a bomb-proof, attack-proof building, but it turned out, when the VC hit us, it wasn't attack-proof enough. Robert Schakne, CBS News, Saigon.

WALLACE: Washington regards the enemy raids as the first step in a strategy aimed at strengthening their hand for any peace talks which may develop, and captured Communist documents lend weight to this theory.

CBS News White House Correspondent Dan Rather reports.

RATHER: We knew this was coming—a well-coordinated series of enemy raids against South Vietnamese cities. Our intelligence even pinpointed the exact day it would happen. What we did not know was where. This is the official story, as given out by White House news secretary George Christian, who went on to say there was no way to completely insulate yourself against this kind of thing if the enemy is willing to sacrifice large numbers of men.

But if we knew it was coming, even to the exact day, Christian was asked, why wasn't extra protection placed around such an obvious place as the Saigon Embassy? The White House spokesman paused, then said, "I just don't know." At the Pentagon a high-ranking source said, "There simply were more of them and they were better than we expected."

Washington is startled but not panicked by the latest series of events. President Johnson privately is warning Congressmen that intelligence reports indicate the whole month of February will be rough in Southeast Asia. Mr. Johnson is emphasizing that the enemy's winter offensive is only beginning. Dan Rather, CBS News, Washington.

WALLACE: The drama of the battle for Saigon captured most attention, but the South Vietnamese capital was only one of the Communist targets. In a moment we'll return with battle film from another city.

(announcement)

WALLACE: The U.S. Command's battle communiqué indicates that the Allied repulsed most of the enemy's attacks, but this success was not universal. In an assault today the Communist captured half of the Central Highlands city of Kontum and the Vietcong flag flies in the center of the northern city of Hue. The enemy claims also to control Quang Tri city, also in I Corps in the north, a claim as yet unconfirmed by the Allies.

But one place where American and South Vietnamese troops turned back the enemy was at Nhatrang, a coastal city about 190 miles northeast of Saigon. In peacetime a pleasant resort city, now Nhatrang is the headquarters for the Fifth Special Forces, the Green Berets; and the Green Berets were in the thick of the fighting. The Communist attack there had begun around midnight, and it developed into a street fight which, as you see here, carried over into the daylight hours. The enemy's apparent goal in this fight, down the street, was a provincial prison where many important Vietcong were being held. During this battle many innocent civilians, friendly to the Allies, were trapped in their homes between the lines of fire between VC and the Green Berets. It was only after twelve hours of battle that the area was secure enough to call those civilians out to safety.

The Communist raids had a stunning impact, all of them, around the world, and the question is, what is it that the enemy is after in these attacks. Certainly he does not believe that these suicide assaults by terrorist squads are going to radically change the course of the war in Vietnam; but there can be no doubt that these attacks are calculated to impress indelibly on public opinion in North and South Vietnam and in the United States the resourcefulness and the determination of the Vietcong and his ability to strike almost at will any place in South Vietnam if he is willing to pay the price.

The story of the past three days, with heavy emphasis, of course, on American and South Vietnamese casualties will be trumpeted throughout Vietnam and around the world by Hanoi. Whether all of this is a prelude to an expression that Hanoi is willing now to go to the negotiation table remains to be seen, but there is little doubt that there will be more such stories from Khesanh and elsewhere in South Vietnam in the bitter month of February that lies ahead.

Mike Wallace, CBS News, New York.

ANNOUNCER: This had been a CBS News Special Report: "Saigon Under Fire."

SOURCE: "Saigon Under Fire," originally broadcast January 3, 1968, over the CBS Television Network; reprinted with permission of CBS News Archive

MEMORANDUM FROM CHAIRMAN OF THE JOINT CHIEFS OF STAFF GENERAL EARLE G. WHEELER FOR THE PRESIDENT, FEBRUARY 12, 1968 (EXTRACT)

2. General Westmoreland repeated over the telephone to me at 0815 hours the gist of his earlier messages; namely, he believes the VC struck out in Phases 1 and 2 of their offensive. He considers he has opportunities available to exploit the enemy's failures. He needs soonest one brigade of the 82d Airborne Division and a Marine Corps Regiment. He considers that he can hold off on a decision to request the remainder of the 82d Airborne Division and the other three battalions of Marines until later. He can absorb logistically the troops he asks for now. It is conceivable that the troops he asks for will be needed only for

six months; he will not bind himself that he will not need more troops at a later time. He pointed out that the forces he is requesting are within the 525,000 ceiling to which he agreed. Parenthetically, he commented that he doesn't know how sacrosanct that figure is. In response to the questions posed in my message to him, attached hereto, he made the following comments:

  a. He does not anticipate "defeat," but he desperately needs the troop elements requested in order to capitalize on opportunities open to him. The enemy has been repulsed in II, III and IV Corps areas, but I Corps must be reinforced. If requested troops are not made available, he would have to undertake an unacceptably risky course of drawing additional forces from elsewhere in South Vietnam.

  b. On balance the ARVN has done a good job. He does not know the status of Regional Force and Popular Force troop elements. He believes it will be 1 April before the status of ARVN is known.

  c. He can support logistically the forces he requested; however, it is mandatory that he open and keep open Highways 1 and 9 and this will cost troops.

  d. Additional forces will give him increased capability to regain the initiative and go on the offensive at an appropriate time.

3. As to paragraph 2 of my cable regarding strategy, General Westmoreland says they are good questions which he will respond to more fully in a message now being drafted. His brief responses to the thoughts expressed in paragraph 2 of my message are as follows:

  a. His Priority One objective is to clear the cities.

  b. He agrees with the expressed Priority Two of giving away no territory of value but he points out that sometimes he must fight in unfavorable terrain and weather in order not to give up important ground.

  c. As to holding Khe Sanh, he has prepared on a close hold basis contingency plans to execute a tactical withdrawal if this becomes desirable and necessary. However, he believes strongly that retention of Khe Sanh will afford him in future opportunities to exploit the enemy's commitment of troops in and around Khe Sanh and deal him a severe and perhaps a knock out blow.

  d. As to the Delta, he does have contingency plans to move forces form there as required. He points out that the battalions committed (US) in the Delta have stiffened the ARVN and have helped him to repulse the enemy with heavy losses. His Riverine Force is now being used in the vicinity of Can Tho with good effect.

5. A senior VC political cadre was captured yesterday at Danang. This man had on him a long document, now being translated, which apparently represents the results of a high level conference of VC officials. The first quick exami-

nation of the document indicates that the VC made a mistake in launching their Tet offensive at the time and in the manner they did. Specifically, the country was not ready for a mass uprising and US/ARVN military strength was seriously underestimated by VC/NVA forces.

SOURCE: Memorandum for the President from General Wheeler, Subject: Reinforcements for South Vietnam, February 12, 1968, declassified by Joint Chiefs of Staff, October 10, 19789; Vietnam Archive (Larry Berman Collection), Texas Tech University, Lubbock, Texas.

WALTER CRONKITE'S "WE ARE MIRED IN STALEMATE" CBS NEWS BROADCAST, FEBRUARY 27, 1968

Tonight, back in more familiar surroundings in New York, we'd like to sum up our findings in Vietnam, an analysis that must be speculative, personal, subjective. Who won and who lost in the great Tet offensive against the cities? I'm not sure. The Vietcong did not win by a knockout, but neither did we. The referees of history may make it a draw. Another standoff may be coming in the big battles expected south of the Demilitarized Zone. Khesanh could well fall, with a terrible loss in American lives, prestige and morale, and this is a tragedy of our stubbornness there; but the bastion no longer is a key to the rest of the northern regions, and it is doubtful that the American forces can be defeated across the breadth of the DMZ with any substantial loss of ground. Another standoff. On the political front, past performance gives no confidence that the Vietnamese government can cope with its problems, now compounded by the attack on the cities. It may not fall, it may hold on, but it probably won't show the dynamic qualities demanded of this young nation. Another standoff.

We have been too often disappointed by the optimism of the American leaders, both in Vietnam and Washington, to have faith any longer in the silver linings they find in the darkest clouds. They may be right, that Hanoi's winter-spring offensive has been forced by the Communist realization that they could not win the longer war of attrition, and that the Communists hope that any success in the offensive will improve their position for eventual negotiations. It would improve their position, and it would also require our realization, that we should have had all along, that any negotiations must be that—negotiations, not the dictation of peace terms. For it seems now more certain than ever that the bloody experience of Vietnam is to end in a stalemate. This summer's almost certain standoff will either end in real give-and-take negotiations or terrible escalation; and for every means we have to escalate, the enemy can match us, and that applies to invasion of the North, the use of nuclear weapons, or the mere commitment of one hundred, or two hundred, or three hundred thousand more American troops to the battle. And with each escalation, the world comes closer to the brink of cosmic disaster.

To say that we are closer to victory today is to believe, in the face of the evidence, the optimists who have been wrong in the past. To suggest we are on the edge of defeat is to yield to unreasonable pessimism. To say that we are mired in stalemate seems the only realistic, yet unsatisfactory, conclusion. On the off chance that military and political analysts are right, in the next few months we must test the enemy's intentions, in case this is indeed his last big gasp before negotiations. But it is increasingly clear to this reporter that the only rational way out then will be to negotiate, not as victors, but as an honorable people who lived up to their pledge to defend democracy, and did the best they could.

This is Walter Cronkite. Good night.

SOURCE: CBS News Special: "Who? What? When? Where? Why? A Report from Vietnam by Walter Cronkite, originally broadcast February 27, 1968, over the CBS Television Network; reprinted with permission of CBS News Archive

REPORT OF THE CHAIRMAN OF THE JOINT CHIEFS OF STAFF GENERAL EARLE G. WHEELER ON THE SITUATION IN VIETNAM AND MACV FORCE REQUIREMENTS, FEBRUARY 27, 1968 (EXTRACT)

1. The Chairman, JCS and party visited SVN on 23, 24, and 25 February. This report summarizes the impressions and facts developed through conversations and briefings at MACV and with senior commanders throughout the country.
2. *Summary*
   —The current situation in Vietnam is still developing and fraught with opportunities as well as dangers.
   —There is no question in the mind of MACV that the enemy went all out for a general offensive and general uprising and apparently believed that he would succeed in bringing the war to an early successful conclusion.
   —The enemy failed to achieve his initial objective but is continuing his effort. Although many of his units were badly hurt, the judgment is that he has the will and the capability to continue.
   —Enemy losses have been heavy; he has failed to achieve his prime objectives of mass uprisings and capture of a larger number of the capital cities and towns. Morale in enemy units which were badly mauled or where the men were oversold the idea of a decisive victory at Tet probably has

suffered severely. However, with replacements, his indoctrination system would seem capable of maintaining morale at a generally adequate level. His determination appears to be unshaken.

—The enemy is operating with relative freedom in the countryside, probably recruiting heavily and no doubt infiltrating NVA units and personnel. His recovery is likely to be rapid; his supplies are adequate; and he is trying to maintain the momentum of his winter-spring offensive.

—The structure of the GVN held up but its effectiveness has suffered.

—The RVNAF held up against the initial assault with gratifying, and in a way, surprising strength and fortitude. However, ARVN is now in a defensive posture around towns and cities and there is concern about how well they will bear up under sustained pressure.

—The initial attack nearly succeeded in a dozen places, and defeat in those places was only averted by the timely reaction of US forces. In short, it was a very near thing.

—There is not doubt that the RD Program has suffered a severe setback.

—RVNAF was not badly hurt physically—they should recover strength and equipment rather quickly (equipment in 2–3 months—strength in 3–6 months). Their problems are more psychological than physical.

—US forces have lost none of their pre-Tet capability.

—MACV has three principal problems. First, logistic support north of Danang is marginal owing to weather, enemy interdiction and harassment and the massive deployment of US force into the DMZ/Hue area. Opening Route 1 will alleviate this problem but takes a substantial troop commitment. Second, the defensive posture of ARVN is permitting the VC to make rapid inroads in the formerly pacified countryside. ARVN, in its own words, is in a dilemma as it cannot afford another enemy thrust into the cities and towns and yet if it remains in a defensive posture against this contingency, the countryside goes by default. MACV is forced to devote much of its troop strength to this problem. Third, MACV has been forced to deploy 50% of all US maneuver battalions into I Corps, to meet the threat there, while stripping the rest of the country of adequate reserves. If the enemy synchronizes an attack against Khe Sanh/Hue-Quang Tri with an offensive in the Highlands and around Saigon while keeping the pressure on throughout the remainder of the country, MACV will be hard pressed to meet adequately all threats. Under these circumstances, we must be prepared to accept some reverses.

—For these reasons, General Westmoreland has asked for a 3 division-15 tactical fighter squadron force. This force would provide him with a theater reserve and an offensive capability which he does not now have.

3. The situation as it stands today:

a. Enemy capabilities
   (1) The enemy has been hurt badly in the populated lowlands, but is prac-
       tically intact elsewhere. He committed over 67,000 combat maneuver
       forces plus perhaps 25% or 17,000 more impressed men and boys, for a
       total of about 84,000. He lost 40,000 killed, at least 3,000 captured, and
       perhaps 5,000 disabled or died of wounds. He had peaked his force total
       to about 240,000 just before TET, by hard recruiting, infiltration, civil-
       ian impressment, and drawdowns on service and guerrilla personnel.
       So he has lost about one fifth of his total strength. About two-third of
       his trained, organized unit strength can continue offensive action. He
       is probably infiltrating and recruiting heavily in the countryside while
       allied forces are securing the urban areas. (Discussions of strengths and
       recruiting are in paragraphs 1. 2 and 3 of Enclosure (1)). The enemy
       has adequate munitions, stockpiled in-country and available through
       the DMZ, Laos, and Cambodia, to support major attacks and country-
       wide pressure; food procurement may be a problem. (Discussion is in
       paragraph 6 Enclosure (1)). Besides strength losses, the enemy now has
       morale and training problems which currently limit combat effective-
       ness of VC guerrilla, main and local forces. (Discussions of forces are
       in paragraphs 2, 5, Enclosure (1)).
       (a) I Corps Tactical Zone: Strong enemy forces in the northern two
           provinces threaten Quang Tri and Hue cities, and US positions at
           the DMZ. Two NVA divisions threaten Khe Sanh. Eight enemy bat-
           talion equivalents are in the Danang–Hoi An area. Enemy losses in
           I CTZ have been heavy, with about 13,000 killed; some NVA as well
           as VC unites have been hurt badly. However, NVA replacements in
           the DMZ area can offset these losses fairly quickly. The enemy has
           an increased artillery capability at the DMZ, plus some tanks and
           possibly even a limited air threat in I CTZ.
       (b) II Corps Tactical Zone: The 1st NVA Division went virtually
           unscathed during TET offensive, and represents a strong threat in
           the western highlands. Seven combat battalion equivalents threaten
           Dak To. Elsewhere in the highlands, NVA units have been hurt and
           VC units chopped up badly. On the coast, the 3rd NVA Division
           had already taken heavy losses just prior to the offensive. The 5th
           NVA Division, also located on the coast, is not in good shape.
           Local force strength in coastal It CTZ had dwindled long before
           the offensive. The enemy's strength in II CTZ is in the highlands
           where enemy troops are fresh and supply lines short.
       (c) III CTZ: Most of the enemy's units were used in the TET effort, and
           suffered substantial losses. Probably the only major unit to escape

heavy losses was the 7th NVA Division. However, present dispositions give the enemy the continuing capability of attacking the
Saigon area with 10 to 11 combat effective battalion equivalents. His
increased movement southward of supporting arms and infiltration
of supplies has further developed his capacity for attacks by fire.

(d) IV Corps Tactical Zone: All enemy forces were committed in IV
Corps, but losses per total strength were the lightest in the country.
The enemy continues to be capable of investing or attacking cities
throughout the area.

(2) New weapons or tactics:

We may see heavier rockets and tube artillery, additional armor, and
the use of aircraft, particularly in the I CTZ. The only new tactic in
view is infiltration and investment of cities to create chaos, to demoral-
ize the people, to discredit the government, and to tie allied forces to
urban security.

4. What does the future hold?

a. Probable enemy strategy. (Reference paragraph 7b, Enclosure (1)). We
see the enemy pursuing a reinforced offensive to enlarge his control
throughout the country and keep pressures on the government and allies.
We expect him to maintain strong threats in the DMZ area, at Khe Sanh,
in the highlands, and at Saigon, and to attack in force when conditions
seem favorable. He is likely to try to gain control of the country's northern
provinces. He will continue efforts to encircle cities and province capitals
to isolate and disrupt normal activities, and infiltrate them to create chaos.
He will seek maximum attrition of RVNAF elements. Against US forces, he
will emphasize attacks by fire on airfields and installations, using assaults
and ambushes selectively. His central objective continues to be the destruction of the Government of SVN and its armed forces. As a minimum he
hopes to seize sufficient territory and gain control of enough people to support establishment of the groups and committees he proposes for participation in an NLF dominated government.

b. MACV Strategy:

(1) MACV believes that the central thrust of our strategy now must be to
defeat the enemy offensive and that if this is done well, the situation
overall will be greatly improved over the pre-TET condition.

(2) MACV accepts the fact that its first priority must be the security of
Government of Vietnam in Saigon and provincial capitals. MACV
describes its objectives as:

— First, to counter the enemy offensive and to destroy or eject the
NVA invasion force in the north.

— Second, to restore security in the cities and towns.

— Third, to restore security in the heavily populated areas of the countryside.

— Fourth, to regain the initiative through offensive operations.

c. Tasks:

(1) *Security of Cities and Government.* MACV recognizes that US forces will be required to reinforce and support RVNAF in the security of cities, towns and government structure. At this time, 10 US battalions are operating in the environs of Saigon. It is clear that this task will absorb a substantial portion of US forces.

(2) *Security in the Countryside.* To a large extent the VC now control the countryside. Most of the 54 battalions formerly providing security for pacification are now defending district or province towns. MACV estimates that US forces will be required in a number of places to assist and encourage the Vietnamese Army to leave the cities and towns and reenter the country. This is especially true in the Delta.

(3) *Defense of the borders, the DMZ and the northern provinces.* MACV considers that it must meet the enemy threat in I Corps Tactical Zone and has already deployed there slightly over 50% of all US maneuver battalions. US forces have been thinned out in the highlands, notwithstanding an expected enemy offensive in the early future.

(4) *Offensive Operations.* Coupling the increased requirement for the cities and subsequent reentry into the rural areas, and the heavy requirement for defense of the I Corps Zone, MACV does not have adequate forces at this time to resume the offensive in the remainder of the country, nor does it have adequate reserves against the contingency of simultaneous large-scale enemy offensive action throughout the country.

5. Force Requirements:

a. Forces currently assigned to MACV, plus the residual Program Five forces yet to be delivered, are inadequate in numbers and balance to carry out the strategy and to accomplish the tasks described above in the proper priority. To contend with, and defeat, the new enemy threat, MACV has stated requirements for forces over the 525,000 ceiling imposed by Program Five. The add-on requested totals 206,756 spaces for a new proposed ceiling of 731,756, with all forces being deployed into country by the end of CY 68. Principal forces included in the add-on are three division equivalents, 15 tactical fighter squadrons and augmentation for current Navy programs. MACV desires that these additional forces be delivered in three packages as follows:

(1) *Immediate Increment, Priority One*: To be deployed by 1 May 68. Major elements include one brigade of the 5th Mechanized Division with a mix of one infantry, one armored and one mechanized battalion; the

Fifth Marine Division (less RLT-26); one armored cavalry regiment; eight tactical fighter squadrons; and a groupment of Navy units to augment on-going programs.

(2) *Immediate Increment, Priority Two*: To be deployed as soon as possible but prior to 1 Sep 68. Major elements include the remainder of the 5th Mechanized Division, and four tactical fighter squadrons. It is desirable that the ROK Light Division be deployed within this time frame.

(3) *Follow-On Increment*: To be deployed by the end of CY 68. Major elements include one infantry division, three tactical fighter squadrons, and units to further augment Navy Programs.

SOURCE: Memorandum of February 27, 1968, from Wheeler to Johnson, declassified by Department of Defense, no date given; Vietnam Archive (Douglas Pike Collection), Texas Tech University, Lubbock, Texas.

SUMMARY OF NOTES FROM MARCH 26, 1968, MEETING BETWEEN PRESIDENT LYNDON JOHNSON AND THE WISE MEN

Summary of Notes

MCGEORGE BUNDY: There is a very significant shift in our position. When we last met we saw reasons for hope.

We hoped then there would be a slow but steady progress. Last night and today the picture is not so hopeful particularly in the countryside.

Dean Acheson summed up the majority feeling when he said that we can no longer do the job we set out to do in the time we have left and we must begin to take steps to disengage.

That view was shared by:

George Ball
Cy Vance
Douglas Dillon
and myself (McGeorge Bundy)

We do think we should do everything possible to strengthen in a real and visible way the performance of the Government of South Vietnam.

There were three of us who took a different position:

General Bradley
General Taylor
Bob Murphy

They all feel that we should not act to weaken our position and we should do what our military commanders suggest.

General Ridgway has a special point of view. He wanted to so strengthen the Army of South Vietnam that we could complete the job in two years.

On negotiations, Ball, Goldberg and Vance strongly urged a cessation of the bombing now. Others wanted a halt at some point but not now while the situation is still unresolved in the I Corps area.

On troop reinforcements the dominant sentiment was that the burden of proof rests with those who are urging the increase. Most of us think there should be a substantial escalation. We all felt there should not be an extension of the conflict. This would be against out national interest.

The use of atomic weapons is unthinkable.

Summary

RIDGWAY: I agree with the summary as presented by McGeorge Bundy.

[ARTHUR] DEAN: I agree. All of us got the impression that there is no military conclusion in sight. We felt time is running out.

DEAN ACHESON: Agree with Bundy's presentation. Neither the effort of the Government of Vietnam or the effort of the U.S. government can succeed in the time we have left. Time is limited by reactions in this country. We cannot build an independent South Vietnam; therefore, we should do something by no later than late summer to establish something different.

HENRY CABOT LODGE: We should shift from search-and-destroy strategy to a strategy of using our military power as a shield to permit the South Vietnamese society to develop as well as North Vietnamese society has been able to do. We need to organize South Vietnam on a block-by-block, precinct-by-precinct basis.

DOUGLAS DILLON: We should change the emphasis. I agree with Acheson. The briefing last night led me to conclude we cannot achieve a military victory. I would agree with Lodge that we should cease search-and-destroy tactics and head toward an eventual disengagement. I would send only the troops necessary to support those there now.

GEORGE BALL: I share Acheson's view. I have felt that way since 1961—that our objectives are not attainable. In the U.S. there is a sharp division of opinion. In the world, we look very badly because of the bombing. That is the central defect in our position. The disadvantages of bombing outweigh the advantages. We need to stop the bombing in the next six weeks to test the will of the North Vietnamese. As long as we continue to bomb, we alienate ourselves from the civilized world. I would have the Pope or U Thant [Secretary-

General of the United Nations] suggest the bombing halt. It cannot come from the President.

A bombing halt would quieten [*sic*] the situation here at home.

CY VANCE: McGeorge Bundy states my views. I agree with George Ball.

Unless we do something quick, the mood in this country may lead us to withdrawal on troops, we should send no more than the 13,000 support troops. . . .

GENERAL TAYLOR: I am dismayed. The picture I get is a very different one from that you have. Let's not concede the home front; let's do something about it.

FORTAS: The U.S. has never had in mind winning a military victory out there; we always have wanted to reach an agreement or settle for the status quo between North Vietnam and South Vietnam. I agree with General Taylor. . . . This is not the time for an overture on our part. I do not think a cessation of the bombing would do any good at this time. I do not believe in drama for the sake of drama.

ACHESON: The issue is not that stated by Fortas. The issue is can we do what we are trying to do in Vietnam. I do not think we can. Fortas said we are not trying to win a military victory. The issue is can we by military means keep the North Vietnamese off the South Vietnamese. I do not think we can. They can slip around and end-run them and crack them up.

SOURCE: "Meeting with Special Advisory Group," March 26, 1968, Meeting Notes File, Box 2, Lyndon B. Johnson Library, Austin, Texas.

PRESIDENT JOHNSON'S ADDRESS TO THE NATION ANNOUNCING HIS DECISION NOT TO SEEK REELECTION, MARCH 31, 1968

President Lyndon B. Johnson's Address to the Nation Announcing Steps To Limit the War in Vietnam and Reporting His Decision Not To Seek Reelection. March 31, 1968. The President spoke at 9 P.M. EST from the oval office in the White House. The address was broadcasted nationally.

Good evening, my fellow Americans:

Tonight I want to speak to you of peace in Vietnam and Southeast Asia.

No other question so preoccupies our people. No other dream so absorbs the 250 million human beings who live in that part of the world. No other goal motivates American policy in Southeast Asia.

For years, representatives of our Government and others have traveled the world—seeking to find a basis for peace talks.

Since last September, they have carried the offer that I made public at San Antonio.

That offer was this:

That the United States would stop its bombardment of North Vietnam when that would lead promptly to productive discussions—and that we would assume that North Vietnam would not take military advantage of our restraint.

Hanoi denounced this offer, both privately and publicly. Even while the search for peace was going on, North Vietnam rushed their preparations for a savage assault on the people, the government, and the allies of South Vietnam.

Their attack—during the Tet holidays—failed to achieve its principal objectives.

It did not collapse the elected government of South Vietnam or shatter its army—as the Communists had hoped.

It did not produce a "general uprising" among the people of the cities as they had predicted.

The Communists were unable to maintain control of any of the more than thirty cities that they attacked. And they took very heavy casualties.

But they did compel the South Vietnamese and their allies to move certain forces from the countryside into the cities.

They caused widespread disruption and suffering. Their attacks, and the battles that followed, made refugees of half a million human beings.

The Communists may renew their attack any day.

They are, it appears, trying to make 1968 the year of decision in South Vietnam—the year that brings, if not final victory or defeat, at least a turning point in the struggle.

This much is clear:

If they do mount another round of heavy attacks, they will not succeed in destroying the fighting power of South Vietnam and its allies.

But tragically, this is also clear: Many men—on both sides of the struggle—will be lost. A nation that has already suffered twenty years of warfare will suffer once again. Armies on both sides will take new casualties. And the war will go on.

There is no need for this to be so.

There is no need to delay the talks that could bring an end to this long and this bloody war.

Tonight, I renew the offer I made last August—to stop the bombardment of North Vietnam. We ask that talks begin promptly, that they be serious talks on the substance of peace. We assume that during those talks Hanoi will not take advantage of our restraint.

We are prepared to move immediately toward peace through negotiations.

So, tonight, in the hope that this action will lead to early talks, I am taking the first step to deescalate the conflict. We are reducing—substantially reducing—the present level of hostilities.

And we are doing so unilaterally, and at once.

Tonight, I have ordered our aircraft and our naval vessels to make no attacks on North Vietnam, except in the area north of the demilitarized zone where the continuing enemy buildup directly threatens allied forward positions and where the movements of their troops and supplies are clearly related to that threat.

The area in which we are stopping our attacks includes almost 90 percent of North Vietnam's population, and most of its territory. Thus there will be no attacks around the principal populated areas, or in the food-producing areas of North Vietnam.

Even this very limited bombing of the North could come to an early end—if our restraint is matched by restraint in Hanoi. But I cannot in good conscience stop all bombing so long as to do so would immediately and directly endanger the lives of our men and our allies. Whether a complete bombing halt becomes possible in the future will be determined by events.

Our purpose in this action is to bring about a reduction in the level of violence that now exists.

It is to save the lives of brave men—and to save the lives of innocent women and children. It is to permit the contending forces to move closer to a political settlement.

And tonight, I call upon the United Kingdom and I call upon the Soviet Union—as cochairmen of the Geneva Conferences, and as permanent members of the United Nations Security Council—to do all they can to move from the unilateral act of deescalation that I have just announced toward genuine peace in Southeast Asia.

Now, as in the past, the United States is ready to send its representatives to any forum, at any time, to discuss the means of bringing this ugly war to an end. I am designating one of our most distinguished Americans, Ambassador Averell Harriman, as my personal representative for such talks.

In addition, I have asked Ambassador Llewellyn Thompson, who returned from Moscow for consultation, to be available to join Ambassador Harriman at Geneva or any other suitable place—just as soon as Hanoi agrees to a conference.

I call upon President Ho Chi Minh to respond positively, and favorably, to this new step toward peace. But if peace does not come now through negotiations, it will come when Hanoi understands that our common resolve is unshakable, and our common strength is invincible.

Tonight, we and the other allied nations are contributing 600,000 fighting men to assist 700,000 South Vietnamese troops in defending their little country. Our presence there has always rested on this basic belief: The main burden of preserving their freedom must be carried out by them—by the South Vietnamese themselves.

We and our allies can only help to provide a shield behind which the people of South Vietnam can survive and can grow and develop. On their efforts—on their determination and resourcefulness—the outcome will ultimately depend. That small, beleaguered nation has suffered terrible punishment for more than twenty years.

I pay tribute once again tonight to the great courage and endurance of its people. South Vietnam supports armed forces tonight of almost 700,000 men—and I call your attention to the fact that this is the equivalent of more than ten million in our own population. Its people maintain their firm determination to be free of domination by the North.

There has been substantial progress, I think, in building a durable government during these last three years. The South Vietnam of 1965 could not have survived the enemy's Tet offensive of 1968. The elected government of South Vietnam survived that attack—and is rapidly repairing the devastation that it wrought.

The South Vietnamese know that further efforts are going to be required:
—to expand their own armed forces,
—to move back into the countryside as quickly as possible,
—to increase their taxes,
—to select the very best men that they have for civil and military responsibility,
—to achieve a new unity within their constitutional government, and
—to include in the national effort all those groups who wish to preserve South Vietnam's control over its own destiny.

Last week President Thieu ordered the mobilization of 135,000 additional South Vietnamese. He plans to reach—as soon as possible—a total military strength of more than 800,000 men. To achieve this, the Government of South Vietnam started the drafting of nineteen-year-olds on March 1st. On May 1st, the Government will begin the drafting of eighteen-year-olds. Last month, 10,000 men volunteered for military service—that was two and a half times the number of volunteers during the same month last year. Since the middle of January, more than 48,000 South Vietnamese have joined the armed forces—and nearly half of them volunteered to do so. All men in the South Vietnamese armed forces have had their tours of duty extended for the duration of the war, and reserves are now being called up for immediate active duty. President Thieu told his people last week: "We must make greater efforts and accept more sacrifices because, as I have said many times, this is our country. The existence of our nation is at stake, and this is mainly a Vietnamese responsibility." He warned his people that a major national effort is required to root out corruption and incompetence at all levels of government.

We applaud this evidence of determination on the part of South Vietnam. Our first priority will be to support their effort. We shall accelerate the reequipment of South Vietnam's armed forces—in order to meet the enemy's increased firepower. This will enable them progressively to undertake a larger share of combat operations against the Communist invaders.

On many occasions I have told the American people that we would send to Vietnam those forces that are required to accomplish our mission there. So, with that as our guide, we have previously authorized a force level of approximately 525,000.

Some weeks ago—to help meet the enemy's new offensive—we sent to Vietnam about 11,000 additional Marine and airborne troops. They were deployed by air in forty-eight hours, on an emergency basis. But the artillery, tank, aircraft, medical, and other units that were needed to work with and to support these infantry troops in combat could not then accompany them by air on that short notice.

In order that these forces may reach maximum combat effectiveness, the Joint Chiefs of Staff have recommended to me that we should prepare to send—during the next five months—support troops totaling approximately 13,500 men.

A portion of these men will be made available from our active forces. The balance will come from reserve component units which will be called up for service.

The actions that we have taken since the beginning of the year:

—to reequip the South Vietnamese forces,

—to meet our responsibilities in Korea, as well as our responsibilities in Vietnam,

—to meet price increases and the cost of activating and deploying reserve forces,

—to replace helicopters and provide the other military supplies we need, all of these actions are going to require additional expenditures.

The tentative estimate of those additional expenditures is $2.5 billion in this fiscal year, and $2.6 billion in the next fiscal year.

These projected increases in expenditures for our national security will bring into sharper focus the Nation's need for immediate action: action to protect the prosperity of the American people and to protect the strength and the stability of our American dollar.

On many occasions I have pointed out that, without a tax bill or decreased expenditures, next year's deficit would again be around $20 billion. I have emphasized the need to set strict priorities in our spending. I have stressed that failure to act and to act promptly and decisively would raise very strong doubts throughout the world about America's willingness to keep its financial house in order.

Yet Congress has not acted. And tonight we face the sharpest financial threat in the postwar era—a threat to the dollar's role as the keystone of international trade and finance in the world.

Last week, at the monetary conference in Stockholm, the major industrial countries decided to take a big step toward creating a new international monetary asset that will strengthen the international monetary system. I am very proud of the very able work done by Secretary Fowler and Chairman Martin of the Federal Reserve Board.

But to make this system work the United States just must bring its balance of payments to—or very close to—equilibrium. We must have a responsible fiscal policy in this country. The passage of a tax bill now, together with expenditure control that the Congress may desire and dictate, is absolutely necessary to protect this Nation's security, to continue our prosperity, and to meet the needs of our people.

What is at stake is seven years of unparalleled prosperity. In those seven years, the real income of the average American, after taxes, rose by almost 30 percent—a gain as large as that of the entire preceding nineteen years.

So the steps that we must take to convince the world are exactly the steps we must take to sustain our own economic strength here at home. In the past eight months, prices and interest rates have risen because of our inaction.

We must, therefore, now do everything we can to move from debate to action—from talking to voting. There is, I believe—I hope there is—in both Houses of the Congress—a growing sense of urgency that this situation just must be acted upon and must be corrected.

My budget in January was, we thought, a tight one. It fully reflected our evaluation of most of the demanding needs of this Nation.

But in these budgetary matters, the President does not decide alone. The Congress has the power and the duty to determine appropriations and taxes.

The Congress is now considering our proposals and they are considering reductions in the budget that we submitted.

As part of a program of fiscal restraint that includes the tax surcharge, I shall approve appropriate reductions in the January budget when and if Congress so decides that that should be done.

One thing is unmistakably clear, however: Our deficit just must be reduced. Failure to act could bring on conditions that would strike hardest at those people that all of us are trying so hard to help.

These times call for prudence in this land of plenty. I believe that we have the character to provide it, and tonight I plead with the Congress and with the people to act promptly to serve the national interest, and thereby serve all of our people.

Now let me give you my estimate of the chances for peace:

—the peace that will one day stop the bloodshed in South Vietnam,

—that will permit all the Vietnamese people to rebuild and develop their land,

—that will permit us to turn more fully to our own tasks here at home.

I cannot promise that the initiative that I have announced tonight will be completely successful in achieving peace any more than the thirty others that we have undertaken and agreed to in recent years.

But it is our fervent hope that North Vietnam, after years of fighting that have left the issue unresolved, will now cease its efforts to achieve a military victory and will join with us in moving toward the peace table.

And there may come a time when South Vietnamese—on both sides—are able to work out a way to settle their own differences by free political choice rather than by war.

As Hanoi considers its course, it should be in no doubt of our intentions. It must not miscalculate the pressures within our democracy in this election year.

We have no intention of widening this war. But the United States will never accept a fake solution to this long and arduous struggle and call it peace.

No one can foretell the precise terms of an eventual settlement. Our objective in South Vietnam has never been the annihilation of the enemy. It has been to bring about a recognition in Hanoi that its objective—taking over the South by force—could not be achieved.

We think that peace can be based on the Geneva Accords of 1954—under political conditions that permit the South Vietnamese—all the South Vietnamese—to chart their course free of any outside domination or interference, from us or from anyone else.

So tonight I reaffirm the pledge that we made at Manila—that we are prepared to withdraw our forces from South Vietnam as the other side withdraws its forces to the north, stops the infiltration, and the level of violence thus subsides.

Our goal of peace and self-determination in Vietnam is directly related to the future of all of Southeast Asia—where much has happened to inspire confidence during the past ten years. We have done all that we knew how to do to contribute and to help build that confidence.

A number of its nations have shown what can be accomplished under conditions of security. Since 1966, Indonesia, the fifth-largest nation in all the world, with a population of more than 100 million people, has had a government that is dedicated to peace with its neighbors and improved conditions for its own people. Political and economic cooperation between nations has grown rapidly.

I think every American can take a great deal of pride in the role that we have played in bringing this about in Southeast Asia. We can rightly judge—as responsible Southeast Asians themselves do—that the progress of the past three years would have been far less likely—if not completely impossible—if America's sons and others had not made their stand in Vietnam.

At Johns Hopkins University, about three years ago, I announced that the United States would take part in the great work of developing Southeast Asia, including the Mekong Valley, for all the people of that region. Our determination to help build a better land—a better land for men on both sides of the present conflict—has not diminished in the least. Indeed, the ravages of war, I think, have made it more urgent than ever.

So, I repeat on behalf of the United States again tonight what I said at Johns Hopkins—that North Vietnam could take its place in this common effort just as soon as peace comes.

Over time, a wider framework of peace and security in Southeast Asia may become possible. The new cooperation of the nations of the area could be a foundation-stone. Certainly friendship with the nations of such a Southeast Asia is what the United States seeks—and that is all that the United States seeks.

One day, my fellow citizens, there will be peace in Southeast Asia.

It will come because the people of Southeast Asia want it—those whose armies are at war tonight, and those who, though threatened, have thus far been spared.

Peace will come because Asians were willing to work for it—and to sacrifice for it—and to die by the thousands for it.

But let it never be forgotten: Peace will come also because America sent her sons to help secure it.

It has not been easy—far from it. During the past four and a half years, it has been my fate and my responsibility to be Commander in Chief. I have lived— daily and nightly—with the cost of this war. I know the pain that it has inflicted. I know, perhaps better than anyone, the misgivings that it has aroused.

Throughout this entire, long period, I have been sustained by a single principle: that what we are doing now, in Vietnam, is vital not only to the security of Southeast Asia, but it is vital to the security of every American.

Surely we have treaties which we must respect. Surely we have commitments that we are going to keep. Resolutions of the Congress testify to the need to resist aggression in the world and in Southeast Asia.

But the heart of our involvement in South Vietnam—under three different presidents, three separate administrations—has always been America's own security.

And the larger purpose of our involvement has always been to help the nations of Southeast Asia become independent and stand alone, self-sustaining, as members of a great world community—at peace with themselves, and at peace with all others.

With such an Asia, our country—and the world—will be far more secure than it is tonight.

I believe that a peaceful Asia is far nearer to reality because of what America has done in Vietnam. I believe that the men who endure the dangers of battle — fighting there for us tonight — are helping the entire world avoid far greater conflicts, far wider wars, far more destruction, than this one.

The peace that will bring them home someday will come. Tonight I have offered the first in what I hope will be a series of mutual moves toward peace.

I pray that it will not be rejected by the leaders of North Vietnam. I pray that they will accept it as a means by which the sacrifices of their own people may be ended. And I ask your help and your support, my fellow citizens, for this effort to reach across the battlefield toward an early peace.

Finally, my fellow Americans, let me say this:

Of those to whom much is given, much is asked. I cannot say and no man could say that no more will be asked of us.

Yet, I believe that now, no less than when the decade began, this generation of Americans is willing to "pay any price, bear any burden, meet any hardship, support any friend, oppose any foe to assure the survival and the success of liberty."

Since those words were spoken by John F. Kennedy, the people of America have kept that compact with mankind's noblest cause.

And we shall continue to keep it.

Yet, I believe that we must always be mindful of this one thing, whatever the trials and the tests ahead. The ultimate strength of our country and our cause will lie not in powerful weapons or infinite resources or boundless wealth, but will lie in the unity of our people.

This I believe very deeply.

Throughout my entire public career I have followed the personal philosophy that I am a free man, an American, a public servant, and a member of my party, in that order always and only.

For thirty-seven years in the service of our Nation, first as a Congressman, as a Senator, and as Vice President, and now as your President, I have put the unity of the people first. I have put it ahead of any divisive partisanship.

And in these times as in times before, it is true that a house divided against itself by the spirit of faction, of party, of region, of religion, of race, is a house that cannot stand.

There is division in the American house now. There is divisiveness among us all tonight. And holding the trust that is mine, as President of all the people, I cannot disregard the peril to the progress of the American people and the hope and the prospect of peace for all peoples.

So, I would ask all Americans, whatever their personal interests or concern, to guard against divisiveness and all its ugly consequences.

Fifty-two months and ten days ago, in a moment of tragedy and trauma, the duties of this office fell upon me. I asked then for your help and God's, that we might continue America on its course, binding up our wounds, healing our history, moving forward in new unity, to clear the American agenda and to keep the American commitment for all of our people.

United we have kept that commitment. United we have enlarged that commitment.

Through all time to come, I think America will be a stronger nation, a more just society, and a land of greater opportunity and fulfillment because of what we have all done together in these years of unparalleled achievement.

Our reward will come in the life of freedom, peace, and hope that our children will enjoy through ages ahead.

What we won when all of our people united just must not now be lost in suspicion, distrust, selfishness, and politics among any of our people.

Believing this as I do, I have concluded that I should not permit the Presidency to become involved in the partisan divisions that are developing in this political year.

With America's sons in the fields far away, with America's future under challenge right here at home, with our hopes and the world's hopes for peace in the balance every day, I do not believe that I should devote an hour or a day of my time to any personal partisan causes or to any duties other than the awesome duties of this office—the Presidency of your country.

Accordingly, I shall not seek, and I will not accept, the nomination of my party for another term as your President.

But let men everywhere know, however, that a strong, a confident, and a vigilant America stands ready tonight to seek an honorable peace—and stands ready tonight to defend an honored cause—whatever the price, whatever the burden, whatever the sacrifice that duty may require.

Thank you for listening. Good night and God bless all of you.

SOURCE: *Public Papers of the Presidents of the United States: Lyndon B. Johnson, 1968-69* (Washington, DC: Government Printing Office, 1970), 1:468–476.

PART VI

Resources

The objective of this section is to provide a guide to references and resources having to do with the Tet Offensive and Khe Sanh and the impact of those events. It is not meant to be an exhaustive and all-inclusive list of every resource on the Vietnam War, but rather focuses on 1968. As such, this section begins with a list of general histories of the war that put the seminal events of that year in proper historical perspective. The other listings focus on various aspects of the Tet Offensive and include books, articles, films, Internet sources, libraries, archives, and other resources.

GENERAL WORKS

Encyclopedias, Bibliographies, Dictionaries, Guides, and Atlases

Anderson, David L. *The Columbia Guide to the Vietnam War*. New York: Columbia University Press, 2002. The author provides a comprehensive guide to the study of the Vietnam War. The guide is divided into three parts. The first is a historical narrative of the war from French occupation through North Vietnam's victory in 1975, organized around key controversial issues. The second part is a mini-encyclopedia of the war that includes key people, places, and events. The third part is an extensive list of resources and documents, plus a detailed chronology that runs from 207 B.C. through President Clinton's recognition of Vietnam in 1995.

Bowman, John S., ed. *The Vietnam War: An Almanac*. New York: Pharos Books, 1985. This reference book covers the military, diplomatic, and domestic events of the war arranged in chronological order. It also includes a number of topical essays, as well as biographical sketches and a bibliography.

———, ed. *The Vietnam War: Day by Day*. New York: Brompton Books, 1989. This is a detailed day-by-day chronology of the war that addresses the key military, political, and diplomatic events from 1857 to 1984.

Burns, Richard Dean, and Milton Leitenberg. *The Wars in Vietnam, Cambodia, and Laos, 1945–1982: A Bibliographic Guide*. Santa Barbara, CA: ABC-CLIO, 1984. An excellent bibliography containing more than 6,200 entries organized by key topics, this book addresses some of the older works but is obviously dated, given the numerous books that have come out since it was published.

Kutler, Stanley I., ed. *Encyclopedia of the Vietnam War*. New York: Macmillan Library Reference, 1996. Containing some 560 articles, this encyclopedia addresses virtually every aspect of the Vietnam War: individuals, places, and events. It also includes ten interpretive essays on key issues of the war.

Moïse, Edwin E. *Historical Dictionary of the Vietnam War*. Lanham, MD: Scarecrow Press, 2001. Moise focuses on the essential elements of the Vietnam War, including significant persons, battles, weapons, places, and events. The book also includes a detailed chronology and a comprehensive bibliography.

Olson, James S., ed. *Dictionary of the Vietnam War*. Westport, CT: Greenwood, 1988. This book provides a good reference that covers key concepts, people, locations, and events of the Vietnam War; it is particularly good on military topics and Vietnam-era terminology.

———. *The Vietnam War: Handbook on the Literature and Research*. Westport, CT: Greenwood, 1993. This book contains twenty-three essays on critical topics about the war; each essay is accompanied by a focused bibliography.

Stanton, Shelby L. *Vietnam Order of Battle*. New York: Galahad Books, 1986. This excellent reference volume addresses U.S. and allied order-of-battle information for all units that participated in the war. It includes unit heraldry, dates of service, geographical areas of operation, and, in many cases, listings of commanders. It also has an extensive set of maps and photographs.

Summers, Harry G., Jr. *Historical Atlas of the Vietnam War*. New York: Houghton Mifflin, 1995. This atlas comprises more than 120 excellent maps accompanied by brief but well-written historical explanations discussing the events that occurred on the respective maps; it includes maps and narratives on the Hill Fights, Con Thien, Dak To, and Tet 1968, including the battles of Saigon and Hue and the siege of Khe Sanh.

———. *Vietnam War Almanac*. New York: Facts on File, 1985. Divided into three parts, this almanac first addresses the background on Vietnam and the war. The second part is a detailed chronology of the war. The third part is a collection of more than three hundred articles on different aspects of the war, including biographical entries, military terms, and geographical locations.

Tucker, Spencer C., ed. *Encyclopedia of the Vietnam War: A Political, Social, and Military History*. 3 vols. Santa Barbara, CA: ABC-CLIO, 1998. This is one of the most comprehensive reference works on the Vietnam War. The first two volumes contain more than nine hundred signed entries ranging in length from several paragraphs to several pages; the third volume provides a representative selection of documents pertaining to the war.

General Histories, Anthologies

Addington, Larry H. *America's War in Vietnam: A Short Narrative History*. Bloomington: Indiana University Press, 2000. This is a brief narrative history of the war in Southeast Asia. It is a good overview, but it does not provide much detail.

Anderson, David L., ed. *Shadow on the White House: Presidents and the Vietnam War, 1945–1975*. Lawrence: University Press of Kansas, 1993. This collection of essays focuses on the presidents who made and executed U.S. policy in Southeast Asia from Truman through Ford, providing useful insights into the conflict and its impact on the presidency. It contains two very good essays on Lyndon Johnson and his handling of the war.

Arnold, James R. *Presidents Under Fire: Commanders in Chief in Victory and Defeat*. New York: Orion Books, 1994. Arnold explores four case studies of presidents and how their administrations handled war. One of those studies addresses Lyndon Johnson, whom Arnold criticizes for failing to deal successfully with the situation in Vietnam.

Bergerud, Eric M. *The Dynamics of Defeat: The Vietnam War in Hau Nghia Province*. Boulder, CO: Westview, 1991. The author analyzes the entire course of the war by examining a single key province, Hau Nghia, northwest of Saigon. He focuses on the operational level, where political policy was translated into military action. The book contains a very good chapter on the Tet Offensive in Hau Nghia, representative of the action seen in many other provinces during the early months of 1968.

——. *Red Thunder, Tropic Lightning: The World of a Combat Division in Vietnam*. Boulder, CO: Westview, 1993. The author provides an account of the operations of a U.S. infantry division. It is a good representation of life in a combat unit that addresses organization, tactics, and the conduct of operations.

Braestrup, Peter, ed. *Vietnam as History*. Washington, DC: Woodrow Wilson International Center for Scholars, 1984. This is a record of the proceedings of a conference of leading historians and analysts of the U.S. experience in the Vietnam War held in early 1983. It is effectively a postmortem on the war, covering a range of topics from military strategy to lessons learned.

Buzzanco, Robert. *Masters of War: Military Dissent and Politics in the Vietnam Era*. New York: Cambridge University Press, 1996. Buzzanco examines the role of senior military leaders and their relationship with the civilian decision makers in the planning and conduct of the war in Vietnam. The book contains a chapter dedicated to the Tet Offensive and its aftermath.

Clarke, Jeffrey J. *Advice and Support: The Final Years, 1965–1973*. Washington, DC: U.S. Army Center of Military History, 1988. Part of the official history of the U.S. Army in Vietnam, this book provides an excellent appreciation of General William Westmoreland's strategy and how that strategy changed under his successor, General Creighton Abrams.

Cohen, Steven, ed. *Vietnam: Anthology and Guide to a Television History*. New York: Knopf, 1983. A companion to the PBS series, *Vietnam: A Television History*, this book includes a number of topical essays and associated documents arranged in chronological order. It includes a lengthy chapter on the Tet Offensive.

Davidson, Phillip B. *Vietnam at War*. Novato, CA: Presidio, 1988. The author, who was senior military intelligence officer under General Westmoreland, provides a comprehensive military history of the war. He maintains that the Tet Offensive was a great victory for the American military but was stolen by the press, who transformed it into a psychological victory for the Communists.

Dawson, Joseph G., ed. *Commanders in Chief: Presidential Leadership in Modern Wars*. Lawrence: University Press of Kansas, 1993. In this book, prominent historians examine various presidents and how they fulfilled their constitutional and political roles during wartime. This book includes an excellent essay on Johnson's wartime leadership by Professor Frank Vandiver.

Dougan, Clark, and Stephen Weiss. *The Vietnam Experience: Nineteen Sixty-Eight*. Boston: Boston Publishing, 1983. This is one in a multivolume series on the Vietnam War. This volume focuses on the dramatic events of 1968 in Vietnam and in the United States, providing very thorough coverage of the Tet Offensive and the siege of Khe Sanh.

Duiker, William J. *The Communist Road to Power in Vietnam*. Boulder, CO: Westview, 1981. This is a general history of the Vietnamese Communist Party's revolutionary strategy with which they prosecuted the war against first the French and then the Americans.

Elliott, Paul. *Vietnam: Conflict & Controversy*. London: Arms and Armour, 1996. The author examines the forces within the U.S. military that contributed to its defeat in the Vietnam War. While putting the war in political context, the emphasis of the book is on how the military fought the war.

Errington, Elizabeth Jane, and B.J.C. McKercher, eds. *The Vietnam War as History*. Westport, CT: Praeger, 1990. Composed of nine topical essays on various aspects of the Vietnam War, this book contains two essays on the Tet Offensive—one addressing how the Communist forces achieved such a stunning surprise and another about Johnson and the media.

FitzGerald, Frances. *Fire in the Lake: The Vietnamese and Americans in Vietnam*. New York: Vintage Books, 1973. The author provides a very biased history of the war from the liberal viewpoint and is very critical of the American government for failing to understand the nature of the revolution in Vietnam.

Gilbert, Marc Jason, ed. *Why the North Won the Vietnam War*. New York: Palgrave, 2002. In this book, nine noted Vietnam scholars discuss how a nominally Third World state defeated a superpower. It addresses foreign and domestic policy issues, military tactics and strategy, and cultural questions surrounding the fall of South Vietnam to the Communist North.

Herring, George C. *America's Longest War: The United States and Vietnam, 1950–1975*. 4th ed. New York: McGraw-Hill, 2002. A very balanced general history of the war, this book is recognized as a major contribution to the study of American involvement in Vietnam. Herring analyzes the ultimate failure in the war and its impact on U.S. foreign policy. The author places the war in the historical context of the Cold War and U.S. containment policy.

Hess, Gary R. *Vietnam and the United States: Origins and Legacy of War*. Rev. ed. Boston: Twayne, 1998. Author places U.S. polices in the context of Vietnamese, Laotian, and Cambodian history. It provides a discussion of how the United States became involved in Southeast Asia.

Hunt, Richard A. *Pacification: The American Struggle for Vietnam's Hearts and Minds*. Boulder, CO: Westview, 1995. Hunt addresses the "other war" and provides one of the best accounts of the pacification program. Within the larger context of the evolution of the pacification effort, Hunt describes the impact of the Tet offensive on the campaign to win the hearts and minds of the South Vietnamese people. The author concludes that the pacification program failed to solve South Vietnam's political and social problems.

Karnow, Stanley. *Vietnam: A History*. 2d ed. New York: Penguin Books, 1997. This comprehensive study of the war looks at the conflict from both sides. Very well documented, this book contains material from extensive interviews with the participants. It includes a thorough discussion of the Tet Offensive and its aftermath.

Kinnard, Douglas. *The War Managers*. New York: Da Capo, 1991 (reprint ed.). The author, himself a general officer, surveyed 173 generals who managed the war in Vietnam. This book is an analysis of the survey responses on a wide range of topics from the quality of both American and Vietnamese troops to U.S. strategy. It includes a very useful chapter on the Tet Offensive.

Lanning, Michael Lee, and Dan Cragg. *Inside the VC and the NVA*. New York: Fawcett Columbine, 1992. The authors provide a comprehensive portrait of America's enemy in the Vietnam War, including a discussion of organization, tactics, recruiting and training procedures, leadership, and fighting ability.

Lewy, Gunther. *America in Vietnam*. New York: Oxford University Press, 1980. The author provides one of the standard defenses of the American effort in Vietnam, which includes a discussion of the post-Tet reassessment of American strategy.

Lind, Michael. *Vietnam, the Necessary War: A Reinterpretation of America's Most Disastrous Military Conflict*. New York: Free Press, 1999. Lind attempts to defend American intervention in Vietnam, but his discussion of the background of the conflict is subject to debate.

Matthews, Lloyd J., and Dale E. Brown, eds. *Assessing the Vietnam War*. Washington, DC: Pergamon-Brassey's, 1987. This is a postmortem on U.S. involvement in Vietnam, which contains several essays on strategy and the nature of the war.

McMahon, Robert J., ed. *Major Problems in the History of the Vietnam War*. New York: Houghton Mifflin, 2003. This textbook, designed to encourage critical thinking about the Vietnam War, consists of a number of recently declassified documents and analytical essays on important topics in the history of the war, including a chapter on the Tet Offensive.

Moss, George Donelson. *Vietnam: An American Ordeal*. 3rd ed. Upper Saddle River, NJ: Prentice Hall, 1998. This is a comprehensive narrative account of America's involvement in Southeast Asia that addresses the political, diplomatic, and military aspects of the war from the 1940s to 1975. It includes a lengthy chapter on the Tet Offensive and its aftermath.

Neu, Charles E. *America's Lost War: Vietnam, 1945–1975*. Wheeling, IL: Harlan Davidson, 2005. Neu, a noted historian, offers a concise, balanced, and well-written narrative history of the war.

Olson, James S., and Randy Roberts. *Where the Domino Fell: America and Vietnam, 1945 to 1990*. New York: St. Martin's, 1991. A concise history of the American experience in Vietnam, this includes a chapter on the psychological impact of the war on the United States and its political legacy.

Palmer, Bruce. *The 25-Year War*. Lexington: University Press of Kentucky, 1984. The author, a retired general, argues that the civilian leaders prevented the military from winning the war.

Palmer, Dave. *Summons of the Trumpet*. San Rafael, CA: Presidio, 1978. An Army colonel when he wrote this book, Palmer provides a good military history of the war, but complains that there was too much interference by civilian leaders in determining how the war was fought.

Pike, Douglas. *PAVN: People's Army of Vietnam*. Novato, CA: Presidio, 1986. A noted expert on both the Viet Cong and the North Vietnamese, Pike describes the creation of the People's Army of Vietnam and how it grew to be one of the largest and most effective armies in contemporary times. He details the militaristic nature of Vietnamese society, describes the organization and functioning of the military forces, and places those forces in a political context.

———. *Viet Cong: The Organization and Techniques of the National Liberation Front of South Vietnam*. Cambridge, MA: MIT Press, 1966. Pike provides a comprehensive discussion of the military army of the National Liberation Front. He describes organization, recruitment, training, and conduct of military operations.

Pimlott, John. Vietnam, *The Decisive Battles*. New York: Macmillan, 1990. This book is an illustrated anthology of seventeen decisive battles in the Vietnam War, including the siege of Khe Sanh and the Tet Offensive. Graphics include photos, computer-generated maps, and specially commissioned paintings that depict critical moments.

———, ed. *Vietnam: The History and the Tactics*. New York: Crescent Books, 1982. An overview of the conflict focusing on how the United States fought the war, this book addresses ground operations, the air war, and the role of U.S. Special Forces. It contains two hundred illustrations.

Podhoretz, Norman. *Why We Were in Vietnam*. New York: Simon & Schuster, 1982. The author sees America's Vietnam effort as a noble cause, but asserts that Johnson failed because he tried to fight the war while keeping his Great Society domestic programs going.

Schulzinger, Robert D. *A Time for War: The United States and Vietnam, 1941–1975*. New York: Oxford University Press, 1997. The author provides a comprehensive overview of the war, including a discussion of Tet and how it changed U.S. strategy in the war.

Sevy, Grace, ed. *The American Experience in Vietnam*. Norman: University of Oklahoma Press, 1989. This book is a collection of essays and articles about the Vietnam War. It contains a very good section on the role of the press in the war.

Sorley, Lewis. *A Better War: The Unexamined Victories and Final Tragedy of America's Last Years in Vietnam*. New York: Harcourt Brace, 1999. The author examines the events that transpired in Vietnam after Creighton Abrams assumed command of MACV from William Westmoreland. He provides a comprehensive examination of the problems that the American army faced in the aftermath of the Tet Offensive as U.S. troops were steadily withdrawn and the responsibility for the war was slowly transferred to the South Vietnamese forces.

Stanton, Shelby L. *Anatomy of a Division: 1st Cav in Vietnam*. Novato, CA: Presidio, 1987. This is a comprehensive history of the 1st Cavalry Division in Vietnam from its arrival in 1965 until its departure in 1972. It includes a discussion of division operations during the Tet Offensive, among them the battle of Hue and the relief of Khe Sanh.

———. *The Rise and Fall of An American Army: U.S. Ground Forces in Vietnam, 1965–1973*. Novato, CA: Presidio, 1985. Author discusses the deterioration of the American Army in Vietnam that gathers momentum after the Tet Offensive.

Thies, Wallace J. *When Governments Collide: Coercion and Diplomacy in the Vietnam Conflict, 1964–1968*. Berkeley: University of California Press, 1980. Author addresses the conflict between the Johnson administration and the North Vietnamese Communists over South Vietnam. He provides a useful examination of North Vietnamese decision making.

Tucker, Spencer C. *Vietnam*. London: UCL Press, 1999. This is a concise, well-documented analytical survey of Vietnamese military history that concentrates on the French and American twentieth-century wars. Unlike many Vietnam war histories, this one begins with a brief account of the earliest recorded days of the Vietnamese people. The author is critical of the way the American military dealt with the Communist strategy of protracted war.

Turley, William S. *The Second Indochina War: A Short Political and Military History, 1954–1975*. New York: Westview, 1986. This book is a very good survey of the war that encompasses not only Vietnam, but also Laos and Cambodia. It provides a particularly useful discussion of Communist policy decisions in addressing how the war began, why its scale outstripped U.S. expectations, and why the Communists prevailed in the end.

Van Dyke, Jon M. *North Vietnam's Strategy for Survival*. Palo Alto, CA: Pacific Books, 1972. This is a comprehensive analysis of North Vietnam's strategy, particularly with regard to their response to the intensive American bombing campaign of 1965 to late 1968.

Warner, Denis. *Certain Victory: How Hanoi Won the War*. Kansas City, KS: Sheed Andrews and McMeel, 1977. Based on a study of General Van Tien Dung's memoirs, Warner, a war correspondent, argues that the North Vietnamese were the aggressors, but that the United States never understood the nature of the war and thus were ultimately defeated.

Werner, Jayne S., and David Hunt, eds. *The American War in Vietnam*. Cornell, NY: Southeast Asia Program, Cornell University, 1993. This is a collection of seven papers presented at a conference held in Hanoi in 1988, during which scholars from Vietnam and the United States met for the first time since 1975 to discuss the war. It contains a particularly useful paper by Ngo Vinh Long of the University of Maine on the Tet Offensive and its aftermath.

Werner, Jayne S., and Luu Doan Huynh, eds. *The Vietnam War: Vietnamese and American Perspectives*. Armonk, NY: M. E. Sharpe, 1993. This is a collection of nineteen papers presented at a conference of prominent American and Vietnamese authorities who met at Columbia University in 1990. It is organized into four sections that address the Vietnamese political/military strategy, the war from the American side, the war in Cambodia, and postwar legacies. It contains an extremely valuable paper by General Tran Van Tra that sheds light on Communists objectives and assessments of the Tet Offensive.

Woodruff, Mark W. *Unheralded Victory: The Defeat of the Viet Cong and the North Vietnamese Army, 1961–1973*. Arlington, VA: Vandemere Press, 1999. The author, a former Marine, seeks to provide a military history of the war and to demonstrate in his opinion that the war was won militarily before the U.S. unilaterally withdrew from the conflict. The author does not sufficiently address why the United States became involved in Southeast Asia in the first place.

Young, Marilyn B. *The Vietnam Wars: 1945–1990*. New York: HarperCollins, 1991. The author analyzes the war in Vietnam and the effect that it had on the home front in the United States. She discusses how the Americans took over after the French defeat at Dien Bien Phu, but, in the end, did no better in dealing with the Vietnamese revolution.

Young, Marilyn B., and Robert Buzzanco. *A Companion to the Vietnam War*. Malden, MA: Blackwell, 2002. This collection of twenty-four historiographical and narrative essays by leading historians examines the war in its most important contexts. It includes an extremely good essay on Lyndon Johnson and the media by Chester Pach.

Biographies

Currey, Cecil B. *Victory at Any Cost: The Genius of Viet Nam's Gen. Vo Nguyen Giap*. Dulles, VA: Brassey's, 1999. Drawing on extensive interviews and material provided by Giap, the author has produced a readable and comprehensive portrait of the Vietnamese military leader and at the same time, a history of the Vietnam War. Currey does not shy away from criticizing Giap for his willingness to sustain appalling casualties in pursuit of his objectives, but he concludes that few in history match Giap's military accomplishments.

Dallek, Robert. *Flawed Giant: Lyndon Johnson and His Times, 1961–1973*. New York: Oxford University Press, 1998. In this definitive biography, Dallek focuses on the White House years and examines Johnson's decisions on Vietnam. He argues that Johnson's handling of the war has obscured many of the good things that he did in Congress and as president.

Duiker, William J. *Ho Chi Minh*. New York: Hyperion, 2000. The author, who served in the U.S. embassy in Saigon during the Vietnam War, has produced the definitive biography of the North Vietnamese leader. Duiker depicts Ho as a nationalist first, but also a convinced Marxist who believed socialism would help his country modernize and correct long-standing social inequities.

Macdonald, Peter. *Giap: The Victor in Vietnam*. New York: Norton, 1993. Written by a British brigadier, this book was one of the first biographies of Vo Nguyen Giap. Macdonald extols Giap's military genius but is uncritical of his shortcomings. The book suffers because of its exclusive reliance on Western sources.

Sheehan, Neil. *A Bright Shining Lie*. New York: Random House, 1988. Sheehan provides a history of the war in Vietnam using as a vehicle the life of John Paul Vann, the legendary American military advisor who became a civilian official and was killed in a helicopter crash during the 1972 North Vietnamese Easter Offensive.

Zaffiri, Samuel. *Westmoreland*. New York: William Morrow, 1994. This is a biography of the commander of U.S. Military Assistance Command, Vietnam. Within the context of his entire professional life, the book provides an appreciation of the Tet Offensive as seen from MACV headquarters.

Memoirs

Clifford, Clark M. *Counsel to the President: A Memoir*. New York: Random House, 1991. Author served as secretary of defense for President Johnson in the aftermath of the Tet Offensive. He advised the president to de-escalate the war in South Vietnam and played a major role in the administration's post-Tet debate following General Westmoreland's request for additional troops.

Hoopes, Townsend. *The Limits of Intervention: An Inside Account of How the Johnson Policy of Escalation in Vietnam Was Reversed*. New York: D. McKay, 1969. Hoopes, who served as undersecretary of the Air Force in the Johnson administration, provides an insider account of the reexamination of U.S. strategy in the period following the Tet Offensive.

Johnson, Lyndon Baines. *The Vantage Point: Perspectives of the Presidency, 1963–1969*. New York: Holt, Rinehart, and Winston, 1971. Johnson explains his thoughts and actions as president, asserting that what he did and what he was trying to do were often misunderstood. This book is useful in understanding and evaluating Johnson's Vietnam policy.

McNamara, Robert S. *In Retrospect.* New York: Times Books, 1995. In this memoir, which was very controversial when it was first published, former Secretary of Defense McNamara discusses his role in American involvement in Vietnam during the Kennedy and Johnson administrations. Admitting part of the blame, he argues that the United States should have withdrawn from Vietnam either in late 1963, after President Diem's assassination, or in late 1964 or early 1965.

Rusk, Dean. *As I Saw It.* Edited by Daniel S. Papp. New York: Norton, 1990. In this book, transcribed from tapes he made for his son, the former secretary of state under President Johnson reminisces about his family, his World War II military experience, and his various government posts. He provides an insider's view of the Johnson White House and defends the correctness of U.S. intervention in Southeast Asia.

Westmoreland, William C. *A Soldier Reports.* Garden City, NY: Doubleday, 1976. In this memoir, the commander of American military forces in Vietnam argues that Tet was a defeat for the Communists, but that the war was lost because the civilian leadership did not provide sufficient resources to win it.

Vietnamese Perspectives

Bui Diem. *In the Jaws of History.* Bloomington: Indiana University Press, 1999. A former high official in the Saigon government who also served as South Vietnamese ambassador to the United States, the author gives his perspective on the Vietnam War and relations between his government and the U.S. He is critical of how the American forces took over the war, exhibiting a blatant disregard of South Vietnamese interests and sensitivities.

Bui Tin. *Following Ho Chi Minh.* Honolulu: University of Hawaii Press, 1995. The author, a former colonel in the North Vietnamese Army, describes his role in the war against the Americans. Interestingly, he eventually leaves Vietnam after the war to become an expatriate in Paris. He provides unique insight into the innermost workings of the Communist decision-making apparatus during the war.

——. *From Enemy to Friend: A North Vietnamese Perspective on the War.* Annapolis, MD: Naval Institute Press, 2002. The author shares additional insights into the Vietnam War. He is relatively evenhanded in his views about the policies and operations of the Vietnamese and U.S. governments during the war.

Carland, John. "An NVA General Looks Back." *Vietnam* (December 2002), 30–36. This is a transcription of an interview with former North Vietnamese General Tran Van Tra, who played a key role in the Tet Offensive of 1968, the Nguyen Hue Campaign of 1972, and the final offensive in 1975. The general's comments during the interview provide extremely valuable insight into how the Communists fought the war.

Chanoff, David, and Doan Van Toai. *Portrait of the Enemy.* New York: Random House, 1986. This is a collection of first-person accounts of life on the other side during the

Vietnam War. It includes the voices of guerrilla fighters, militant monks, propaganda chiefs, village party officials, and many others, providing a wide variety of perspectives from those who fought against U.S. troops and the Saigon government.

Guan, Ang Chen. "Decision-Making Leading to the Tet Offensive (1968)—The Vietnamese Perspective." *Journal of Contemporary History* 33 (July 1998): 341–353. The author provides a very good account of the decisions that led to the launching of the Tet Offensive.

Hoang Ngoc Lung. *The General Offensives of 1968–69.* Washington, DC: U.S. Army Center of Military History, 1981. Written by a former ARVN colonel, this is one in a series of monographs written after the war that provide the South Vietnamese military perspective. Author addresses the Tet Offensive and the "Mini-Tet" offensive that followed.

Lam Quang Thi. *The Twenty-Five Year Century: A South Vietnamese General Remembers the Indochina War to the Fall of Saigon.* Denton: University of North Texas Press, 2001. A former general in the South Vietnamese army, the author describes his life and participation in the Vietnam War. His narrative includes a vivid description of his experiences during the Tet Offensive.

McGarvey, Patrick J., ed. *Visions of Victory: Selected Vietnamese Communist Military Writings, 1964–1968.* Stanford, CA: Hoover Institution, 1969. This collection includes translations of articles and broadcasts from 1966 to 1968 that cover such topics as the effectiveness of American tactics and the successes and failures of the Tet Offensive.

Military History Institute of Vietnam. *Victory in Vietnam: The Official History of the People's Army of Vietnam, 1954–1975.* Translated by Merle L. Pribbenow. Lawrence: University Press of Kansas, 2002. This is an English translation of the 1994 official history of the North Vietnamese Army. Pribbenow, a former CIA officer who served five years in Vietnam, has performed an invaluable service by translating this history, which answers many lingering questions from the war.

Ngo Vinh Long. *The Tet Offensive and Its Aftermath.* Ithaca, NY: Cornell University Press, 1991. The author seeks to examine the aftermath of the offensive and how it changed the conduct of the war. It is particularly notable for its reliance on Vietnamese language sources and interviews. He maintains that the National Liberation Front recovered from the losses it incurred during the Tet Offensive and, contrary to what most Western historians have written, played an important role in the military successes of 1972 and 1975.

——. "The Tet Offensive and Its Aftermath." In March Jason Gilbert and William Head, eds., *The Tet Offensive,* 89–123. Westport, CT: Praeger, 1996. Long asserts that the Tet Offensive, though it did not overthrow the Saigon government, was successful in accomplishing its main objective of forcing the United States to de-escalate the war and to begin negotiations.

Nguyen Cao Ky. *Buddha's Child: My Fight to Save Vietnam.* New York: St. Martin's, 2002. The former prime minister of South Vietnam recounts his rise and fall from power and the errors great and small that led to his nation's defeat. This autobiography offers valuable insight into the history of the war as seen from the South Vietnamese side.

Page, Tim. *Another Vietnam: Pictures of the War from the Other Side*. Washington, DC: National Geographic, 2002. This book is a remarkable pictorial record of the war in Vietnam seen from the other side. Taken by North Vietnamese combat photographers, the images provide a comprehensive portrait of America's heretofore largely faceless enemy.

Pham Van Son. *Tet—1968: The Communist Offensive That Marked the Beginning of America's Defeat in Vietnam*. 2 vols. Salisbury, NC: Documentary Publications, 1980. This is an English edition of an earlier official history written by a South Vietnamese lieutenant colonel in the Military History Division of the Joint General Staff of the Republic of Vietnam Armed Forces. It describes the action from the South Vietnamese perspective.

Tran Van Tra. *Vietnam: History of the Bulwark B2 Theater, Volume 5: Concluding the 30-Years War, Southeast Asia Report No. 1247*. Washington, DC: Foreign Broadcast Information Service, February 2, 1983. This book was written by a PAVN general who commanded the forces that attacked Saigon from the north during the Tet Offensive.

Truong Nhu Tang. *A Vietcong Memoir*. New York: Harcourt Brace Jovanovich, 1985. Written by a founding member of the Viet Cong, this book provides a unique perspective on the war from the other side that is generally free of the strident socialist dogma that normally accompanies many Vietnamese Communist accounts of the war.

Vo Nguyen Giap. *Big Victory, Great Task*. New York: Praeger, 1968. This book provides Giap's assessment of the situation of the war in South Vietnam. It includes a series of articles broadcast over Hanoi Radio in 1967 that provided insight into the thinking that led to the decision to launch the Tet Offensive.

——. *The Military Art of People's War*. New York: Monthly Review Press, 1970. A collection of speeches and essays, this book gives an appreciation for the tactical doctrine of insurgency operations and the political guidelines for enlisting the people in the insurgency.

Oral Histories

Denenberg, Barry. *Voices from Vietnam*. New York: Scholastic, 1995. This is a collection of accounts of the Vietnam War told in the voices of the participants. Arranged chronologically, it includes a variety of perspectives, including government officials, political leaders, diplomats, soldiers, war protestors, reporters, and Vietnamese citizens and soldiers on both sides.

Kellen, Konrad. *Conversations with Enemy Soldiers in Late 1968/Early 1969: A Study of Motivation and Morale*. Santa Monica, CA: Rand Corporation, 1970. This book collects interviews Rand Corporation analysts conducted with Communist soldiers in the period following the Tet Offensive.

Maurer, Henry. *Strange Ground: Americans in Vietnam, 1945–1975*. New York: Henry Holt, 1989. This oral history traces the evolution of American involvement from the last days of World War II to the fall of Saigon three decades later. It includes a number of accounts of the fighting during the Tet Offensive.

Steinman, Ron. *The Soldier's Story: Vietnam in Their Own Words*. New York: TV Books, 1999. This oral history contains the vivid recollections of seventy-seven veterans who recall their wartime experiences. It contains sections on those who participated in the fighting during the Tet Offensive and the siege of Khe Sanh.

Verrone, Richard Burks, and Laura M. Calkins. *Voices from Vietnam: Eye-witness accounts of the War, 1954–1975*. Newton Abbot, UK: David and Charles, 2005. This book includes first-person accounts of the Vietnam War drawn from the Oral History Project at the Vietnam Archive, Texas Tech University, Lubbock, Texas. It contains twenty-eight pages of accounts by participants in the Tet Offensive.

Willenson, Kim. *The Bad War: An Oral History of the Vietnam War*. New York: New American Library, 1987. This is a collection of oral histories of those with many different views and perspectives on the war. There are several entries on the Tet Offensive as viewed by journalists, politicians, and soldiers.

Document Collections

Barrett, David M., ed. *Lyndon B. Johnson's Vietnam Papers: A Documentary Collection*. College Station: Texas A&M University Press, 1997. This collection of documents focuses on Johnson's Vietnam policy and provides provide an excellent insight into what President Johnson's advisers told him about the Viet Nam from November 22, 1963, to January 20, 1969.

Gettleman, Marvin E., Jane Franklin, Marilyn B. Young, and H. Bruce Franklin, eds. *Vietnam and America: A Documented History*. Rev. ed. New York: Grove Press, 1995. A history of the war told in essays by leading experts on the war accompanied by original source material, this book includes documents such as speeches, messages, and official records from both sides of the conflict.

Goodwin, Doris Kearns. *The Johnson Presidential Press Conferences*, 2 vols. New York: E. M. Coleman Enterprises, 1978. This is a collection of the transcripts of the president's press conferences. It includes those conducted prior to, during, and after the Tet Offensive.

Katsiaficas, George, ed. *Vietnam Documents: American and Vietnamese Views of the War*. New York: M. E. Sharpe, 1992. This collection contains fifty-two documents that present a complete picture of the war from 1954 to 1975 and includes seven entries on the Tet Offensive.

Moss, George Donelson, ed. *A Vietnam Reader: Sources and Essays*. Englewood Cliffs, NJ: Prentice Hall, 1991. This book includes a collection of five essays and more than sixty primary source documents.

The Pentagon Papers: The Defense Department History of United States Decisionmaking on Vietnam—The Senator Gravel Edition. Boston: Beacon Press, 1972. Senator Mike Gravel of Alaska read this version of the Pentagon Papers into the congressional record. It contains four volumes of text, including two thousand pages of narrative, seven hundred pages of documents, and two hundred pages of statements by government officials. An additional volume contains notes and commentary.

Porter, Gareth, ed. *Vietnam: A History in Documents*. New York: Earl M. Coleman, 1979. This collection includes key documents on the Vietnam War from 1941 to 1975.

Public Papers of the Presidents: Lyndon Baines Johnson, 1968–69. 2 vols. Washington, DC: U.S. Government Printing Office, 1970. This is the official compilation of President Johnson's public writings, addresses, and remarks. These volumes contain all of Johnson's speeches and remarks about Vietnam in the 1968–69 period, including his comments about the situation just before the Tet Offensive and, of course, the famous address when he announced that he would not run for reelection.

Sheehan, Neil, Hedrick Smith, E. W. Kenworthy, and Fox Butterfield. *The Pentagon Papers—as published by The New York Times*. Chicago: Quadrangle, 1971. This version of the Pentagon Papers includes 134 documents.

Williams, William Appleman, Thomas McCormick, Lloyd Gardner, and Walter LaFeber, eds. *America in Vietnam: A Documentary History*. New York: Norton, 1975. The editors compiled a collection of documents, including some from the 1950s that emphasize the origins of the war and U.S. commitment of troops.

LYNDON JOHNSON AND THE WAR

Barrett, David M. *Uncertain Warriors: Lyndon Johnson and His Vietnam Advisors*. Lawrence: University Press of Kansas, 1994. Barrett examines President Johnson's relationship with his advisors and how this relationship resulted in a flawed strategy in Vietnam.

Berman, Larry. *Lyndon Johnson's War: The Road to Stalemate in Vietnam*. New York: Norton, 1989. Berman examines Johnson's management of the war, focusing on what he describes as the flawed decision making that resulted in a bloody stalemate in Vietnam. He also faults senior military officers and presidential advisors who, in Berman's opinion, did not serve the president well.

Brands, H. W. *The Wages of Globalism: Lyndon Johnson and the Limits of American Power*. New York: Oxford University Press, 1995. Brands places Johnson's wartime policies in the context of the many international crises he faced, not just Vietnam, and the policy of global containment of Communism that he inherited from his predecessors.

Clifford, Clark. "A Vietnam Reappraisal." *Foreign Affairs* 47 (July 1969): 601–623. Former Secretary of Defense Clark Clifford provides a blueprint for changing strategy in Vietnam published only a few months after President Johnson left office.

Gardner, Lloyd C. *Pay Any Price: Lyndon Johnson and the Wars for Vietnam*. Chicago: Ivan R. Dee, 1995. An examination of Johnson's juggling of military strategy, international diplomacy, and domestic politics during the Vietnam War. Author asserts that Vietnam was not solely Lyndon Johnson's war, but rather a series of inevitable conflicts rooted in New Deal liberalism and Cold War diplomacy.

Herring, George C. *LBJ and Vietnam: A Different Kind of War.* Austin: University of Texas Press, 1994. Herring maintains that Johnson's leadership style adversely affected the Vietnam War's outcome. He asserts that Johnson discouraged the open exchange of ideas in discussions with advisers and failed to encourage cooperation among those directing the war effort. In the end, his flawed management failed to meet the challenges encountered.

LaFeber, Walter. *The Deadly Bet: LBJ, Vietnam, and the 1968 Election.* Lanham, MD: Rowman & Littlefield Publishers, 2005. The author examines the political ramifications of Johnson's decision in the wake of the Tet Offensive not to run for reelection. The result was the turmoil of the 1968 presidential election, a crisis for the United States that, LaFeber argues, was more severe than any since the Civil War.

Schandler, Herbert Y. *Lyndon Johnson and Vietnam: The Unmaking of a President.* Princeton, NJ: Princeton University Press, 1977. This book examines the events that led up to the day when Lyndon Johnson made the dramatic announcement that he would not be a candidate for reelection. It focuses on the Tet Offensive and its political ramifications.

Vandiver, Frank E. *Shadows of Vietnam: Lyndon Johnson's Wars.* College Station: Texas A&M University Press, 1997. Vandiver provides an empathetic portrait of a besieged commander-in-chief who had to deal with Vietnam, the Great Society, the Six-Day War, the Dominican Republic and other crises. This revisionist look at Johnson lays some of the blame for the president's difficulties on the legacy of John F. Kennedy, fears of communism and nuclear confrontation, the impact of the media, and the motives and methods of Johnson's advisors.

THE TET OFFENSIVE

Arnold, James R. *Tet Offensive 1968: Turning Point in Vietnam.* London: Osprey, 1990. One of the Osprey Campaign Series, this book provides a brief, but detailed depiction of the fighting during the Tet Offensive. It includes very good maps and photographs of the combat action.

Bradford, Zeb B. "With Creighton Abrams During Tet." *Vietnam* (February 1998), 43–49, 66. The author was aide-de-camp to the deputy commander of MACV during the Tet Offensive.

Brodie, Bernard. "Tet Offensive." In Noble Frankland and Christopher Dowling, eds., *Decisive Battles of the Twentieth Century: Land-Sea-Air*, 320–334. New York: David McKay, 1976. The author, a renowned political scientist, discusses his thesis that the Tet Offensive changed the course of the war, analyzing the decisiveness of the offensive and its short-term and long-term effects.

Coan, James P. "Tet Attack at Cam Lo." *Vietnam* (February 2004), 34–40. A former Marine recounts the Communist attack on Cam Lo, a district capital near Quang Tri, during the Tet Offensive.

Daugherty, Leo J. III. "Post One at War: Marine Security Guards and the Vietnam War, 1963–1975." *Vietnam* (February 2006), 43–47. Within the larger story of Marine security guards at the American Embassy in Saigon, the author relates the events of the early morning hours of January 31, 1968, when Viet Cong sappers breached the embassy grounds.

Falk, Richard. *Appropriating Tet*. Princeton, NJ: Princeton University Center of International Studies, 1988. Author discusses how historians and commentators on both sides have appropriated Tet to describe their overall interpretations of the war and its meaning.

Gilbert, Marc Jason, and William Head, eds. *The Tet Offensive*. Westport, CT: Praeger, 1996. An excellent collection of essays and commentary, this book provides unique and valuable perspectives of noted Vietnam War scholars on the various aspects of the Tet Offensive and its aftermath.

Goldsmith, Wynn A. "River Rats to the Rescue at Ben Tre." *Vietnam* (February 1998), 26–32. This is an account of the role of the "Brown Water Navy" in the battle of Ben Tre during the Tet Offensive.

Gross, John E. "The Tet Battles of Bien Hoa and Long Binh." *Vietnam* (February 2006), 18–26. The author, who served as a company commander in the 9th Infantry Division, provides a firsthand account of the battles of Bien Hoa and Long Binh during the opening hours of the Tet Offensive.

Hanson, Victor Davis. *Carnage and Culture: Landmark Battles in the Rise to Western Power*. New York: Anchor Books, 2002. The author examines nine battles to determine why Western culture has spread so successfully across the world. He maintains that military power was the primary reason. Among the battles he explores is the Tet Offensive.

Kerwin, Walter T. "Desperate Hours During Tet: Inside MACV Headquarters." *Vietnam* (February 2001), 27–32. This is an account of the Tet Offensive as told by General Westmoreland's chief of staff.

Kneipp, Nancy V. *The Tet Offensive and the Principles of War*. Newport, RI: Department of Joint Military Operations, Naval War College, 1996. The author, a professor at the Naval War College, seeks to discuss the successes and failures of the Tet Offensive in terms of the principals of war.

Lomperis, Timothy J. "Giap's Dream, Westmoreland's Nightmare." *Parameters* 18 (June 1988), 18–32. Lomperis address Giap's plan for the General Offensive–General Uprising of 1968. The author, a political scientist, analyzes U.S. and Communist strategies. He maintains that Tet ended Giap's dream of winning a Dien Bien Phu–like victory against the Americans, but that ultimately Hanoi "achieved success in failure."

McManus, John C. "Battleground Saigon." *Vietnam* (February 2004), 26–33. This article recounts the battle fought by a battalion of the U.S. 7th Infantry Regiment, 199th Infantry Brigade, to retake part of Saigon during the Tet Offensive.

Nolan, Keith W. *The Battle for Saigon: Tet 1968.* New York: Pocket Books, 1996. This history of the battle chronicles such events as the assault on the American Embassy and the ground attacks on Bien Hoa and Tan Son Nhut airbases.

North, Don. "VC Assault on the U.S. Embassy." *Vietnam* (February 2000), 38–47, 72. The author, a reporter, witnessed the attack on the U.S. Embassy in Saigon.

Oberdorfer, Don. *Tet! The Turning Point in the Vietnam War.* Baltimore, MD: Johns Hopkins University Press, 2001. The author, a journalist who covered the Vietnam War, provides one of the more comprehensive accounts of the Tet Offensive, covering the decisions and events that led up to the offensive, the bitter fighting during the offensive, and its dramatic aftermath.

———. "Tet: Who Won?" *Smithsonian* (November 2004), 117–123. The author addresses the various interpretations of who won the Tet Offensive. This is a very balanced and objective essay.

Pohle, Victoria. *The Viet Cong in Saigon: Tactics and Objectives During the Tet Offensive.* RM-1799-ISA/ARPA. Santa Monica, CA: Rand Corporation, 1969. This Rand study provides great insight into how and why the Viet Cong attacked Saigon during the Tet Offensive.

Schmitz, David F. *The Tet Offensive: Politics, War, and Public Opinion.* Lanham, MD: Rowman & Littlefield, 2005. This book seeks to reexamine the Tet Offensive in the context of American foreign policy, the state of the war up to 1968, and the impact of the media on public opinion. It is extremely well documented and makes extensive use of primary source material. It concludes with a very useful bibliographic essay on the offensive and its aftermath.

Shiels, Frederick L. *Preventable Disasters: Why Governments Fail.* Savage, MD: Rowman & Littlefield, 1991. The author, a political scientist, looks at three case studies of governmental failure, one of which is the Tet Offensive and its aftermath.

Spector, Ronald H. *After Tet: The Bloodiest Year in Vietnam.* New York: Free Press, 1993. The author, who served as a Marine historian in Vietnam, addresses the year after Tet, maintaining that the offensive was only the beginning of what he describes as the bloodiest of the war for American forces.

Tonsetic, Robert. *Warriors: An Infantryman's Memoir of Vietnam.* New York: Ballantine, 2004. The author served in Vietnam as a company commander in the 199th Infantry Brigade during the Tet Offensive and provides a detailed account of his unit during the fighting in 1968.

Worth, Richard. *Tet Offensive.* Philadelphia: Chelsea House Publications, 2002. A very brief overview of the offensive and its aftermath, this book does not include detailed analysis about Communist planning and objectives.

THE BATTLE OF HUE

Annenberg, Robert. "Intelligence Team Under Siege." *Vietnam* (February 2001), 34–42. This is a firsthand account of the experiences of an Army intelligence officer in Hue during the Tet Offensive.

Brown, Richard L. *Palace Gate: Under Siege in Hue City, Tet, January 1968*. London: Schiffer, 1997. An Air Force officer who served as an adviser to the South Vietnamese division commander in Hue during the Tet Offensive, the author was present for the first seventeen days of the bitter fighting within the ancient Citadel of Hue.

Bullington, James. "And Here, See Hue!" *Foreign Service Journal* (November 1968), 18–49. The author was a foreign service officer who successfully hid during the Communist occupation of Hue during the Tet Offensive.

——. "Trapped Behind Enemy Lines." *Vietnam* (February 1999), 18–24. This is an account of the author's experiences as a diplomat trapped in Hue after the Communists captured the city in February 1968.

Clifford, James O. Sr. "Forgotten Massacre at Hue." *Vietnam* (February 2002), 26–32, 63. The author, a journalist, asserts that the U.S. news media did not thoroughly report the deaths of civilians in Hue at the hands of the Communists.

Dix, Drew. *The Rescue of River City*. Fairbanks, AK: Drew Dix Publishing, 2000. A Special Forces staff sergeant who won the Medal of Honor for his actions in the defense of Chau Phu during the Tet Offensive writes this account.

Eby, Omar. *A House in Hue*. Scottsdale, PA: Herald Press, 1968. The author is a Mennonite who was in Hue during the North Vietnamese occupation. He describes what happened when the Viet Cong took control of the city.

Flores, John W. "Marine's Sacrifice at the Battle of Hue." *Vietnam* (February 1999), 26–32. This article provides an account of Marine Sergeant Alfredo Gonzales, recipient of the Medal of Honor, who gave his life during the battle for Hue.

Hammel, Eric. *Fire in the Streets: The Battle for Hue, Tet 1968*. Chicago: Contemporary Books, 1991. In a definitive combat narrative of the bloody battle for Hue in 1968, Hammel gives a vivid and up-close account of the house-by-house, block-by-block fighting.

Krohn, Charles A. *The Lost Battalion: Controversy and Casualties in the Battle of Hue*. Westport, CT: Praeger, 1993. Written by the unit's intelligence officer, this is the story of a battalion from the 1st Cavalry Division and its attack on a North Vietnamese force on the outskirts of Hue in 1968.

Laurence, John. *The Cat from Hue: A Vietnam War Story*. New York: Public Affairs, 2002. Author was a war correspondent in Hue during the Tet Offensive. He provides a vivid description of the battle as well as insight into the life of a reporter in war.

Maslowski, Peter, and Don Winslow. *Looking for a Hero: Staff Sergeant Joe Ronnie Hooper and the Vietnam War*. Lincoln: University of Nebraska Press, 2005. Sergeant Hooper was awarded the Medal of Honor for action near Hue on February 21, 1968. The book describes the action within the larger context of Hooper's life before and after he received the medal.

Nolan, Keith W. *Battle for Hue: Tet 1968*. Novato, CA: Presidio, 1983. New York: Dell, 1985. This is a comprehensive and detailed account of the fight for control of Hue during the Tet Offensive.

Pike, Douglas. *The Viet Cong Strategy of Terror*. Saigon: U.S. Mission, 1970. Within the larger context of Viet Cong strategy and its implications, Pike asserts that the

Communists massacred more than two thousand civilians during the occupation of Hue during the Tet Offensive.

Porter, D. Gareth. "The 1968 'Hue Massacre.'" *Indochina Chronicle* 33 (June 24, 1974). Challenging Douglas Pike's assertion about the nature of the civilian deaths in Hue in 1968, the author maintains that there was no systematized massacre by the Communists.

Porter, D. Gareth, and Len E. Ackland. "Vietnam: The Bloodbath Argument." *The Christian Century*, November 5, 1969. The authors challenge the claim that the Communists massacred civilians during the Battle of Hue. They also say that the argument that the Communists would do the same thing on a grander scale if they took over the entire country added to the panic of the South Vietnamese populace in the northern provinces during the North Vietnamese offensive in 1975 that led to the collapse of the Saigon government and its forces.

Smith, George W. *The Siege at Hue*. Boulder: Lynne Rienner, 1999. The author was an Army captain and intelligence adviser to the 1st ARVN Division during the battle for Hue. He provides a detailed account of the South Vietnamese participation in the bloody fighting to retake control of the Citadel, a story not covered in most accounts of the battle.

Warr, Nicholas. *Phase Line Green: The Battle for Hue, 1968*. Annapolis, MD: Naval Institute Press, 1997. The author was a platoon commander in the 1st Battalion, 5th Marines, during the battle for Hue. He describes what it was like to deal with the savage house-to-house fighting.

THE SIEGE OF KHE SANH

Archer, Michael. *A Patch of Ground: Khe Sanh Remembered*. Central Point, OR: Hellgate Press, 2005. The author, a Marine radioman during the siege, provides his perspective on the fighting at Khe Sanh.

Boyne, Walter J. "Airpower at Khe Sanh." *Air Force Magazine* 81, no. 8 (August 1998), 82–88. Boyne describes the various aspects of airpower that had such a significant impact on the outcome of the fighting at Khe Sanh in 1968.

Brush, Peter. "Aerial Lifeline to Khe Sanh." *Vietnam* (December 1999), 30–37. Brush discusses the airlift that kept Khe Sanh supplied during the siege.

——. "Perspectives: Khe Sanh Could Have Been Another Dien Bien Phu if the NVA Had Cut Off the Marines' Water Supply." *Vietnam* (August 1997), 58–60. Brush questions why the North Vietnamese failed to attack the Marine water supply at Khe Sanh.

Corbett, John. *West Dickens Avenue: A Marine at Khe Sanh*. New York: Ballantine Books, 2003. The author was Marine gunner in the 26th Marines at Khe Sanh during the siege. He describes his days there in dispassionate, but detailed prose, providing a vivid account of what life was like for the Marines during the desperate battle there.

Drez, Ronald J., and Douglas Brinkley. *Voices of Courage: The Battle for Khe Sanh, Vietnam*. New York: Bulfinch Press, 2005. This account is a narrative of the bitter fighting at Khe Sanh that draws on the firsthand experiences of the Marine who fought there. Two audio discs that include some of the interviews used to compile the narrative accompany the book.

Ewing, Michael. *The Illustrated History of Khe Sanh*. New York: Bantam Books, 1987. This book provides a brief narrative and an extensive collection of photos and maps.

Hammel, Eric. *Siege in the Clouds: An Oral History*. San Francisco: Pacifica Press, 2000. This book is a collection of first hand accounts of the seventy-seven-day siege.

Nalty, Bernard C. *Air Power and the Fight for Khe Sanh*. Washington, DC: Office of Air Force History, United States Air Force, 1973. This book is the official history of U.S. Air Force support to the Marines during Operation Niagara and the siege of Khe Sanh.

Phillips, William R. *Night of the Silver Stars: The Battle of Lang Vei*. Annapolis, MD: Naval Institute Press, 1997. This is the story of the North Vietnamese attack on the Special Forces camp at Lang Vei, in which the Communists used tanks for the first time in the war.

Pisor, Robert. *The End of the Line: The Siege of Khe Sanh*. New York: Norton, 1982. A war correspondent for the *Detroit News*, Pisor discusses the history, politics, and strategies of the battle of Khe Sanh, but also gives an appreciation of the nature of the desperate fighting there. He is very critical of General Westmoreland for underreporting the American casualties and overestimating the North Vietnamese dead after the battle.

Prados, John, and Ray W. Stubbe. *Valley of Decision: The Siege of Khe Sanh*. Boston: Houghton Mifflin, 1991. Based on interviews, documentary research, and the personal experiences of one of the authors, this is a comprehensive history of the battle for Khe Sanh in 1968. The authors also address the larger political context that led to the decision to stand and fight there.

Rottman, Gordon S. *Khe Sanh 1967–68*. London: Osprey, 2005. This excellent volume in the Osprey series addresses the siege of Khe Sanh and the battles that preceded it. It provides a detailed narrative, excellent maps, and a number of photographs.

Shore, Moyers S. *The Battle of Khe Sanh*. Washington, DC: History and Museums Division, Headquarters U.S. Marine Corps, 1969. The official Marine Corps history of the battle, this is based on extensive interviews of the survivors of the seventy-seven-day siege.

Shulimson, Jack, Leonard A. Blasiol, Charles R. Smith, and David A. Dawson. *U.S. Marines in Vietnam: The Defining Year 1968*. Washington, DC: History and Museums Division, Headquarters U.S. Marine Corps, 1997. A volume in the official history of the Marine Corps in Vietnam, the authors address Marine operations in I Corps, among them the earlier battle for the hills around Khe Sanh, the siege and the bitter fighting at Hue, and the siege of Khe Sanh. This is an extremely detailed and thoroughly documented account based on interviews and official records.

Simmons, Edwin H., et al. *The Marines in Vietnam 1954–1973: An Anthology and Annotated Bibliography*. Washington, DC: Headquarters, U.S. Marine Corps, 1974. An anthology of articles about the Marines in Vietnam that includes one on the battle for Khe Sanh.

Spencer, Ernest. *Welcome to Vietnam, Macho Man: Reflections of a Khe Sanh Vet*. Alamo, CA: Corps Press, 1987. A company commander in the 26th Marines, Spencer tells what it was like to endure the fight for Khe Sanh at the ground level. Extremely well written, this book is a no nonsense account of life in the "mud and blood."

Stockwell, David B. *Tanks in the Wire: The First Use of Enemy Armor in Vietnam*. New York: Jove Publications, 1990. Written by an Army armor officer, this is a narrative of the attack on the Special Forces camp at Lang Vei in which the Communists used tanks.

THE HILL FIGHTS AND BORDER BATTLES

Coan, James P. *Con Thien: The Hill of Angels*. Tuscaloosa: University of Alabama Press, 2004. The author, a decorated Marine, describes his experiences while assigned as a tank platoon leader stationed at Con Thien for eight months during the period 1967–68.

Hammel, Eric. *Ambush Valley: I Corps, Vietnam, 1967, the Story of a Marine Infantry Battalion's Battle for Survival*. Novato, CA: Presidio, 1990. Hammel describes the vicious fighting by the 3rd Battalion of the 26th Marines near the DMZ in September in the words of the survivors of the bitter fighting that preceded the siege of Khe Sanh.

Hemingway, Al. "Hell on the Hill of Angels." *Military Heritage* 7, no. 4 (February 2006): 40–45, 74. The author addresses the siege of Con Thien.

Murphy, Edward F. *Dak To: The 173d Airborne Brigade in South Vietnam's Central Highlands, June-November 1967*. Novato, CA: Presidio, 1993. The author tells the story of the U.S. paratroopers in the desperate fight for Hill 875 in the Central Highlands. This battle was a result of General Giap's strategy to pull U.S. units away from the populated areas as the Communist forces prepared for the Tet Offensive.

——. *Semper Fi: From Da Nang to the DMZ, Marine Corps Campaigns, 1965–1975*. Novato, CA: Presidio, 1997. Murphy seeks to provide a history of Marine Corps operations in Vietnam, but may have thrown his net too wide for a book of this length. He does address the Hill Fights of 1967, the siege of Khe Sanh, and the Battle of Hue.

——. *The Hill Fights: The First Battle of Khe Sanh*. Novato, CA: Presidio, 2003. This book addresses the firefights, ambushes, and other battlefield action of the vicious actions that took place in the hills around Khe Sanh for several months before the siege of the Marine base that began on January 21, 1968.

Pearson, Willard. *The War in the Northern Provinces, 1966–1968*. Washington, DC: Department of the Army, 1975. An official U.S. Army history, this book addresses operations in the area just south of the DMZ in the years prior to the 1968 Tet Offensive, including the "border fights" of 1967.

Simmons, Edwin H. "Marine Corps Operations in Vietnam, 1967." In *The Marines in Vietnam, 1954–1973*. Washington, DC: History and Museums Division, Headquarters, U.S. Marine Corps, 1985. Simmons describes the Marine Corps operations at Con Thien and in the hills surrounding Khe Sanh in 1967.

Telfer, Gary F., Lane Rogers, and Victor K. Fleming. *U.S. Marines in Vietnam, Fighting the North Vietnamese Army, 1967*. Washington, DC: History and Museums Division, Headquarters U.S. Marine Corps, 1984. An official Marine Corps history, this book examines the fighting in 1967 when the Marines first took on the People's Army of Vietnam.

PRESIDENT LYNDON B. JOHNSON AND THE MEDIA

Adams, Eddie. "The Pictures That Burn in my Memory." *Parade Magazine* (15 May 1983), 4–6. The photographer who took the famed photograph of General Loan shooting a Viet Cong suspect reflects on the effect of the photograph.

Arlen, Michael J. *Living-Room War*. New York: Penguin Books, 1982. Arlen examines television reporting on the war, 1966–1968.

Arnett, Peter. *Live from the Battlefield: From Vietnam to Baghdad, 35 Years in the World's War Zones*. New York: Simon & Schuster, 1994. About half of this book covers Arnett's career and controversial coverage as an Associated Press reporter in Vietnam from 1962 to 1975. He was present in Vietnam during the Tet Offensive and attributed the infamous quote about "destroying Bet Het to save it" to an unnamed American major.

——. "Tet Coverage: A Debate Renewed." *Columbia Journalism Review* (January/February 1978), 44–47. A review of Peter Braestrup's *Big Story* that challenges Braestrup's conclusions.

Braestrup, Peter. *Big Story: How the American Press and Television Reported and Interpreted the Crisis of Tet in Vietnam and Washington*. 2 vols. Boulder, CO: Westview, 1977; one-volume abridgment, New Haven, CT: Yale University Press, 1983. Providing a very detailed study with voluminous documentation, Braestrup is very critical of the performance of the press during the Tet Offensive. He concludes that media reporting helped transform a tactical disaster in a strategic psychological victory for the Communists.

Elegant, Robert. "How to Lose a War: Reflections of a Foreign Correspondent." *Encounter* 57 (August 1981), 73–90. Elegant argues that a hostile media seized defeat from the jaws of victory by turning public opinion against the war and limiting the government's freedom of action.

Halberstam, David. *The Powers That Be*. New York: Knopf, 1979. Halberstam examines the American news media, focusing on *Time* magazine, CBS, the *Washington*

Post, and the *Los Angeles Times*. He includes a discussion of the coverage of the Vietnam War.

Hallin, Daniel C. *The "Uncensored War": The Media and Vietnam*. Berkeley: University of California Press, 1989. The author provides a balanced analysis of the *New York Times* and network coverage of the war from 1961 to 1973. He concludes that the media generally accepted official explanations of the war up until the Tet Offensive, but then began to reflect rather than drive growing public disaffection with the war.

Hammond, William H. *Reporting Vietnam: Media and Military at War*. Lawrence: University Press of Kansas, 1998. A senior historian at the U.S. Army's Center of Military History, Hammond examines the tense relationship between the armed services and the media during the Vietnam War. An abridgement of Hammond's earlier two-volume work, this book challenges the assertions of many military leaders that the media lost the war by swaying public opinion.

Mohr, Charles. "Once Again—Did the Press Lose Vietnam?" In Grace Sevy, ed., *The American Experience in Vietnam*, 143–152. Norman: University of Oklahoma Press, 1989. Mohr argues that the media, and in particular television reporters, did not slant the news but rather only reported what they saw.

Pach, Chester J., Jr. "The War on Television: TV News, the Johnson Administration, and Vietnam." In Marilyn B. Young and Robert Buzzanco, eds., *A Companion to the Vietnam War*, 450–469. Malden, MA: Blackwell, 2002. The author provides a balanced account of the impact of the television media on Johnson and his conduct of the war. Pach concludes that the president thought that his problem was that he had failed to win the war on television when the real problem was the war that television showed.

Reporting Vietnam. 2 vols. New York: Library of America, 1998. This two-volume anthology is a collection of newspaper and magazine reports and book excerpts from more than eighty reporters and writers that cover the entire period of American involvement in Vietnam. Volume 1 contains a number of articles and reports on the Tet Offensive and Khe Sanh.

Salisbury, Harrison, ed. *Vietnam Reconsidered: Lessons From a War*. New York: Harper & Row, 1984. This compilation of essays contains two essays by Peter Braestrup and Keyes Beech respectively that take the media, and particularly television, to task for having a negative impact on American perceptions of the fighting and outcome of the Tet Offensive.

Turner, Kathleen J. *Lyndon Johnson's Dual War: Vietnam and the Press*. Chicago: University of Chicago Press, 1985. Author argues that Johnson did not do a good job of explaining U.S. actions to the press and increasingly lost press support.

Wyatt, Clarence R. *Paper Soldiers: The American Press and the Vietnam War*. New York: Norton, 1993. The author seeks to counter the widespread belief that the American press was a major factor in the U.S. failure in Vietnam. He reveals that the record shows instead a fluctuating mix of cooperation and confrontation between journalists and the government and military.

MILITARY INTELLIGENCE AND TET

Adams, Sam. "Vietnam Cover-up: Playing War with Numbers." *Harper's*, May 1975. Adams was an analyst for the Central Intelligence Agency analyst during the Vietnam War. He charged that MACV headquarters in Saigon deliberately downplayed the number of guerrillas in South Vietnam and that this deception played a major role in the surprise of the Tet Offensive. Adams helped produce a CBS television documentary about American intelligence failures in Vietnam that was the subject of a lawsuit brought by William Westmoreland, former MACV commander.

——. *War of Numbers: An Intelligence Memoir*. South Royalton, VT: Steerforth, 1994. This is Sam Adams's unfinished memoir, in which he expands on the charge originally made in the article above that MACV headquarters deliberately altered enemy order of battle figures. His wife published it after Adams died.

Adler, Renata. *Reckless Disregard: Westmoreland v. CBS et al; Sharon v. Time*. New York: Vintage Books, 1988. The author, a lawyer, analyzes the Westmoreland trial and a similar suit brought by Israeli General Ariel Sharon against *Time* magazine. The Westmoreland trial evolved from the CBS television documentary that charged MACV had altered the order of battle accounting in order to show progress in the war. Adler is very critical of both CBS and *Time*.

Allen, George W. *None So Blind*. Chicago: Ivan R. Dee, 2001. The author, a former career officer in the Central Intelligence Agency who served in Vietnam for a number of years. He criticizes American leaders, who he asserts were unwilling to confront reality when presented with bad news from intelligence sources and insisted in making their own strategic and tactical decisions. It includes a lengthy chapter on the Tet Offensive.

Blood, Jake. *The Tet Effect: Intelligence and the Public Perception of War*. London: Routledge, 2005. Blood, a retired military intelligence officer, examines what he calls "the Tet Effect," which he describes as the loss of credibility that results with the public is given "skewed," or "just plain bad," intelligence. After discussing the impact of intelligence failures during the Tet Offensive, he asserts that the "Tet Effect" was also operable when the United States went to war in Iraq in 2003.

Brewin, Bob, and Sydney Shaw. *Fair Play: CBS, General Westmoreland, and How a Television Documentary Went Wrong*. New York: Atheneum, 1987. This book, by two journalists, provides a generally impartial and thorough account of the landmark legal case. The book examines the making of the documentary, the history of the war, and finally the trial itself.

Davidson, Phillip B. *Secrets of the Vietnam War*. Novato, CA: Presidio, 1990. This book addresses the experiences of the author who served as the chief United States military intelligence office in Vietnam (MACV J-2) from May 1967 until May 1969. Among a wide array of issues, the author addresses the enemy troop-strength controversy in the months leading up to the Tet Offensive. Not surprisingly, Davidson assumes a very pro-Westmoreland stance.

Ford, Harold P. *CIA and the Vietnam Policymakers: Three Episodes, 1962–1968.* Washington, DC: History Staff, Center for the Study of Intelligence, Central Intelligence Agency, 1998. A historian for the CIA, the author examines three episodes between 1962 and 1968, one of which is the Tet Offensive, to determine the information and judgments the CIA provided senior decision makers. The author assesses the impact these inputs had or did not have on policy decisions.

Ford, Ronnie E. *Tet 1968: Understanding the Surprise.* London: Frank Cass, 1995. The author, an Army captain, examines the role played by U.S. intelligence in the Tet Offensive and demonstrates how the Communists were able to achieve such a stunning level of surprise when they launched the offensive.

Handel, Michael I., ed. *Leaders and Intelligence.* London: Frank Cass, 1989. This is a book of essays on leadership and strategic intelligence. It includes an essay on Westmoreland and intelligence by T. L. Cubbage.

Jones, Bruce. *War Without Windows.* New York: Vanguard, 1987. Jones was a junior officer who worked in military intelligence in Saigon during 1967–68. He asserts that he participated in the falsification of enemy order of battle figures.

Kowet, Don. *A Matter of Honor.* New York: Macmillan, 1984. This book purports to be the inside story of the CBS documentary about the "uncounted enemy" in Vietnam and its repercussions.

President's Foreign Intelligence Advisory Board. "Intelligence Warning of the Tet Offensive in South Vietnam." Issued on April 11, 1968, and declassified and released to the U.S. House of Representatives Pike Committee in 1975, this is the report of the president's select advisory board on the failure of U.S. intelligence to anticipate the scope and magnitude of the Tet Offensive.

Wirtz, James J. "Deception and the Tet Offensive." *Journal of Strategic Studies* 13 (June 1990): 82–98. Wirtz discusses the role of deception in the ability of the Communists to achieve the stunning surprise they achieved with the launching of the Tet Offensive.

——. "Intelligence to Please?—The Order of Battle Controversy During the Vietnam War." *Political Science Quarterly* 106 (Summer 1991): 239–263. Wirtz addresses the order-of-battle controversy that erupted when CIA analyst Sam Adams charged that MACV was deliberately underestimating the number of Viet Cong and PAVN forces in the field before and during the Tet Offensive.

——. *The Tet Offensive: Intelligence Failure in War.* Ithaca, NY: Cornell University Press, 1994. Wirtz examines the Communist deception plan that preceded the Tet Offensive and addresses why American and South Vietnamese intelligence failed to see what was happening.

U.S. STRATEGY IN VIETNAM

Krepinevich, Andrew F., Jr. *The Army and Vietnam.* Baltimore, MD: Johns Hopkins University Press, 1986. In this critical analysis of U.S. military strategy in Vietnam from 1954 to 1973, the author charges that the Army mistakenly applied the doctrine that had been developed for a conventional war in Europe to the unique situation in Vietnam, while ignoring the demands of fighting a counterinsurgency.

Sharp, U. S. Grant. *Strategy for Defeat.* San Rafael, CA: Presidio, 1978. The former commander-in-chief in the Pacific (CinCPac) maintains that the United States was not doomed to failure in Vietnam, but lost because the White House prosecuted a fatally flawed strategy.

Summers, Harry C., Jr. *On Strategy: A Critical Analysis of the Vietnam War.* Novato, CA: Presidio, 1982. The author argues that the Vietnam war was winnable, but that a misunderstanding of classical military theory and its connection to policy led to a fatally flawed strategy and subsequent defeat for the United States in Vietnam.

Thayer, Thomas C. *War Without Fronts: The American Experience in Vietnam.* Boulder, CO: Westview, 1985. The author provides a quantitative analysis of the critical dimensions of the war. He concludes that the war was so different from anything that the United States had previously fought that the public and that this difference made it difficult for Washington and the military to comprehend. According to Thayer, the flaws in strategy stemming from this lack of comprehension made U.S. failure in Vietnam inevitable.

COMBAT AFTER-ACTION REPORTS AND COMMAND HISTORIES

1st Battalion, 14th Infantry, Combat After Action Report, 3–28 February 1968, dated 13 April 1968.

1st Battalion, 22nd Infantry, Combat After Action Report, 30 January–12 February 1968, undated.

1st Brigade, 101st Airborne Division, Combat After Action Report, February 22–March 2, 1968.

1st Cavalry Division, 14th Military History Detachment, Combat After Action Report—Op Hue, Period 2–26 February 1968, dated 16 August 1968.

1st Marine Division, 1st Mar Div Commander's AAR, Tet Offensive, 29 January–14 February 1968, dated 25 May 68.

1st Marine Division, TF X-Ray, AAR, Operation Hue City, with enclosures, dated 14 April 1968.

1st Marines (Rein), 1st Marine Division (Rein), Combat Operations After Action Report (Operation HUE CITY), dated 20 March 1968.

4th Battalion, 12th Infantry, 199th Infantry Brigade (Sep)(Light), Combat After Action Report, 14 January–17 February 1968.

199th Infantry Brigade (Separate) (Light), After Action Report, Long Binh/Saigon, Tet Campaign, 12 January–19 February 1968.

II Field Force Vietnam, After Action Report—Tet Offensive, 31 January–18 February 1968.

II Field Force Vietnam, Operational Report—Lessons Learned, Period Ending 30 April 1968.

U.S. Military Assistance Command, Vietnam. Command History, 1967.

U.S. Military Assistance Command, Vietnam. Command History, 1968.

MICROFILM/MICROFICHE

Lester, Robert E., ed. *Records of the Military Assistance Command Vietnam*. 3 parts. 90 microfilm reels. Bethesda, MD: University Publications of America, 1988.

——. *Records of the U.S. Marine Corps in the Vietnam War*. 3 parts. 78 microfilm reels. Bethesda, MD: University Publications of America, 1990.

——. *U.S. Army Build-up and Activities in South Vietnam, 1965–1972*. 3 parts. 29 microfilm reels. Bethesda, MD: University Publications of America, 1989.

——. *The War in Vietnam: The Papers of William C. Westmoreland*. Part I: History, Statements, and Clippings Files. 25 microfilm reels. Bethesda, MD: University Publications of America, 1993.

The Lyndon B. Johnson National Security Files, 1963–69: Agency File. 34 microfilm reels. Bethesda, MD: University Publications of America, 1977.

The Lyndon B. Johnson National Security Files, 1963–69: Vietnam: First Supplement. 18 microfilm reels. Bethesda, MD: University Publications of America, 1996.

Pike, Douglas, ed. *The History of the Vietnam War*. 10 units. Microfiche. Ann Arbor, MI: UMI Research Collections, 1988.

Stubbe, Ray W., ed. *Khe Sanh: A Collection of Research Documentation*. 10 microfilm reels.

DOCUMENTARY FILMS

Air Power at Khe Sanh. VHS, 30 minutes. Brentwood Communications, 1990.

Battlefield Vietnam, Episode 1: *Countdown to Tet*. VHS, 58 minutes. Time Life Video, 1998.

Battlefield Vietnam, Episode 2: *The Tet Offensive*. VHS, 58 minutes. Time Life Video, 1998.

Battlefield Vietnam, Episode 6: *Siege at Khe Sanh*. VHS, 58 minutes. Time Life Video, 1998.

Bloody Sieges of Khe Sanh & Con Thien: Miscalculation in Vietnam. VHS, 44 minutes. A&E Television Networks, 1996.

History Alive: Unsung Heroes—The Battle of Khe Sanh. VHS, 50 minutes. A&E Television Networks, 2002.

To Hell and Beyond: Air Power at Khe Sanh. VHS, 30 minutes. Brentwood Home Video, 1989.

The Vietnam War with Walter Cronkite. DVD, 11 hours. CBS Video Library, 2003.

The Vietnam War with Walter Cronkite: The Tet Offensive. VHS, 55 minutes. CBS Video Library, 1985.

20th Century with Mike Wallace: Vietnam Dilemma: Tet Offensive and the Anti-War Movement. VHS, 55 minutes. The History Channel, A&E Television Networks, 2000.

Vietnam, Episode 8: *The Tet Offensive.* VHS, 61 minutes. CBS Video, 1987.

Vietnam: A Television History, Episode 7: *Tet 1968.* DVD/VHS, 60 minutes. PBS, 2004.

Vietnam: Battle of Khe Sanh. VHS, 60 minutes. MPI Home Video, 1989.

Vietnam: On the Frontlines, Volume 2: *Tet in Saigon and Hue.* VHS, 50 minutes. The History Channel, A&E Television Networks, 2000.

Vietnam: The Ten Thousand Day War, Episode 7: *Siege.* VHS, 49 minutes. Embassy Home Entertainment, 1980.

War Stories: The Siege at Khe Sanh. VHS, 50 minutes. Fox News, 2001.

War Stories: The Tet Offensive. VHS, 50 minutes. Fox News, 2002.

Why Vietnam & Why Khe Sanh? VHS, 55 minutes. United American Video, 1998.

ELECTRONIC RESOURCES

Web Sites

The American Experience—Vietnam. http://www.pbs.org/wgbh/amex/vietnam/index. html. A companion to the PBS series *Vietnam: A Television History,* this site includes maps, primary sources, bibliography, and transcripts of the television programs.

Documents Relating to the Vietnam War. http://mtholyoke.edu/acad/intrel/vietnam. htm. This site contains many primary- and secondary-source documents, with links to documents on other sites.

Edwin Moïse Bibliography of the Vietnam War. http://www.clemson.edu/caah/history/ FacultyPages/EdMoise/bibliography.html Prepared and maintained by a nationally recognized Vietnam scholar, this site provides an extensive, annotated bibliography arranged topically. It includes links to other Vietnam sites.

Khe Sanh Declassified Documents. http://members.easyspace.com/airdrop/index. html. This site includes a number of declassified documents having to do with Khe Sanh.

Texas Tech University Vietnam Center, Virtual Archive. http://www.vietnam.ttu.edu/ virtualarchive. This site offers an extensive collection of primary sources online and includes access to documents, photos, oral history interviews (both audio files and transcripts), and a wide range of media formats.

Vietnam: Echoes from the Wall. http://www.teachvietnam.org. This site, maintained by the Vietnam Veterans Memorial Fund, provides an educational curriculum and associated links for teaching about the Vietnam War.

Vietnam War Internet Project. http://www.vwip.org/vwiphome.html. Maintained by the Lyndon Baines Johnson Presidential Library, this site offers an extensive array of links to documents, memoirs, photos, bibliographies, and other sources.

The Wars for Vietnam: 1945–1975. http://students.vassar.edu/~vietnam/. This site provides links to a wide selection of primary source documents, bibliographies, and other sites.

CD-ROMs

American Journey: The Vietnam Era (1999). Edited by George Herring, Clarence Wyatt, and Robert K. Brigham. Published by Primary Source Media (Woodbridge, CT) for Mac and Windows, it provides primary source material organized around thematic essays. It also includes links, timelines, maps, pictures, and full-text search capability.

USA Wars: Vietnam (1994). Published by Quanta Press (Minneapolis) for Mac and Windows. Distributed by WAE (Clarkson, WA). This CD has a large amount of text from primary source documents and secondary documents plus images, tables, maps, and a section on the Vietnam War Memorial.

War in Vietnam: A Multimedia Chronicle (1995). Published by Macmillan Digital (New York) for Mac and Windows. CD provides more than a thousand articles from the *New York Times*, an hour of film footage from CBS News, 35 maps, 800 photographs, and the Vietnam War Memorial database.

Wings: Korea to Vietnam (1995). Published by Discovery Multimedia (Bethesda, MD) for Mac and Windows. CD includes information on five hundred aircraft of all types flown during the wars in Korea and Vietnam. It also includes interactive base tours, war reports with video, and many other features.

ARCHIVES AND LIBRARIES

U.S. Army Command and General Staff College, Combined Arms Research Library, Eisenhower Hall, 250 Gibbon, Ft Leavenworth, KS 66027; tel. 1 (913) 758–5053

Lyndon Baines Johnson Presidential Library, 2313 Red River Street, Austin, TX 78705; tel. 1 (512) 482–5137

Marine Corps Historical Center, 1254 Charles Morris Street SE, Washington Navy Yard, D.C. 20374, tel. 1 (202) 433–0731

U.S. Army Military History Institute, 22 Ashburn Drive, Carlisle, PA 17013, tel. 1 (717) 245–3711 (facsimile inquiries only)

Vietnam Archive, The Vietnam Center, Texas Tech University, Special Collection Library, Room 108, Lubbock, TX 79409, tel. 1 (806) 742–9010

INDEX

replaced by General Abrams, 156; authorizes the use of U.S. ground troops, 3; calls for 10 percent surtax, 143; concerned about Khe Sanh, 58; convenes the "Wise Men," 157; declining public support after Tet, 70, 73, 74, 157; directs Clifford to form task force, 155; halts bombing of North Vietnam, 77; meets with President Thieu, 141; on Khe Sanh and Dien Bien Phu, 25, 58; orders "Success Campaign," 6–7, 27, 111; predicts Communist offensive, 27; remarks about failure of Tet Offensive, 58, 152; replaces William Westmoreland, 76; responds to report by "Wise Men," 75–76; response to additional troop request, 120–121; response to Tet Offensive, xvi; "San Antonio Formula," 145, 191–193

Joint Chiefs of Staff (JCS), 174

Joint General Staff, 32, 174

Joint General Staff headquarters, attack on, 33–34

Jorden, William, 95

Junction City, Operation. See Operation, Junction City

Karnow, Stanley, 11, 31, 83

Kennedy, Robert F., 73, 74–75, 77, 148, 153, 156, 158, 174

Khe Sanh, xvi, 12, 15, 17–19, 150, 175; abandoned by Marines, 77, 109, 158; aerial resupply of, 61; Cronkite prediction about, 60; compared to Dien Bien Phu, 21–22, 25, 57, 60, 62, 64, 105, 107–108, 113–114, 129 n 3; Communist build-up at, 23; Communist objectives at, 104–109; fire support, 19; coordination at, 61–62; Hill 558; Hill 861, 14, 23, 24; Hill 861A, 58–59; Hill 881 South, 19, 23, 24; Hill 881N, 19; impact of fighting at Hue, 60; media coverage of, 36, 113–114; purpose of

siege, 104–109; siege of, 23–25, 56–65; siege lifted, 63–64; tactical air support, 61–62, 64; water supply at, 107

khoi nghia, 14

Kien Tuong, 31

King, Martin Luther, Jr., 6, 142, 152, 157

Kitt, Eartha, 150

Kontum, 175

attacks on, 29, 40

intelligence about, 21

Korea, Republic of, 8, 175

Korea, South. See Korea, Republic of

Krainick, Horst Gunther, 100

Krepinevich, Andrew F., Jr., 119–120

Krulak, Victor, 107

Ky, Nguyen Cao. See Nguyen Cao Ky

LaHue, Foster C., 45, 48, 49, 52, 175

Lai Khe, 38

Lam, Hoang Xuan. See Hoang Xuan Lam

Lang Vei Special Forces Camp, 18, 22; fall of, 59–60, 152, 175–176

Lao Dong (Workers') Party, xvii, 9, 76, 141, 152, 176; decides to launch Tet Offensive, 142; resolution calling for Tet Offensive, 90–91; Resolution 13, 10, 182; Resolution 14, 146, 182; Thirteenth Plenum, 9, 10, 141, 182

Laos, 7

Le Duan, 9, 90, 176

Le Duc Tho, 176

Le Thanh Tonc, 23–24, 105

Le Thanh Nghi, 142

Lewy, Gunther, 101

"Liberation Radio," 14

Life, 145

Lind, Michael, 122

Loan, Nguyen Ngoc. See Nguyen Ngoc Loan

Loc Ninh, battle of, 16, 17, 27, 146, 176

Lodge, Henry Cabot, 75

Long Binh, attack on, 37, 38–39, 176

Long, Ngo Vinh. See Ngo Vinh Long.